BY THE SAME AUTHOR

Gunners at War
(*Arms and Armour Press*)

Swords for Hire

Swords for Hire

EUROPEAN MERCENARIES
IN EIGHTEENTH-CENTURY INDIA

Shelford Bidwell

JOHN MURRAY

© Shelford Bidwell 1971

Printed in Great Britain by
William Clowes & Sons Limited
London, Colchester and Beccles
0 7195 2432 6

For P.M.B.

Contents

Illustrations

* From the Department of Prints and Drawings in the India Office Library, reproduced by kind permission of the Secretary of State for Foreign and Commonwealth Affairs.

Acknowledgments

I THINK it proper to begin by acknowledging my debt to Herbert Compton, whose book I took idly from the shelves of the Secunderabad Club library when I was a subaltern and which has held my interest ever since. Nearly ninety years ago Compton collected every available scrap of information about the military adventurers of northern India who served in the Moghul and Mahratta armies. His book is an invaluable source and but for his industry the modern writer would find only the coldest of scents to follow.

Mr. Dineen, the ever-helpful librarian of the Royal United Services Institute for Defence Studies, allowed me to keep his copy of Compton's *Particular Account* for over a year.

I would like to thank Mr. Farrington of the India Office Library for his help with other sources and Mrs. Mildred Archer of its Department of Prints and Drawings for finding most of the illustrations.

Mr. King and his staff at the Army branch of the Ministry of Defence Library are the great stand-by and support of military authors and I must record my gratitude to them and especially to Mr. Potts for drawing my attention to Dundas' *Principles of Military Movement*.

Major-General B. P. Hughes gave me the benefit of his expert knowledge on the artillery of the period and also some helpful advice about the composition by caste and race of the Indian armies of those days.

Colonel Bonnafant, Military Attaché at the French Embassy in London and Colonel Hurbin of the French Army's Historical Service kindly provided me with useful and interesting information.

The correct way to spell Indian words and proper names in English is always a problem as no two authorities seem to agree. In general I have not attempted to be orthographically correct, but at the same time have avoided the phonetic attempts of our ancestors such as 'Oogyne' for 'Ujjain'. I have throughout preferred what is likely to be familiar to the English reader, such as 'sepoy' for 'sipahi' and 'Muttra' for 'Mathura', and so on.

I   *The Mercenaries*

IN the middle of the eighteenth century, when the great Empire founded in India by Babur the Tiger and Akbar was in decline, the commanders of the armies of India became perplexed. They themselves, they believed, were past masters of the art of war. Their armies were numerous and powerful. Their soldiers were drawn from castes and races who delighted in war and were bred for it. Yet, when they met ridiculously small armies from the two races of European traders who had been allowed to settle on their coasts and who were becoming increasingly ambitious and truculent they were defeated, sometimes ignominiously. It was not only the white soldiers who overthrew them. The bulk of the armies of the foreigners was made up of native *sipahis*, or sepoys, of the same races as their own, but led by white officers. Their guns, their muskets, their swords were no better than the native models. Clearly they had some mysterious secret of victory the Indian generals did not possess. It lay, they saw, in European method, order, drill and discipline; simple qualities but alien to the native military genius. Accordingly from the mid-century onwards they began to pay foreign officers to raise and train battalions and brigades of regular infantry on the European pattern. As the eighteenth century wore on and the Moghul Empire continued to crumble the Imperial army and the successor states which were carved out of its ruins all raised corps of regular troops commanded by Europeans of varying military ability: French, Dutch, Swiss, Armenian, German, Italian, English, Scots, Irish, American and Eurasian. The earliest were French-trained and in the Imperial armies of Delhi; later the Nawab-Wazir of Oudh and the Subahdar of the Deccan, the family of the Nizam-ul-Mulk of Hyderabad, the Moghul viceroys who now ruled virtually independent states, Haidar Ali, the usurper of Mysore and petty Jat and great Rajput chieftains all had their corps of regular troops. Later, in the nineteenth century, the Sikh ruler Ranjit Singh employed a few French professional soldiers, not to command his wild irregulars, but to convert them into a formidable army.

Swords for Hire

The high period and the greatest achievements of the European mercenaries, or 'military adventurers' as they were called, however, was from 1784, when the great Mahratta leader Madhaji Sindia discovered a brilliant French soldier and employed him to lay the foundation of a mercenary regular army of northern Indians to supplement his swarms of Mahratta guerrillas; to 1803, when this 'Army of Hindustan', as it was sometimes called, succumbed after the most desperate fighting to Wellesley and Lake. These 'trained brigades', as the British often called them were not 'Mahrattas' any more than the Swiss or the German *lanzknechts* of the sixteenth-century French army were French, but before we explore their now obscure history it is necessary to glance at the Indian military scene.

Why was it necessary for so great and gifted a group of peoples, heirs of a brilliant civilisation, and whose martial qualities are second to none, to rely for their defence on mercenaries officered by foreigners; and, moreover, foreigners without a vestige of Indian patriotism who when the hour of decision arrived so often deserted them? The answer lies in a complex of factors, political, religious, military, reaching back into the Moghul past, and the great difficulty is to avoid the temptation to go back further and further in an attempt to make the background clear, and to stray away from the main theme. The simplest, perhaps over-simple, answer to this question is that Islamic, Moghul India, its Muhammedan rulers and its Hindu subjects alike, had long since stagnated, and its military system with it.

In the eighteenth century the 'Moghul' armies, to use a loose but convenient term, were still essentially the same as they had been in the early sixteenth century.[1] They were completely untrained, except in skill-at-arms; they were without regular sub-divisions, subordination of command, staff, any supply or medical services, and were quite incapable of manoeuvre. The two important striking arms were the cavalry, the great majority being Moghuls, or Hindustani Muhammedans, and the artillery. The Moghuls were by this century very different from the savage, fair-skinned troopers from Balkh and Samarkand who had ridden into India behind Babur the conqueror in 1529. They no longer carried the deadly Mongol bow, and they were softer, no longer inclined to ride thirty or forty miles in a day and sleep with their saddles for pillows;

2

but well led and in sufficient numbers their headlong charge could still decide a battle. Cavalry was also the traditional arm of the western clans of Rajasthan, or Rajputana. The Rajput horsemen were apparitions from ancient India. They dressed in armour like knights, over which they wore long yellow gowns, the *maranacha poshak* or 'clothes of the dead', as a sign that they had 'washed their hands of life'. They were thus officially already dead and battle was a sacrament to celebrate their glorious sacrifice. Their only tactic was to form the *ghol*, or dense circle, and charge and charge again until their enemy broke or they were all killed. Few troops could stand up to these suicidal Don Quixotes.

The Moghuls were great artillerymen, and an army was accompanied by a long train of cannon of every size, but the bigger and heavier the better. It moved slowly, the principal draught animal being the bullock, and like the rest of the army could not manoeuvre; but planted wheel to wheel in long rows and well entrenched it was a formidable arm. In addition to the guns there would be whole battalions of rocket-men carrying bundles of iron rockets with sticks, not unlike the ones we still use on Guy Fawkes night. Their fire if dense enough could be effective and was certainly alarming.

The infantry were recruited from every tribe and caste, and broadly speaking each group had its own specialty. Some, like the Rohillas, specialised in the defence of forts, others in mountain or jungle warfare. The fanatical Ghosais and Bairagis, wandering religious beggars who worshipped Siva, the god of destruction, and sought release in death were used for 'forlon hopes' and suicidal attacks. They were the berserkers of India and went into action stark naked and smeared with ashes, their hair flying loose, and worked themselves up to a frenzy of wild howling as they flung themselves on the enemy. In the ranks of the foot every weapon and type of soldier could be seen; little jungle-axes, crossbows, bows, spears, pikes, matchlocks and swords and round shields. The general principle was the ancient one of recruiting by tribes and aptitudes rather than of training soldiers comprehensively for their military tasks. The nearest approach to a regular infantry were the battalions of Muslim *Najibs*, the fore-runners of the solid 'Punjabi Mussulmans' of the later British Indian army. Later there could be seen wedged into this picturesque and polyglot horde the ordered ranks of sepoys in cross belts and European coats under the command of a white mercenary: added to the military fruit salad in the hope that it would be a strengthening ingredient.

With this host travelled another equally huge one of camp-followers. The humblest trooper had his groom and grass-cutter, the officers had their cooks and tent-coolies and baggage drivers as well, and the commanders were accompanied by whole convoys of bullock carts and pack-animals moving their households and wives and children. As well there were merchants selling grain and food, the stalls of shop-keepers, cattle on the hoof, the gypsy drivers of baggage animals, sellers of arrack and *bhang* (or cannabis) and opium; conjurors, dancing girls and prostitutes. There were even professional camp-thieves, licensed to ply their trade by the provost-martial. Halted to camp or to give battle a Moghul army resembled a huge country fair or the site of a gold-rush; on the move it straggled across the country like a large tribe in the process of migration.

The great weakness of these armies in the field was the absence of any proper division into subordinate formations and of any hierarchical chain of command. Leadership was heroic and kingly and all turned on the leader's presence. In spite of the individual courage of the soldiers they were subject to the most violent panic which struck like lightning. It could easily be caused by the leader being struck down or simply disappearing from view. This could be a sign of ill-omen. Alternatively the troops might reasonably conclude that they had been betrayed, as it was a habit of their generals to gallop off the battlefield and to abandon them if things did not go well. Time and again we read of a native Indian army suddenly breaking apart as the result of such an unexpected shock. Indeed, the whole fate of India was once decided by just such a panic a century before; at the battle of Samulgarh, when Prince Darya Shukoh was contesting the succession with his brother Aurungzeb. When victory was in his grasp Darya dismounted from his elephant for some trivial reason. His troops saw the howdah empty, the cry went up: 'the Prince is dead', and in a matter of minutes they began to flee in disgraceful *sauve-qui-peut* which no one could check. Such troops, so volatile and so incapable of manoeuvre were very vulnerable to a sudden setback, or to a surprise or a flank attack, from which they found it hard to recover.

Their other great weakness lay in the feudal system by which they were maintained. The basic revenue of India was rent paid to the crown for land tenure: all land belonging to the crown. The army was a militia maintained by officials called *mansabdars* who in exchange for their salary undertook to bring into the field a fixed number of soldiers according to their rank. In practice, and this was the general rule in the period of the European mercenaries, they were given estates or territories for the purpose in *mansab* called *jaghirs*, and they were also known therefore as *jaghirdars*, the general term for a landed man. It was their business to administer the district, collect the revenue, reward themselves, pay and maintain their troops and to pass over a fixed percentage to the Governor above or to the central government.

Jaghirdarships and mansabdarships were not hereditary as were their equivalents under the European feudal system. On the contrary, it was the Moghul principle to change the holders round from time to time to prevent any ambitious man digging himself in too securely or obtaining too loyal a following and entertaining thoughts of independence. It is impossible to think of a worse system. Too great military efficiency led to suspicion and removal. There was every temptation to fudge the military returns, to use the troops, who themselves were underpaid or in long arrears, to squeeze the last penny out of the peasant sub-tenants—the *'ryats'*—and amass as much money as possible by extortion and embezzlement and misapplying the military funds for as long as the appointment was held. The troops brought hastily into the field were therefore deficient in numbers, underpaid, badly equipped and often mutinous. Mutiny was endemic in the armies of India—'strikes' we would call them today—for the ill-used sepoys had no other way to obtain redress. Although the land revenue had been justly fixed in Akbar's time, in the anarchy of the declining empire its collection by a demoralised soldiery according to:

'The good old rule, the ancient plan,
that he who has the power shall take
and he shall keep who can'

often degenerated into mere pillage which was resisted by the more warlike or truculent communities. Such was the system the mercenary officers found that they had to operate to fulfil their contracts.

2

There was another military movement—the term 'army' is hardly appropriate—the Mahratta guerrillas. In the previous century the Muslim bigot Aurungzeb when he became Emperor had abandoned the tolerance of the wise Akbar and imposed a number of galling and insulting restrictions on the Hindu majority of his subjects. It was not the intellectual Brahmins nor the chivalrous Rajputs who fought effectively for Indian and Hindu freedom but a mid-caste race of wiry Hindu mountaineers who lived in the ranges of west-central India under a leader of genius called Shivaji. They were a shrewd, cunning, unscrupulous, ruthless, intelligent and down-to-earth people. One of their great folk-tales is of how Shivaji enticed a Muslim general to a peace conference and stabbed him to death as he embraced him in greeting, while his comrade Ambaji ambushed and destroyed his waiting army. In the course of time these mountaineers had descended to the plain of the Deccan and had discovered the advantages to be gained from uniting guerrilla tactics with the horse. Their armies consisted entirely of swarms of light cavalry, undisciplined and loosely grouped under their chiefs; each horseman with a lance or a sabre, sitting on a rubbishy saddle tied up with string, a bag of meal or cold rice for rations, and mounted on a weedy little pony which could go all day with a little dusty grass and a handful of peas for forage. The Mahratta armies paid themselves by a system of universal 'danegeld' or blackmail called the *chauth*. There was no infantry and no artillery. They learned to use this mobility to wear down the ponderous Moghul armies by constantly attacking their outposts, ambushing small parties, cutting off supply-columns and endlessly evading battle until their opponents were worn out by marching and mad with frustration. For guile and stratagem they had no equals. In a short space of time, less than a century, they succeeded in wrecking the Empire and came within an arms length of becoming its heirs. On one fatal day in 1761 however, they forsook their traditional method of warfare and suffered a terrible defeat at the hands of an invading Afghan army from which they never fully recovered. They then reverted to their original system of warfare until in the 1770s the great chief Madhaji Sindia was severely defeated by small forces of British regulars and decided the time had come to have after all some proper infantry and guns of his own.

The first impact of European arms, however, was not in 1779 when Goddard defeated Sindia on the Narbada river or in 1780 when two companies of Popham's sepoys escaladed his fortress of Gwalior. It had been long before in 1746, when Dupleix defied the great Moghul official, the Nawab (or 'Deputy') of the Carnatic. This was in the early stage of the struggle between the British and French for control of southern India. Dupleix had attacked the British, captured Fort St. George, now Madras, and carried its occupants off to Pondicherry as prisoners. The British appealed most piteously to the Nawab of the Carnatic as their protector, but unfortunately for them they had recently offended him and in his oblique Asian way he let Dupleix at first have a free hand in the hope that the humiliation would teach the British a much-needed lesson in good manners. Then, when he had thought that matters had gone far enough, he sternly ordered Dupleix to cease to make war on Moghul territory, and to withdraw. Dupleix, who was the only man in India to have taken the true measure of a Moghul army, prevaricated. He told the commander of the garrison he had put into Fort St. George, a civilian called Duval d'Empresnil, to stand fast, while to the Nawab he gave his promise that he had only taken the place from the British to return it to him, but in Pondicherry he gave orders for reinforcements to be sent up to d'Empresnil. After a time the Nawab became angry and decided on a show of force. He sent his son, an unfortunate and feeble creature called Maphuz Khan, with an army of ten thousand strong in cavalry, the traditional arm of the Moghuls, and with forty cannon to take the place over as Dupleix had promised. D'Empresnil shut the gates of the fort in his face. In spite of this piece of insolence Maphuz Khan did not assault the place, or bombard it or even invest it closely. The weakness of Fort St. George was that the water supply lay some distance outside the defences, and Maphuz Khan perceiving this put a guard on the wells and retired his army to a position in observation. He had not much stomach for fighting and in any case by the conventions of Asian warfare the offender should be given time to react. A little skirmishing followed, but nothing serious happened until the garrison began to feel the lack of water. D'Empresnil sent out a convoy of water-carts and carriers, and as an escort a small force of infantry and two guns, with the aim of replenishing his supplies and, possibly, of testing the temper

7

of his hesitant opponent. The Moghul troops observed this move with astonishment. According to their experience of warfare it was impossible for infantry to stand up to cavalry, and for this absurdly tiny force to defy the whole army was a piece of impudence. Almost contemptuously some squadrons of cavalry were ordered to charge, drive off the infantry and capture the guns.[2]

The point of this anecdote is this. As has been said, collective training and drill were things unknown to the armies of ancient India. Like their Turkish ancestors, the Moghuls were great artillerymen, but they relied on numbers and weight of metal; but as for the service of the piece, or 'gun-drill', for loading, 'pointing' (or 'laying'), for firing, for running up the carriage after recoil, and for sponging and ramming home the charge and the projectile and so on, it was an excitable, noisy and slow process in their armies. Cavalry tactics against guns were therefore to draw the first salvo and then to gallop in and sabre or spear the gunners while they fumbled with rammer and handspike to re-load the empty guns. What Maphuz Khan's troopers did not realise (and the modern reader may perhaps be surprised to learn) was that as early as 1746 Western gunners as the result of discipline and unceasing drill could fire a field-piece once every fifteen seconds, or with really good 'detachments' (crews) even once every twelve seconds.[3] They could fire faster than the man armed with a musket, because he had to perform all the actions single-handed, whereas in the artillery the work was methodically shared among a number of operators drilled until they moved automatically, like clockwork. For distant targets artillery relied on cannon-balls or 'shot', for those closer in, 'grape', or clusters of iron shot about the size of golf-balls done up in netting bags; and for targets at muzzle-point 'case', or lead musket balls the size of marbles in cylindrical containers. The infantry, if equally well-drilled, were indeed capable of a damaging fire, but their principal weapon was the bayonet and they were still really pike-men. The main source of fire power were the infinitely more destructive guns which were justly regarded as the decisive weapon.

In India all this was still unknown, therefore when a couple of round-shot ploughed into the horsemen as they formed up, they for their part regarded it as the signal that they had five minutes or more pleasurably to settle the hash of the gunners; but as they charged the French changed to grape and case and began to fire as fast as possible without the need for any precise aim. The effect on the approaching squadrons was to empty seventy saddles, and the survivors turned tail. The moral effect was even more severe. The cavalry were the elite: they had been seen to fly by the whole army: their faces, as Indians say, had been 'made black'. They could not understand what had happened, and finally came to the conclusion that they had been led into an artillery ambush and the rolling fire which had thrown them back had come from a number of artfully concealed guns. Nevertheless, Maphuz Khan raised the siege, such as it was, and moved off to observe these dangerous people from a greater and safer distance. Worse for him was to come.

He learned that Dupleix had ordered up reinforcements from Pondicherry so on the 4th November, 1746 leaving Fort St. George without a force to cover it, he took up a strong position to bar their approach at the point where the road from Pondicherry to Madras crosses the River Adyar at a ford under the walls of a small town called St. Thomè. According to custom he put the infantry who, as stated, were poorly regarded in Moghul armies, behind the decrepit walls of the town. He planted his batteries on the northern and higher bank of the river to cover the approaches to the crossing, and behind them he deployed his horsemen. It was thus a strong and well-organised position in three lines and in depth. All these preparations were to meet the advance of a thousand men: two hundred and fifty French regulars and the remainder French-trained sepoys.

Dupleix's daring plans depended from a military shoe-string. He could spare no guns or cavalry from Pondicherry, or even an experienced field officer, and had entrusted the command of the march to a civilian called Paradis: which was the name of the Swiss civil engineer who emerges briefly into history to initiate an explosion whose reverberations were eventually to be felt all over Moghul India. Having no cavalry to reconnoitre for him Paradis blundered into Maphuz Khan's position without warning. The first intimation he had of the presence of the enemy was a cannonade from the farther bank of the Adyar, fortunately ill-directed, the shot flying overhead. Behind the batteries he could see something even more disturbing; dark masses of mounted troops, the light glittering from their lance points, extending far to the right and to the left.

Paradis' best hope, had he but known in time, would have been to try to slip round Maphuz Khan and join hands with the garrison of the fort, or failing this to retreat, but he was now in a trap. If he remained where he was it would only be a matter of minutes before the gunners found his range. If he attempted to move away or manoeuvre and if there was a cavalry leader worth a farthing in front of him he would, without any cavalry or guns of his own to support him, be in deadly danger. Paradis did not hesitate. He shook his troops out into assault formation, ordered them to fix their bayonets, placed himself in front, and calling on them to follow splashed across the shallows and scrambled up the far bank and into the enemy batteries. In war the crudest and most direct tactics, if also the promptest and most daring, are often the best. The French entered the batteries without firing a shot, the gunners fled and Paradis, reforming his men, continued his advance in a more orthodox way against the apparently hypnotised cavalry by alternate companies, firing and charging, and charging and firing.

They were up to the wall of the town and over it when a tumult of shouting and firing broke out in the enemy rear. D'Empresnil, a man who had the root of the military matter in him, had marched out from Madras to the sound of the guns and fallen on the rear of the enemy position. The army of the Carnatic dissolved in panic led by Maphuz Khan himself, who climbing on to a fast dromedary, left the scene followed by anyone who had a horse to ride, and the infantry running. The French stood rubbing their eyes, having with two battalions caused a large army literally to disappear, the only evidence of its former existence being a long row of abandoned guns, a mass of carts and baggage ready to be plundered and a few dead and wounded men.

The rout of St. Thomè could be called one of the decisive battles of Indian history. It was in a way like Majuba, or Jitra in Malaya in 1941, when a despised enemy overthrew with ignominy the army of a powerful empire with a long tradition of victory. Its news must have spread through India only slowly, carried by travellers along the roads, in the letters of merchants and by gossip from village to village, but with profound effect. Then in 1757 came the British victories of Plassey and later in the 1760s Undwa Nala and

Buxar, or Baksar. No Indian Cromwell or Frederic arose to lead the brave Indian armies in their fight against the ever-encroaching British. The only thing that occurred to the Moghul viceroys and deputies, the Nawabs and Subahdars, was to copy and to hire Europeans to do it for them. Even so, they were used more to fight each other than the invaders.

The earliest mercenary officers were all French, and were not originally, strictly speaking, 'adventurers' or 'mercenaries' at all. The French, perhaps with the lessons of the American wars in mind, sought to strengthen their Indian allies in their war against the British by training them in European warfare as they had the Canadians. They sent the Moghul rulers what we would now call 'military missions'. French-trained batteries opposed Clive at Plassey. The troops of the Nawab-Wazir of Oudh opposing the British in Bengal were assisted, to very little effect as it turned out, by a group under a Franco-Scot called Law,[4] formerly of Dillon's Regiment in the famous Irish Brigade of the French Army. Law could achieve nothing in the face of Moghul chaos and Moghul irresolution and in any case was soon removed from the scene when he was captured by the British. It was from the men he left floating about in the Moghul armies that the first true mercenaries, resembling the Italian *condottieri* emerged; men fighting for any master who would pay their wages and virtually the owners of their little private armies, or 'parties' as they were sometimes called. It is in the British accounts of the severe fighting of 1763 at Patna and later at Baksar that the shadowy figures of Markur, reputedly an Armenian, and the more substantial ones of Reinhardt and of Madec appear.

Walter Reinhardt was from Strasbourg and originally a private in one of the British East India Company's polyglot European battalions from which he deserted to join Law as a sergeant.[5] He was a man of some energy and force of character, for he later promoted himself and some fellow Frenchmen to the rank of officer and persuaded the Amir Kassim Ali Khan—Macaulay's 'Meer Cossim'—to employ him to raise a brigade of sepoys trained in the French style. With this he earned the distinction, which he was to share later only with the French regular officers with Tipu Sultan and a cavalry commander called Fleury in the Army of Hindustan, of actually defeating a British force. It is not for this he is remembered by the British, however, but because it is his name that is the answer to Macaulay's rhetorical question, in his essay on Warren Hastings, concerning the responsibility for the massacre of Patna. Kassim Ali had actually been installed as Governor of Bengal by the British only to find that he was expected to be their 'quisling', to use a modern term, and to put up with the Company's high-handedness and also its extreme dishonesty towards his people in a transaction concerning customs dues. Reinhardt's victory had put about forty British officers and civilians and some one hundred soldiers into his hands. Enraged by the British in general and their success in capturing his fortress of Mongir in particular, Kassim Ali gave orders for his prisoners to be slaughtered.

Such an act of course was not regarded as absolutely outrageous by Asian custom. Only two years previously Ahmed Shah Durrani had massacred thousands of his Mahratta prisoners after his victory at Panipat. Tipu Sultan thought it reasonable enough to order the slaughter of the British survivors of Baillie's and Brathwaite's forces after their defeat, but was fortunately restrained by his French officers. Kassim Ali's own Indian soldiers, however, demurred: executions, they felt, were the concern of butchers and low-caste men and not theirs. The job was done by Reinhardt's sepoys. The rank and file were shot through the windows of their goal. The officers Reinhardt invited to dinner, they imagining that they were being placated in view of the British victories and perhaps were about to be released when the murder squads rushed in and began to cut them down. According to one story the dismayed and astonished men defended themselves desperately with fists and even knives and forks, until all were left weltering in blood, wine and gravy mixed. After this Reinhardt was somewhat shy of meeting the British, and at the critical battle of Buxar he remained cautiously deaf to all orders to advance and engage them and withdrew his brigade in timely fashion and intact to avoid the rout; a manoeuvre which was to become a habit with his force. Reinhardt died in 1778, and his native wife took over his brigade which continued to supply a disgraceful and occasionally comic accompaniment to the history of the mercenaries until it was disbanded in about 1805.

Madec was a far more respectable character, although he, too, was a deserter from the Honourable East India Company's army, which he left during the mutiny which took place shortly before

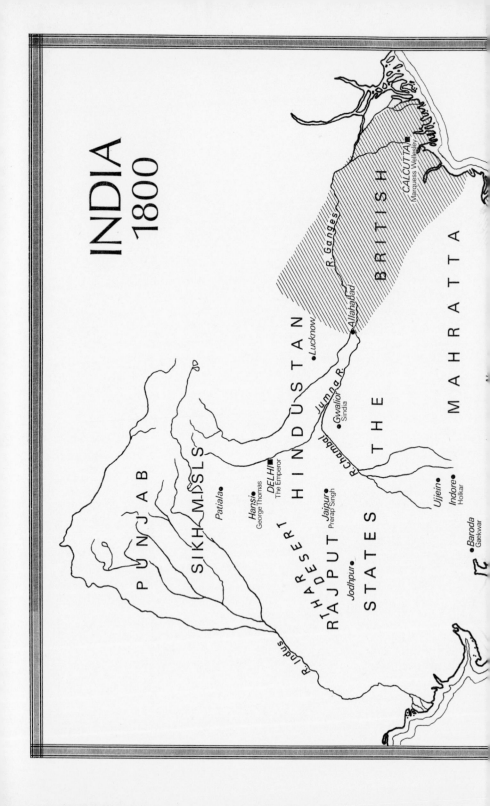

INDIA
1800

PUNJAB

SIKH MISLS

R. Indus

THAR DESERT

Patiala•

Hansi•
George Thomas

DELHI■
The Emperor

HINDUSTAN

Jodhpur•

RAJPUT

Jaipur•
Prerap Singh

STATES

THE

Ujjein•

Indore•
Holkar

Baroda•
Gaekwar

R. Chambal

Gwalior•
Sindia

Jumna R.

MAHRATTA

•Lucknow

•Allahabad

R. Ganges

BRITISH

CALCUTTA■
Marquess Wellesley

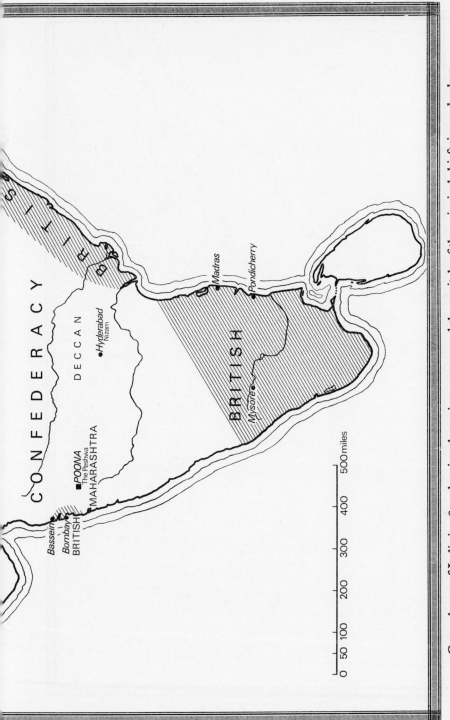

General map of India in 1800 showing the major powers, and the capitals of the principal chieftains and rulers

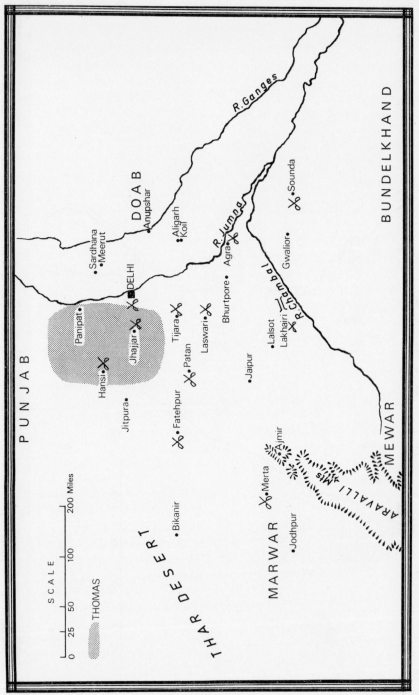

Hindustan and Rajasthan

the battle of Buxar. He became involved in numerous intrigues whose aim was to establish French influence in northern India, but he proved ineffective both as an amateur diplomatist and as a commander in the field. He was hardly a great soldier, but as a businessman, and after all a mercenary is simply a businessman who deals in warfare, he was more successful. After a number of unprofitable adventures, including losing his whole force in an ambush, he raised another and sold it, literally lock, stock and barrel, to say nothing of the sepoys, their uniforms, the guns and the transport, to Chettri Singh, the Rana, or King, of Gohad from whose service it eventually passed into the Army of Hindustan. Madec's and Reinhardt's brigades were the earliest of the European-led and owned mercenary forces of Moghul India. Madec, sad to say, did not live long to enjoy his affluence, for after retiring to France he was killed in a duel, doubtless the victim of what one account of him describes as his 'reckless impetuosity'.[6]

The successors of Reinhardt and Madec fall broadly into three classes. First there was a solid core of trained regular officers, mainly French, but as well there were Europeans of all nations who had wandered into Moghul India from the Company's service looking for better terms of employment, or simply through restlessness. Among them were men like the Dutchman Hessing and the Frenchmen Fremont and Chevalier Dudrenac; Sutherland, who was cashiered out of a Highland regiment; and probably many like the attractive Bellasis, an Engineer officer who found like other young officers who were to follow him to India that it was a land of fatally easy credit and who turned mercenary to pay his debts. He was killed, poor fellow, storming a fort, much admired and regretted by all the fraternity who noted with awe that apart from his soldierly qualities he could actually speak Greek and Latin and play the violin.

Next came the British. Some, like William Gardner or Felix Smith were regulars of the King's, as opposed to the Company's service, who threw up their commissions for adventure or in the hope of achieving the promotion they were denied. They were all honest professionals with a strict code of honour and of conduct involving absolute loyalty to their often highly unreliable masters while under contract. Few were able to do more than defend a fort or command a battalion, or at a pinch a brigade, but they gave good value for money. The lower tier of junior officers, the 'regimental' officers who stood in the ranks, was recruited very largely from the sons of British officers born in the country, some of mixed blood. As we shall see, the battalions in the Mahratta service were not French, but British-trained and facsimiles of the Company's sepoy regiments.

Then there were the deserters, genuine soldiers of fortune; often illiterate men of obscure origin escaping from the brutal and degrading slavery of life on the lower deck of an eighteenth-century warship or in the ranks of an eighteenth-century battalion. The Victorian writers tended to purse their lips at their military pretensions, their 'low' birth, their dissolute habits and their deplorable practice of co-habiting with low-caste native women. 'An inferior specimen of a class generally inferior,' says Colonel Malleson severely of the ex-private, ex-chef Louis Bernard, alias 'Bourquin'. Louis Bourquin was admittedly an ass and a poltroon, but low birth does not obviate courage or skill.[7] Such men also became Marshals of France. Today it is impossible not to admire those men who tramped off penniless into a continent whose languages and customs were as strange to them as if they had travelled to another planet, and as in as great a state of confusion and danger as Laos or Africa or Vietnam are today. Among them were Thomas and Cuiller-Perron, both seamen; one from the fleet of Admiral Sir Edward Hughes, the other from that of Hughes' rival Suffren; there were Michael Filose, who started life as a muleteer in Italy, and his two half-caste sons; and James Shepherd who arrived in Hindustan as 'batman' or valet to an officer, who 'rose from obscurity to consequence by his bravery, his perseverance and his fidelity,' and after some time in the Mahratta service became a colonel in the East India Company's army. Many died after humble and hard lives as drill-sergeants or gunners, others commanded forces greater than those they had deserted, and sometimes to better effect than the officers of the armies they had fled. Adventurous, romantic, perilous and sometimes disgraceful or squalid as the lives of these men were, individually they amounted to nothing. The Indians did not find in them the answer to the British, and the British did not attach much importance to them, except perhaps for one or two good French regular officers in the service of Haidar Ali, and they were only auxiliaries. In northern India they would have remained nothing more than an interesting minor episode in military history had it not been for one man. In 1784 there arrived among the Mahrattas a mercenary officer seeking employment who had already served in the French and Russian armies and with the British in a sepoy battalion of the Honourable East India Company's forces. He was a Savoyard called Benoit la Borgne.

Benoit de Boigne

THE PORTRAIT of de Boigne was made for the citizens of his native Chambery, in Savoy, when he was in the autumn of his life; the vastly wealthy and successful General Count de Boigne, friend of kings, and the town's most distinguished citizen. The severely handsome face is of a commander or a pro-consul; the expression a little humourless, calm, lofty and aristocratic. Aristocrat, however, he was not: his origin was bourgeois. He was born on the 8th March, 1751, the son of Monsieur la Borgne, a trader in hides, who planned that his young Benoit should move up the social ladder slightly and become a lawyer. The boy thought differently. He was restless and romantic, and not so much ambitious as dreaming of fame and distinction. He set his heart on becoming an officer in the army. This, he believed, would be his road to greatness, and he was to cling to this idea in the face of every disappointment and frustration. It was not long before he met his first. An officer in the army of the kingdom of Sardinia (of which Savoy then formed a part) had to be of noble descent: only the ranks were open to the sons of shopkeepers and hide merchants. Here, of course, Benoit was lucky. Apart from providing young Italian counts with the opportunity to wear beautiful uniforms, the sole historic purpose of the Sardinian army seems to have been to provide a victim for a demonstration of the genius of Napoleon in his debut as a general in 1796. What sort of life a young, keen professional soldier without birth or money would have had in it is almost too disagreeable to imagine. To be thus rudely reminded of his proper station, however, was a bitter humiliation, and the bogus 'de' and the spelling 'Boigne' probably date from this rejection. It is not without significance that when he finally attained high command some twenty years later and thousands of miles away in Asia the colours he chose for his new model army bore the white cross of ungrateful and unappreciative Savoy.

Fortunately there was another opening available for a would-be professional soldier across the border, in France. In 1770 the famous Irish Brigade of the French army still existed, and service in it no longer confined to Irishmen or exiled Jacobites; it was a worthy predecessor of the Foreign Legion and an admirable school for soldiers. De Boigne (as he is best known, and as it is convenient to call him), left home and in his nineteenth year was commissioned into Clare's Regiment. There he received a good grounding in his chosen profession and also in the behaviour of an officer and French gentleman; in the Brigade's code of conduct and in the stately formal manners of the day, which were to enable him to be at ease with English noblemen and in Indian courts alike. There too he probably learned his English, which he spoke with the brogue: there was a joke about the Army of Hindustan that although the drill-manual was in English the orders were in Irish. All this was to be of great advantage to him, but it was with less satisfaction that he discovered, like many other young officers, that the life of a soldier far from being adventurous or exciting is eternally occupied with parades, drills, inspections and guard duties, and that he is more concerned in seeing that his men have cleaned their fire-arms and have the correct number of cartridges in their pouches and a bread ration in their haversack, than in storming batteries or other heroic deeds. Even in war there was little glory for a subaltern, whose duty it was to stand wedged into the ranks of his platoon and to turn left or right or advance or retire with them like an automaton. Not that de Boigne saw any active service, for Clare's was stationed most of the time in France. Bored after six years of garrison duties and seeing no hope of promotion or glory he resigned. It is one of the remarkable features of de Boigne's early career that he seems to have missed seeing any serious active operations until he was over thirty and commanding a brigade.

His next move was to obtain a commission in a battalion of Greeks being raised in the Russian army by an Admiral Orloff to fight the Turks, and in the somewhat predictable fiasco that followed he was made a prisoner of war. This temporarily disgusted him with soldiering. In Turkey he had heard great stories about India from merchants returning from the East. De Boigne had an inspiration. He would acquire fame by travelling overland in the footsteps of Alexander from Syria to the Hydaspes; and once there he would make his fortune: de Boigne was never avaricious, but to be both poor and ambitious forces a man to see the advantages of wealth. His first attempt to reach India starting from Aleppo proved abortive as the master of the caravan he joined abandoned his journey on learning of war on the frontiers of Persia which made it unsafe to travel. His second was equally unfortunate. Egypt seemed to be on the way to India, so he set off there, only to be ship-wrecked in the Nile delta, and he arrived in Cairo penniless.

Here at last he had a piece of luck. When de Boigne had still been in the Russian service he had been detached to escort a son of the Earl of Northumberland, who was travelling in the Near East, while he was visiting the sites of classical Greece, and they had become friends. Lord Percy had gone on to Egypt, and de Boigne to his great relief ran into him in Cairo. In those days no one felt any embarrassment in asking a great man for a favour: indeed, it was regarded as the obligation placed on rank and wealth. Lord Percy was delighted to help this charming young French officer on his way to India, and introduced him to the British consul, lent him money and helped him obtain a passage in a ship from Suez. Most important, he provided him with letters of introduction: one to no less than Warren Hastings, the Governor of Bengal, and the other to the Town-Major of Fort St. George; 'Town-Majors' being then, of course, officers of some consequence, and not the petty administrators of our day. De Boigne then set off gratefully down the Red Sea in what his biographer calls a 'country boat', probably one of those big ocean-going dhows or 'booms' which until quite recent years used to sail from Aden to Bombay. It is disappointing that he left no description of his voyage, but unfortunately all the local and intimate details we would value so much were either omitted in contemporary accounts, or later suppressed or ignored as a result of Victorian prudery. All we know is that he finally arrived in Madras in the January of 1778, with a little money, clutching his two precious letters and full of hope.

In the imagination of eighteenth-century Europeans the East was a marvellous world, a compound of Marco Polo, the Arabian Nights and Il Seraglio. In India splendid and barbaric kings sat on thrones made of ivory and lapis lazuli over cellars full of pearls and diamonds, who went to war on elephants, and when they were killed their distraught queens threw their jewels to the poor and climbed on to their husband's pyres and burned themselves alive. Even Napoleon was seduced by this fantasy. 'I saw myself,' he admitted late in life, 'marching into India, riding on an elephant, wearing a turban, bearing my own version of the Koran, and exploiting for my own profit the theatre of all history....' India, alas, was not the theatre of all history but its *cul-de-sac*. Even Babur the Conqueror thought it a poor swap for Samarkand: the climate horrible, the people tiresome idolaters, no wine and not even any good melons. By the end of the century the empire of Babur and Akbar, 'The Great', was in ruins; grass and shrubs sprouted from the cracks in its monuments and palaces, the whole country was seedy and run-down, and cursed with an incessant and complicated civil war.

Nevertheless there was still life and movement in the ruin of the Empire of the Moghuls, and still some residual glamour in that vast and bizarre country. Although a thieving Persian King had stolen the Peacock Throne and the huge diamond called 'the Mountain of Light' there was still an Emperor in his palace in Delhi; tigers, bandits, Kings, Queens, elephants, castles, and naked fakirs who lay on nails or walked on fire. None of this, however, was visible from Madras. Life in an Indian 'station' or 'cantonment' in the twentieth century was bad enough, although the English had learned by then how to make the best of things with the club and healthy opium of exhaustion from sport and with frequent leave to the cool hills or to Europe. In those days it was excruciating. There was nothing to do except to make money, or talk about making it, quarrel, gossip, intrigue and drink to insensibility. To read the diary of William Hickey is to have a glimpse of hell. One cannot help feeling that the zest for combat shown by British soldiers in their eastern battles was simply joy at the relief from the appalling boredom of their lives. Clive was so wretched that he tried to kill himself. For de Boigne his Madras period was one of loneliness, disappointment and finally of frustration and despair. No one seemed at all elated by the arrival of a young foreigner, with or without letters to the right people, an odd accent and no money. No one offered to help him make a fortune. It required the capital he had not got, and also the dull grind at a desk or in the warehouse he had run away from Chambery to avoid. He was reduced to giving fencing lessons to earn a few rupees and finally he decided to turn mercenary once more.

The Company's army was not much concerned about nationality. Its white regiments contained every nationality in Europe, and at that moment any trained officer was welcome. The final battle with the French for India was beginning, with the Company against the French and their ally Haidar Ali of Mysore on land, and Admiral Hughes and the Royal Navy against the great Suffren and the French Navy at sea. De Boigne was able to obtain a lieutenant's commission in the Company's Sixth Native Infantry. He had arrived at the very moment for a man thirsting for military glory, but once again he seemed fated to miss all action. The Sixth were with Baillie's force when it was trapped and destroyed by Tipu, the ferocious son of Haidar Ali, but de Boigne was, luckily for him, on detached duty at the time escorting a supply column. He was then selected by the Governor to command his bodyguard, which was flattering as it was an appointment reserved for good officers equipped with the social graces, but a Governor's Bodyguard, splendid though it appears to be, is ornamental rather than militarily useful, and the worst risk it faced was a shower of rain. He occupied himself in military study of the most practical nature: he left Madras with a detailed knowledge of the British organisation and system of training and tactics which he was later to copy almost exactly. He also made himself agreeable and angled for promotion. He had his eye on the vacancy for the adjutancy of a battalion. It was not a very grand appointment, but it meant a little more money, a captaincy and possibly the way forward, as the adjutant was the trainer, the executive and the disciplinarian of a battalion. A successful adjutant meant a good battalion, and he could earn a grateful colonel's recommendation for a majority. He missed it through an indiscretion.

As Byron once remarked, the adultery curve tends to rise in the tropics. Every cantonment had its current flirtations and sometimes its current scandal, but even in that permissive age the army did not approve of tinkering with the wives of brother officers. It affected discipline and made for bad feeling in a regiment. Normally a discreet warning was enough but for some reason in de Boigne's case the stupid and clumsy device of a court-martial or a court of inquiry or of honour or something of that sort was decided upon. Of what de Boigne was actually suspected has been glossed over, except that it was something to do with an officer's wife (he 'took undue liberties' with her and as it would be out of character for him to have physically molested her against her will—although

Benoit de Boigne

Madhaji Sindia

one can never be sure in that climate—this means presumably he was enjoying a liaison). He was acquitted, but this was no solace to him.[1] He was furious that his private behaviour had been discussed publicly and pompously by a panel of officers—he might have understood a challenge to a duel—and even more angry when he learned that he was not being given the adjutancy in spite of his innocence. He resigned, for the third time. His friend the Governor advised him not to be so foolish, and to wait for things to blow over, but de Boigne was adamant. He was by then thirty-one, he had achieved nothing, and also he was feeling once more the itch to move. He decided he would attempt his overland journey again, this time from India to Europe, or to Russia. He obtained another letter recommending him to Warren Hastings from the Governor, and set off for Calcutta. By the August of 1783 he had reached Agra, in the heart of the sub-continent, equipped with money, letters of credit and travel documents signed by the Governor-General, and was ready to advance at last into his central Asian goal.

Even if de Boigne had never succeeded as a commander in the field he would still have been a truly remarkable man. He arrived in Calcutta an utterly undistinguished ex-lieutenant, no longer young, without money, without friends and equipped only with his boundless self-confidence and an introduction to a great man whom he had never set eyes on and who had no reason to be interested either in him or his plans. His projected journey offered no commercial prospects, and if it was a question of intelligence of central Asian affairs there were other and cheaper ways to obtain it, apart from the fact that the Company had its own political officers. Yet in a month or so he obtained the support of Warren Hastings, who fitted him out with letters requesting both the Company's residents and the native rulers along his route through India to give him assistance and he made friends who gave him shelter and who lent him money, or at least put him into the way of borrowing it. This was sufficient to carry him as far as the city of Lucknow, on the western limit of the British sphere of influence. There it was his intention to present his credentials to the Nawab-Wazir of Oudh, and to contact an influential man at his court, a French adventurer called Major-General Martine.[2]

If Martine's name is remembered at all it is because of the building of a convent school he gave the city called La Martinière, which was later a hotly contested strong point in the great siege of Lucknow in the Mutiny of 1857, and by his grotesque tomb; the corners guarded by the life-size effigies of four sepoys with their arms reversed and bearing the inscription: 'Claude Martine, arrived in India a common soldier, and died a Major-General; pray for his soul', which can still be seen in the city. He had never in fact commanded much more than a company, and his rank was an honorary one conferred on him by the Board of Directors of the Company for services rendered. Originally he had come to India in the ranks of the Bodyguard of the French Governor of Pondicherry, Lally. This fine body of men, recruited largely from criminals and debtors in France and disliking Lally's ideas of discipline, deserted *en bloc* to the British, and Martine with them. Martine suggested to his captors that in exchange for a commission he would raise a unit of renegade Frenchmen to fight for the Company. Happily this disreputable project failed when Martine's men mutinied in their turn, and were disbanded, but Martine stayed on to make himself useful to the Company in various ways and ended up with their blessing in command of the Nawab-Wazir of Oudh's forces. Militarily the Major-General had little to occupy him, but he was a shrewd and energetic fellow, and established himself as the Nawab's unofficial adviser, and also his banker and money-lender. He set up as a trader, and he also had a lucrative practice as an agent and a contact-man for European merchants dealing in Moghul India. De Boigne seems to have captivated him as he had everyone else—perhaps Martine, who had never really mastered English, was delighted to talk French again—and it is highly likely that it was he who was behind the rather odd transaction that followed.

The Nawab-Wazir of Oudh was still nominally the Moghul Governor of the province, but for the past twenty years he had been appointed at the behest of the British and enjoyed his salary as long as he behaved himself. He could really do little more for de Boigne than graciously permit him to pass through his territory, and if he had refused the British Resident would have contradicted him. To call on him was merely a polite formality. The Indian custom when making such a visit was for the visitor to offer a *nazzar*, a formal present, as according to the Indian code of manners it was discourteous to approach a great man for a petition or any other reason empty-handed: the poorest would bring a basket of fruit, or a few eggs. (This the later British often crudely confused with a bribe, which of course would be much more delicately offered.) In de Boigne's case all that would have been necessary would have been to offer a gold coin, which would be touched in token of acceptance and returned. An important visitor would offer a present consonant with his rank and receive something valuable in exchange; while a really distinguished one, such as the envoy of a rajah or a general after a victory, would be given a 'robe of honour', in the form of a gown of rich material worked with precious stones and gold thread.

The Nawab in his innocence had no notion that the handsome and dignified man before him was in fact a penniless adventurer. One of the difficulties Indians had in their dealings with the *'Feringhis'* was in telling one from another. Between themselves the status, caste, race and religion of each man could easily be distinguished by dress or by speech or by caste-mark, but the white men all looked alike and in the main were equally brash, equally offensive and equally ignorant of Indian language and custom. De Boigne, to the Nawab, seemed a superior sort of person, as indeed he was, and had a letter showing him to be the protégé of the Nawab-Wazir's paymaster and real master, the great Governor in Bengal. He invested de Boigne in a robe of honour and also arranged for him to have letters of credit on bankers in Kabul and Kandahar to the tune of no less than twelve thousand rupees, or about fifteen hundred pounds sterling at the value of those days. De Boigne promptly went to the bazaar and sold his khilut or robe for a large sum in cash. No one was particularly squeamish about money matters in those days, but there can be no doubt that the Nawab-Wazir had been the victim of a confidence trick, and that Martine, who probably took a percentage, assisted in it. It is significant that he remained de Boigne's banker and business partner for the rest of his career.[3]

De Boigne was now in funds, and was able to proceed to his next step which was characteristic of the thoroughness with which he set about everything that he did. He settled down in Lucknow for five months, thus avoiding the extreme heat and the heaviest of the monsoon rains, and studied the languages that would be most useful to him. The actual ones he does not mention, but an obvious choice would be Persian, the court language of the Moghuls and also of

Afghanistan, and which therefore would carry him to the borders of Turkey. Of the Indian languages Punjabi would be too local and Pashto too difficult; and we know that he never learned Rajasthani. (Later, when he was a general, he undertook a mission of some delicacy at a Rajput court, and in a rather hostile atmosphere he noticed an officer whispering in the Raja's ear, and the Raja shake his head. Afterwards he asked one of his staff what had been said. 'He was asking permission to draw his sword and kill you,' was the reply.) The next most and immediately useful language would have been Urdu, the *lingua franca* of the Moghul armies, closely cognate with the language of Hindustan which of course was Hindustani, but with a simple grammar and with many Arabic, Persian and Portuguese words and written in the same script as Persian. A *munshi* to teach both languages would be easily found in Lucknow, and these are the two he certainly learnt, and a priceless advantage they were to prove in the next year, but not for the reasons he expected then. Thus equipped financially and mentally, and having acquired servants, horses and baggage animals de Boigne set off on his next leg to Delhi and the imperial court.

If he had ever had his horoscope cast it would make interesting reading. All our lives have turning points and strokes of luck, but in de Boigne's it is uncanny how his every move which might have deflected him away from his destiny was blocked or deflected in some way so that he was returned to his correct path. His caravan turns back, a chance meeting with Lord Percy gives him an introduction to Warren Hastings, one chance prevents him from being killed in southern India, and another from becoming successful and remaining there. His next misfortune served to throw him into contact with the man who put his feet on the rungs of the ladder to fame and success.

When de Boigne reached Agra he found that the name of Warren Hastings was not as magical as it had been in Lucknow and that the Moghul officials were suspicious of him. To them an explorer was simply a spy. The Emperor would not see him, neither would the chief minister. De Boigne then thought of the British envoy, the 'political agent', accredited to the great Mahratta chieftain Madhaji Sindia whom, he heard, was at present in camp besieging the fortress of Gwalior. De Boigne was sure that Mr. Anderson would help him to obtain a *laisser-passer* from the Moghul authorities and set off to Gwalior to find him. On the way thieves held up the caravan with which he was travelling and rifled his bullock-cart, stealing all his baggage and his strong-box with his precious papers and bills of exchange.

De Boigne was now in a fix, adrift without money or passport, far from British help in a country torn by civil war and banditry. A less determined man might have made his way as best he could to Lucknow, where Martine would have given him asylum, and made a fresh start from there. At this point his good sense in learning the language paid off. He was not cut off from his fellow travellers in the caravan by having to speak through an interpreter and he was a man who made friends. Someone hinted to him that there was a purpose behind the robbery. The thieves were Madhaji Sindia's men. Madhaji had chosen this typically Mahratta way of finding out who the mysterious stranger was and what he was doing. De Boigne rode straight on to Madhaji Sindia's camp, determined to force him to restore his property. De Boigne was a shrewd and diplomatic man. He knew that in Asia dignity, calmness and patience coupled with the manifest intention of obtaining a reasonable object is as effective as a display of wrath, however justified. Like all strong-minded, self-confident men he assumed that it was the duty of everyone to help him; something that gives them uncanny powers of persuasion. It made a deep impression on the Mahratta chief. With Anderson's help he recovered all of his property except his precious papers. He was therefore stumped. He was worldly enough to realise that great men like Warren Hastings do not like being asked for favours twice. Nor could he and Martine hope to milk the Nawab-Wazir of Oudh a second time.

Go back he would not. His only remaining marketable commodity was his sword, so he resolved to become a mercenary for the third time. He had heard that the pickings in Hindustan—the name given to the part of India at whose centre is Agra and Delhi and is now called Uttar Pradesh—were good and that there were already several mercenary corps. The Rana of Gohad now owned Madec's former regiment, Ali Bahadur of Bundelkand had one, and he heard that the Raja of Jaipur was looking for a mercenary captain. De Boigne did not find it easy to obtain a post because he was ambitious. He wanted to command an army, not some ragged battalion, and he set a high price on his services. He nearly came to an agreement with the Raja of Jaipur, but the Raja withdrew. He ran into unexpected objections from the Company: Warren Hastings himself became suspicious of his motives. He had only agreed to help de Boigne cross India. It all looked hopeless when de Boigne's persistence was rewarded from an unexpected quarter. Madhaji Sindia sent for him and made him an offer.

Madhaji was a tough, rather dark, common little man with a rough manner, a limp, and no pretentions.[4] He liked to call himself the *patel*, the chairman of a village council, and in the democratic Mahratta tradition never adopted any rank or royal style. The limp dated from a wound at the battle of Panipat, where Ahmed Shah Durrani had smashed the combined Mahratta, Jat and Rajput armies, and he had ordered all the prisoners to be lined up and beheaded. 'Two pearls have been dissolved, twenty-seven gold coins lost, and silver and copper past counting,' ran the encoded letter that brought the terrible news to the Mahratta capital. Madhaji, then a man of twenty, was one of the few pearls which escaped. He had spent the years since slowly, but with great determination and political skill, building up the strength of the house of Sindia, to whose leadership he had succeeded. He had foresight beyond any other Indian of his day, and saw that disunited as India was it would fall to the British, who had already seized Bengal and Oudh, were wrestling with the French for the south, and were interfering everywhere. His life's aims were threefold: to unite the Mahrattas, to seize whatever remained of the Empire and to resist the British advance. He had already had a brush with their trained sepoys. As previously mentioned, three years before two or three thousand under a Major Popham had chased his troops out of Gohad and stormed in one night the fortress of Gwalior which he was at this moment so laboriously besieging, and a Colonel Goddard had handled his cavalry extremely roughly.

Madhaji was a good soldier and free from the innate conservatism from which good soldiers suffer. He saw that the swarms of Mahratta light horse, supremely adapted for raiding, could speedily occupy a country, but were themselves an ungovernable menace to their masters. They lived by plunder and had to be kept at war to be paid. The Mahratta conquests were hopelessly unstable. Madhaji saw what he required was an army like the British; disciplined, reliable, always in readiness and one that could hold and consolidate as well as conquer. He had observed that no one has ever prised anything loose the British had once gained. One of the qualities of great men is the ability to recognise great qualities in others. He saw that the tall and dignified *Feringhi* (European) who spoke Persian and Urdu correctly and politely was a man of very different character from the dim and seedy officers who hawked their swords around the Indian courts. He made de Boigne a businesslike offer. He was to raise, train and command a force of two strong battalions with artillery for which he would be allowed funds of eight rupees per man on the strength, and a personal salary of one thousand rupees a month. Everything would be left to him, the choice of men and officers, equipment and control of the finances. It was a princely offer, and de Boigne accepted at once. We do not know whether he had been finally seduced by his dreams of military glory, or whether at the time he merely intended to make enough money to start on his travels again.

In the event he remained in the service of Madhaji Sindia and his successor Daulat Rao Sindia for eleven years. He raised for him what came to be called the Army of Hindustan and led it in a series of victorious battles. He rose even higher than this to become Sindia's governor of Hindustan, that last remaining province of the Moghul Empire.

De Boigne was one of those rare men who do not require to serve an apprenticeship and who on reaching the heights spring into top gear as if all their lives had been spent in the habit of command. The nearest modern parallel to de Boigne is Wingate, who also was one minute a junior officer who had not commanded so much as a battery in his own Regiment, and then suddenly a Brigadier raising a small army. He, like de Boigne, was a man of unlimited energy and boundless self-confidence, but unlike de Boigne he was able to gather a group of brilliant men around him and had the help of a trained staff. De Boigne was entirely alone. The man with the nearest resemblance to a staff officer he was ever to have was the able Scotsman Sangster, who became in effect his chief ordnance officer and his virtual quartermaster-general. In an environment in which for anyone with access to stores or to public money it was the accepted thing to embezzle part of them, and in a climate which can grind down the most industrious and conscientious man, and eventually force him to choose between indolence or a breakdown, de Boigne had to be his own quarter-master, his own adjutant, his own accountant and his own drill-sergeant. His appetite for work was prodigious. He started in the cool hours of dawn, which was usual in India, and then toiled on through mid-day and the deadly afternoons far into the night, which was unheard of. He had first of all to fill his ranks, and this he did by promising each trained infantry sepoy five and a half rupees per month, which was as good as the Company's pay; and, what was more, he saw that each man had it and that none of it stuck to the fingers of others.

It was the habitual practice in India to defraud the men or pay them in long arrears so that they were usually in a state of mutiny or on the point of mutiny. Even the Company's troops were not free from it. (The Mutiny, although of course it had deep political and national roots, was caused in part by the Company's meanness over allowances; and the smaller but almost fatal mutiny before the crucial battle of Buxar in 1764, by its actual dishonesty.) It is a remarkable tribute to de Boigne's administration that the Army of Hindustan never once mutinied. The basic soldier's pay having been settled and with his total strength on establishment fixed at seventeen hundred, there remained left four thousand two hundred and fifty rupees a month to pay the European officers, the *sirdars*, or Indian officers, and the European gunners a high enough salary to attract the best. There were very few Europeans; a captain to command each battalion with a second in command, and a sergeant-major to command the artillery company which was part of the battalion, and a European, in charge of each gun. Judging by his later pay scales, which seem to have been based on service and ability rather than the appointment, the captains may have received four hundred rupees a month, the equivalent of twenty pounds sterling at the value of those days and an enormous sum; but it must be remembered that the life was hard, dangerous and probably short. It is worth noting that the battalion accountant, an Indian, was paid sixty; the same as the artillery sergeant-major and nearly double the senior Indian officer, or Subahdar. There was no shortage of excellent Indian officers or of good recruits for the ranks but clearly an honest accountant was worth his hire.

Benoit de Boigne

For senior European officers he won over Sangster, who was at
that time commanding Madec's old corps in Gohad, who was able
to take off his shoulders all the details of equipping the force; and
for battalion commanders he engaged Hessing, a tough old Dutch
mercenary; and Frémont, a Frenchman of Royalist sympathies who
had left his own army after the Revolution. With these three, and
his Indian accountants and 'writers' he set to work to recruit, to
draw up rolls and pay-lists, to allot men to companies and battalions,
to engage tailors for the uniforms and to issue them, and to begin the
detailed work of buying and issuing arms and equipment. Later,
Sangster, who was a trained gun-founder and manufacturer and an
excellent organiser, set up factories and arsenals for the Army of
Hindustan: but for the moment everything had to be bought and
carefully inspected—muskets, bayonets, cannon, camels, bullocks,
carts, cymbals, drums, fifes, tools for carpenters, blacksmiths and
armourers, harness, good quality gunpowder, shot, shell for the
howitzers, and man-killing grape-shot.

While this was going forward the business of training began,
first by squads, and then by platoons and companies and finally by
battalions. De Boigne, we know, favoured the British organisation,
and the details of the establishments and their tables of equipment
and pay for his later brigades survive, but about this early brigade,
the nucleus of the later army, we are less sure. It is said to have
consisted of two battalions each of eight hundred and fifty men plus
artillery. This is nearly double the size of contemporary British
battalions, which were designed to be small and flexible. However,
at Lalsot, as will be seen later, de Boigne formed one large square
and was able to put all his guns inside; and calculations based on this
point to the larger battalion. It is possible, of course, that the force
consisted of two British type battalions each about five hundred
strong, and two batteries of five guns (as in the Army of Hindustan)
of about one hundred and forty men, and that the balance of two
hundred odd men were taken up in barrack duties, recruit squads,
baggage guards and so on, but this is all conjecture. We cannot be
certain until the formation of de Boigne's famous First Brigade of
the Army of Hindustan proper in 1790, whose establishments,
tables of equipment and pay scales are exactly known. What is
certain is his system of manoeuvre and his tactics, which he took
straight out of the British manual.[5]

The infantry were primarily pike-men. Although the volleys of disciplined musketeers could be formidable, especially from the British regulars, the main source of fire-power was short-range artillery using grape or case. The decisive weapon was the bayonet, especially in the assault. Often in the old accounts of actions occurs some such phrase as; 'Our brave fellows never took their fire-locks from their shoulders until they reached the entrenchments, and then giving one huzza they charged home with the bayonet.' The point was that to pause in the attack to fire, and then go through the elaborate business of reloading, simply exposed the attackers to the fire of the defence. It also took the momentum out of the attack and it might be difficult to persuade the men to advance again. All drill and discipline were directed towards flexibility in manoeuvring, a rock-like immobility in defence and an unwavering advance in the assault. The basic formation was in four lines. The first three were the firing and fighting lines; one pace between ranks and twenty-one inches for each man in the rank. This made a solid wall of men presenting a hedge of a triple row of bayonets. Firing was by platoon volleys, a platoon being about thirty men; or by 'files', the front, middle and rear rank man in each file loading by turns and keeping up a rolling fire. The fourth rank stood three paces farther back. If there were spare men available they stood in this rearward rank, ready to take the place of men who fell, for no gap must ever be allowed to appear; and also there stood all the non-commissioned officers. The essential use of the fourth rank, as Dundas' manual bluntly explains, was to keep the attacking ranks closed up, and prevent any attempt to break towards the rear. We nowadays tend to dwell on the horrors of modern war, but the modern soldier is positively encouraged to scatter or lie down to avoid fire. Our forebears were not even allowed to move out of the path of the clearly visible round-shot, and had to stand absolutely motionless, except in obedience to a sharp command to close up into the gaps of the fallen, splashed with the blood and brains of their neighbours and listening to the shrieks of those cut in half or dismembered by shot. (The extreme 'steadiness on parade' demanded by modern drill sergeants, even forbidding the eyes to move in the head, is the legacy of the psychological conditioning for an obsolete type of combat, which has survived well into the twentieth century.) It was recognised that there was a danger of the men breaking, and the

N.C.O.'s (not enough allowed on the British establishments, complains Dundas) were there to keep the men in place with a sharp word or even a poke from a sword or bayonet.

Manoeuvre was simple in theory; it was rather more perplexing on broken ground, under fire, in clouds of smoke and with hostile cavalry hanging about waiting to catch a commander changing from one formation to another. A battalion consisted of eight companies each of two platoons of two sub-divisions; one of these companies being the light, or skirmishing and scouting company, and the other the grenadier, or special assault company of tall and especially brave men. On the march the battalion moved in column of sub-divisions, six or seven men abreast. When musketry fire was needed the battalion was drawn out in its long line of four ranks, and to change to column the companies or sometimes the 'grand divisions', or pairs of companies, would on the order swing to the right or left pivoting on one end like gates. Movement on the battlefield was in 'open column', the distances being so exactly maintained that the 'gates' could swing back to form a line facing to either flank; or, a more difficult manoeuvre, the rear companies would range up alongside the leading one and form a line to the front. The usual formation for the attack was the line, from which volleys of musketry from the whole battalion would be followed by a charge. If the front was narrow, or when attacking a gap, the attack would be made in column, the companies closed up so that a solid block of men hit the enemy position, cheering and stabbing, with the rear companies going on over the front ones as they fell. The flanks and rear of these rigid lines of robot-like men were extremely vulnerable and to be caught defenceless from those directions was an absolute disaster. Accordingly, if threatened by cavalry, which was invariably the case in Indian warfare, squares were formed, so presenting an unbroken front in every direction. These were not the little battalion-size squares familiar to us from pictures of the Battle of Waterloo, but large, irregular rectangles of infantry, sometimes of brigade size and sometimes, as at Buxar, of the whole army.

De Boigne's artillery was not in a separate corps, but part and parcel of the battalions, although later the Army of Hindustan had its separate siege train of heavier, battering guns. Its main component was of three-pounder and six-pounder guns each drawn by eight bullocks or sometimes by the gun coolies called *kelasis* using drag-ropes. A *golandauz*, or gunner proper, was paid from six to eight rupees, a kelasi four and a half to eight. Caste entered into it. Neither the infantry sepoys nor the gunners proper would willingly pull the guns, which made matters awkward if the gun-bullocks or kelasis were killed, or if the kelasis ran away, which sometimes happened. Moving as they did at walking pace it was impossible to mass the guns rapidly at a decisive point. Accordingly in the defence they were scattered along the line; as one tactical authority put it, 'the infantry form the curtain wall, the guns the bastions'. In the attack they went forward with the battalions to drop into action and bombard the defenders at close range. Each artillery company or, in modern terms, battery, was of four guns and a light howitzer to fire shells in a high curve to drop into trenches or behind walls. (They could also fire case shot in close action.) Its establishment included an ammunition wagon for each gun, drivers, wheelwrights, carpenters and smiths and a platoon of sappers to make gun platforms and emplacements.

Gunners and infantry alike had to be drilled and drilled again, until however tired or terrified they were they performed their specific movement exactly and automatically. In European armies the effect of drills was fortified by the drill-sergeant's cane, and by flogging inattentive soldiers senseless. This would not do in India. Indian soldiers could accept punishment, if it was deserved and sufficiently dramatic. When Munro of the Company's army was faced with a mutiny in Oudh he had the men tried by a court-martial of his Indian officers who sentenced the ring leaders to be blown from muzzles of guns, a death terrible in this world and damning for both religions in the next. The grenadier company of the guilty battalion demanded to die first, as it was also their privilege in battle. This was one thing, but cursing or kicking or beating were quite another, apart from which the sergeant or subaltern who struck a Pathan or a Rajput was unlikely to survive to do it a second time. (In a much later war a foolish British officer unfamiliar with Indian troops kicked a sepoy who appeared to hesitate to obey an order. The man instantly, and some would say rightly, bayoneted him.) Honour, or *izzat*, which meant little or nothing to some European goal-bird or some ploughboy dragged into the ranks and grossly misused was the mainspring of these warriors, who were soldiers both by tradition and caste. Sepoys could only be managed by respecting their izzat, by personal example, discipline that was manifestly just and by close attention to the customs, religion and prejudices of each man. It was not easy for Europeans and mistakes could be made. (In 1916, for instance, the vastly experienced British-Indian army gave orders for a regiment of Baluchis, many of whom were recruited from a heretical Muslim sect for whom the soil of Iraq was peculiarly sacred, to go to Mesopotamia which completely upset them. A Pathan company, always touchy, murdered their officers for some imagined slight in 1936.) De Boigne recruited the bulk of his troops from the area between the Jumna and the Ganges called the Doab, from Oudh and Rohilkand, with a sprinkling of Rajputs and Afghans. It was an explosive mixture, as the Company was to find in 1857. The greatest tribute to de Boigne is that their morale and discipline never failed and was maintained long after he had gone.

These labours occupied de Boigne for most of the year 1784. Then in October of that year Madhaji Sindia ordered him to bring his brigade into the field. It had always been his ambition to gain political control of the rump of the Empire, which was roughly coincident with Hindustan, through the person of the Emperor, Shah Alam II. That poor man was at the moment prisoner of his quarrelling *amirs*, or nobles, and was driven to distraction. Two of his *wazirs*—chief ministers—had been murdered by them one after another. He appealed to Madhaji to intervene. This is what he had been waiting for, and with his army of irregular Mahratta horsemen and his new brigade of regular infantry under de Boigne he crossed the Chambal river which marked the northern boundary of his own territory and marched to Agra to meet the Emperor.

3   De Boigne's First Campaign

MADHAJI SINDIA'S advance on Delhi in answer to the fugitive Emperor's appeal was a step in an ambitious and, indeed, a noble plan. Madhaji was no ordinary man. He was a Mahratta, with all the characteristics of that energetic race, but unlike his fellows he was not obsessed with intrigue for intrigue's sake, or the acquisition of power and money because of sheer cupidity. To de Boigne he was the most generous and loyal of masters, and his rise to fame was due to Madhaji's confidence in him and the part he was to play in furthering his ambitions. The two men were interdependent: one could not have succeeded without the other. This is therefore a convenient moment to leave de Boigne and his uniformed columns marching north in company with the disorderly squadrons of Mahratta irregular horse and look briefly at the political scene as it appeared in Moghul India in 1784, and to consider what Madhaji's intentions really were.[1]

The Empire had in fact ceased to exist. Its condition resembled Byzantium in the last years of the Paleologues. There was an Emperor, a palace, and a capital; but the area under imperial control was a fluctuating one, sometimes as big as Yorkshire, sometimes no larger than the suburbs of Delhi. All the great provinces had fallen away. The Punjab was in anarchy. The British were in control of all Bengal and Oudh, and were wresting control of the Carnatic and of Mysore from the French and Haidar Ali. The great Subahdar of the Deccan—the Viceroy of the South—had broken away and his children, adopting his style of Nizam-ul-Mulk, sat as kings in Hyderabad. All central India was ruled, or infested, by the Mahrattas, who under their peculiar constitution had divided up the spoils of Shivaji as follows. The house of Sindia, of which Madhaji was an illegitimate scion, held Gwalior and Ujjain; the Bhonslas, Berar and Nagpur; the Holkars, Indore; and the 'Gaekwar', Baroda. None had yet arrogated to himself the style of Rajah or Maharajah. Madhaji himself was nicknamed 'the old Patel', and 'gaekwar' is another nickname meaning 'the cowherd'. They had in the past set up in Poona, Shivaji's old capital, a Prime

34

Minister for their Confederation to whom they all agreed to defer, called the 'Peshwa', but by some curious Indian alchemy this office had become hereditary, and he was now almost as powerless as a constitutional monarch. At this time the Peshwa, a young man, was a puppet in the hands of, so to speak, a prime minister's prime minister, at that time the able Nana Farnavis. Nana Farnavis was no friend of Madhaji's, and neither was the reigning Holkar, Tukaji. It must always be borne in mind, and this was the Mahratta tragedy, that all these great chiefs and the robber barons, like Appa Khandi Rao, who followed them were as mutually dangerous and as ready to devour one another as a knot of snakes in a basket.

All that remained of the Empire was the vague loyalty of Rajputana, whose chiefs still looked towards Delhi; and the Subah, or Viceroyalty, of Hindustan, which was bounded roughly by the northward bend of the Ganges in the east, Hariana in the west, the Chambal in the south and the Sutlej in the north-east. It too was in anarchy, with the great amirs of the court in a sort of perpetual Asian version of the Wars of the Roses, fighting each other for its spoils; for in spite of all the troubles there was still trade, and the groaning peasants—the ryats—still tilled the rich soil. 'If the rains come', runs the Hindustani proverb, 'and the tax-gatherer stays away, who cares who the hell reigns in Delhi?' The Jumna 'Doab'—the area between the Jumna and the Ganges: it means 'Two Waters'—was especially rich and worth many lacs of rupees in revenue. Apart from the fact, therefore, that Hindustan and in particular the quadrilateral of Agra, Aligarh, Meerut and Delhi is the strategic centre of India, the possession of Hindustan was not to be despised.

There was another and even more powerful factor. The Emperor in terms of political power was a cipher: a poor studious man in his sixties, often a prisoner in his palace, dragged from pillar to post by whoever constituted the ruling junta among the amirs, and who had only been thrust on to the throne when Alamgir II had been murdered in a palace revolution many years before. (Except that he was by no means so simple, the nearest English equivalent to Shah Alam II is our King Henry VI.) He had however *charisma*, in the exact sense of that overworked word: by virtue of his office he had grace. The Indians, apart from being among the most sensible of peoples, had, like all who have lived for long periods in a time of troubles, a great respect for order and authority. This was personified by the Emperor: he was the 'Jehangi-Lat-Saheb'—the Victorious War Lord; 'Khudawund'—the Born of Heaven; or, in the humbler speech of the people, 'Mabap'—their Father-Mother. In the eyes of both religions there still resided in him some of the magic of the wise and illustrious Akbar, who had Hindu as well as Muslim generals, Brahmins for counsellors and took Rajput princesses into his harem. This feeling was still so strong among the people that all rule was by the virtue of the Emperor's authority and he alone could legally appoint or dispossess. Even the British made a point of arranging for their puppet Nawabs to be approved of by the Emperor. Indian politics, therefore, was like chess, which after all is an Indian game, and he who held the king was the winner.

For an outsider—a Hindu and a Mahratta—this was politically difficult and dangerous. It would indeed be fascinating to know for certain how Madhaji Sindia saw the problem and what were his plans. Unfortunately Madhaji's thoughts remain a secret. He made no speeches, wrote no memoirs and said little to anyone. Mahrattas used to boast in a self-deprecating way of their cunning and treachery and lack of candour. Madhaji, a Mahratta peasant at heart and proud of the fact, had his share of these characteristics. His objectives have to be inferred from his actions. He wished first of all to unite the Mahrattas and believed that this could best be done by preserving the office of Peshwa. The power and leadership would be that of Sindia, but he was always at pains to show himself the Peshwa's subordinate, vesting him ceremonially in the delegated authority he, Madhaji, would in reality exercise. After he had gained his object he carefully preserved the fiction that it was the Peshwa not he who was the Imperial Regent. At the same time he had to wrest control of the Emperor's person from the amirs, the great Moghul nobles, who were usually fighting among themselves for the privilege. Were he successful he would control with the Imperial and Peshwa's blessing the strong central part of all India and eventually perhaps the Deccan. He did not wish, at least not then, to arouse or to challenge the British, but with the rump of the Empire as base their encroachments could be arrested. Two things he had to have: a reliable army and a source of regular revenue.

He already had the basis of a regular army in de Boigne's corps of regular infantry, too small to be decisive, but it was all he could

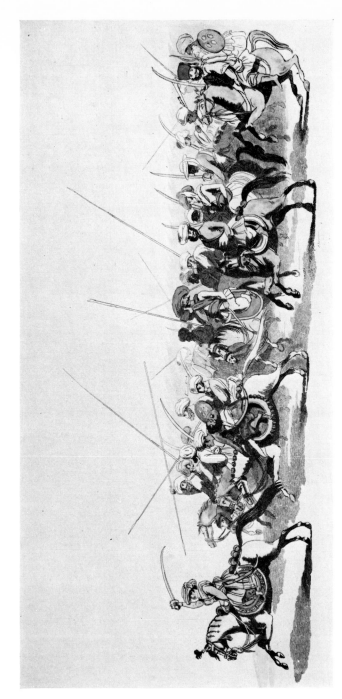

Mahratta irregular cavalry on the march

A Najib, armed with a matchlock

A regular sepoy of the East India Company's army, late eighteenth century: the model for de Boigne's infantry

De Boigne's First Campaign

afford for the moment. The Mahratta fiscal system was chaotic. It was only a form of blackmail by which a quarter of the declared revenue—the chauth—was paid over under the threat of pillage and massacre. Madhaji was anxious to lay his hands on the lush provinces of Hindustan to provide the financial backing for his army and his plans generally. Next, he had to introduce himself somehow into Imperial affairs until he could work himself into a commanding position and become the *de facto* ruler of Hindustan and strong enough to defy his rivals. All this was surrounded by political difficulties through which Madhaji threaded his way with great skill. Having met the British once or twice he determined to avoid at all costs any conflict with them, and also the temptation to take advantage of their involvement in the far south with the French. He had to keep his fellow chiefs off his back, and to avoid giving the impression that he was becoming too big for his boots. He resolutely refused, therefore, the offices and honorific titles the Emperor Shah Alam II pressed on him on his arrival. Shah Alam wanted to appoint him *Amir-ul-Umara*, or Chief of the Nobles. This he declined. He planned to divide and rule among the amirs, and had no intention of becoming, metaphorically speaking, Lord Chancellor to a House of Lords prepared, if given half a chance, to drag him from the Woolsack and assassinate him. He accepted on behalf of his suzerain the Peshwa the title of *Vakil-ul-Mutluq*; freely, the 'Imperial Legate'. (A *vakil*, means 'pleader' or 'envoy'.) He had also, and this was a delicate business, to reward his rapacious generals so as to keep their loyalty; and this meant the presentation of jaghirs for them to fleece which could only be taken from the Moghul nobles he had put down to restore the Emperor to his palace in Delhi and to safety. This proved too difficult, and was what led to his initial reverse and to de Boigne's first essay in command.

Madhaji met the Emperor at Agra in the October of 1784, and after some bloodless manoeuvres restored him to his throne in January 1785. For the next two years he managed affairs with adroitness, avoiding trouble and managing to place two of his men as garrison commanders in the fortresses at Aligarh and Agra. He then overreached himself.

He suspected the Rajput rulers of Jodhpur and of Jaipur were in communication with the disaffected Amirs. There was a special

4   37

relationship between the great Rajput princes and the Moghul emperors. Their territories were surviving fragments of the ancient Hindu civilisation broken up by the Muslim conquerors. The word Rajput applies equally to caste and race. The Rajputs of Rajasthan, or Rajputana, were both Rajputs by caste, and were also Rajputs by race and language. For them courage and loyalty were the highest virtues. After their defeat the wise Emperor Akbar who tolerated Hinduism and wished to attach the best non-Muslim soldiers in India to his throne favoured them, employed Rajputs as generals and took a Rajput princess into his harem. Their princes paid tribute to the Moghuls and continued to rule their lands. They remained loyal to the Moghul emperors even after the anti-Hindu follies of Aurungzeb and the later decay of Imperial rule, for they had 'eaten the Emperor's salt', as the saying went. The Rajputs despised the Mahrattas, for all their Hinduism, because of their pretensions to Rajput caste, and they hated them because they had suffered in the past from their raids and rapacity. In the politics of Hindustan, therefore, the Rajputs were always ready to combine with the Moghuls against the Mahrattas, whom the Rajputs saw as usurpers of the Imperial power. To pay the Imperial tribute to the low-born bastard who was the hereditary slipper-bearer of the Peshwa was intolerable. This was felt most keenly in Jaipur and in Jodhpur, or Marwar, where the great fighting clan of Rathors lived.

Allied with the Amirs these princes could be very dangerous to Madhaji. His first move therefore was in his capacity as the Imperial Vakil to call on them for unpaid tribute owing to Delhi. This was not a mere fiscal measure: it was a political move demanding that they should acknowledge the authority of Delhi and Madhaji's right to exercise it. Then without waiting for an answer he mobilised and marched down into Rajputana. His army was in three contingents. He had with him the usual mass of irregular light horse, de Boigne's brigade, and a strong force of cavalry, infantry of all sorts and guns from the Imperial levies led by two Muslim nobles, Mohammed Beg Hamadani and his nephew Ismael Beg. Ismael Beg was, after his uncle, one of the most powerful and successful of the Moghul amirs. He was a brave and determined man and a bold leader of cavalry; one of the last of the old school of Moghuls and more like a Turk than a Hindustani. Had Madhaji not intervened it might have been he who held the Emperor and ruled the Empire. When Madhaji ordered him and his squadrons into the field against the Rajputs Ismael Beg felt that he was ranged on the wrong side and decided to remedy this when opportunity offered. He found the army of the two Rajput chiefs drawn up to meet him near a small town called Lalsot.

The affair at Lalsot is worth describing in detail, because apart from being the debut of de Boigne it is an excellent example of the warfare of Moghul India and of the impact of European troops on their unreformed armies: much more so than St. Thomè, because the soldiers of northern India were far more formidable than the feeble troopers of Maphuz Khan. Moghul generals, however, did not believe in fighting for fighting's sake. Both Liddell Hart and Sun-Tzu would have found much to approve of in their strategy, for they were believers in deception and the indirect approach, and never saw any profit in storming a fort if they could bribe the *kiladar*, or seneschal. Madhaji first realised that he had been outwitted when the two Begs followed by all the Moghul cavalry rode straight across the plain to where Jaipur and Jodhpur were waiting and amid loud cheers wheeled about and took up a position extending the Rajput line. At this sight the Moghul infantry became unsteady and there was a great deal of confusion and shouting among their leaders. Madhaji saw that the longer he hesitated the less likely they were to fight, and immediately ordered the whole line to advance, which it did until within cannon-shot where it halted to open the conventional preliminary bombardment. At this point Madhaji nearly won by a fluke. A lucky shot killed Mohammed Beg and, as so often happened in Indian warfare, the death of a leader was interpreted as a bad omen. The Moghul horse with cries of dismay began to turn the heads of their horses and to ride off the field. Ismael, however, rallied them; and with great judgment charged the Mahratta wing on the right and driving them without trouble from the field rode after them like Prince Rupert with such dash and so far that when he returned the battle was over. The Moghul infantry and artillery, although not under attack, prudently withdrew to a safe distance.

De Boigne had been posted on the extreme left, and was now left standing with his little cluster of red-coated sepoys alone on the plain. To a soldier of his upbringing, to withdraw, to turn his

back on an enemy, was ignoble; and moreover, he had had no order
to do so. Facing him was a mass of cavalry, all yellow like a field of
mustard, whom he presumed were the *jerd kopre wale* or the *pela
kopre wale*, the 'Yellow Jackets': men of the great fighting clan of
Rathor wearing the garb of death: yellow being the colour of both
mourning and of royalty. De Boigne was looking at a spectacle few
Europeans had ever seen and one which was soon never to be seen
again: the chivalry of ancient India emerging from their native
deserts, incredibly handsome men, descended, so they believed,
from the Sun and the Moon; of a caste so strict that they could not
sit at table with even the kings of another people; plumed, helmeted,
glittering in mail and their chiefs hung with jewellery like women.
He did not waste much time in admiring them, however. He
estimated there were ten thousand in front of him, and while
Madhaji was trying to infuse some spirit into the Imperial infantry
behind him he formed a hollow square. Knowing the bald sequence
of events and that he had trained his battalions strictly according
to the British manual we can reconstruct the picture of his first
battle with some accuracy.

He had a total establishment of 1700 men according to his contract. By the ordinary course of military events some of these must
have been guarding his baggage, some absorbed in headquarters,
some of the reserves and the non-commissioned officers who stood
in the fourth or reserve line, and possibly some 100 per battalion
may have been taken up in the two artillery companies, or batteries
as we would now call them, say altogether 400. This would leave
1300 bayonets, if the battalions were up to strength and the light
and grenadier companies stood in the line, or roughly 320 men, of
three ranks of 106, in each face. At twenty-one inches to a file this
gave a frontage of about sixty yards. This at close gun-intervals—
six yards—would just accommodate the guns (we can assume that
he had left his howitzers somewhere in the rear, keeping eight guns
with him). A variation of these figures one way or another does not
make a great deal of difference. What the Rathor leaders looked at
was a ridiculous little clump of infantry standing alone in the vast
brown plain. It would have fitted on to one half of a full-sized
Rugby football ground. They were puzzled at first, hesitated, and
then finally decided to charge it. In all probability they did not
think there would be much resistance so they did not perhaps ride

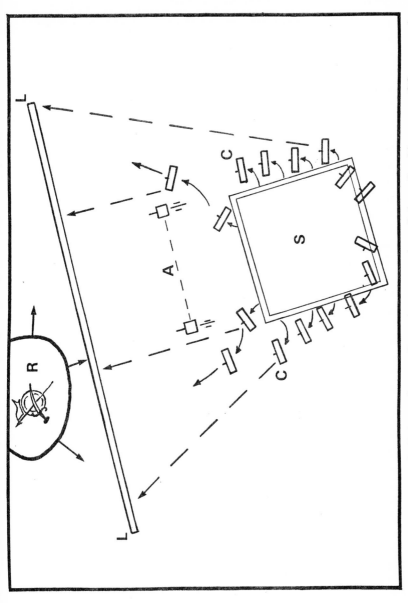

A daring manoeuvre: de Boigne changes formation to attack at Lalsot. S, old square; CC, companies breaking into column; A, artillery; LL, new line; R, Rathor Cavalry

in with their usual suicidal elan and their discomfiture was correspondingly greater.

The inside of the square of course would be crowded. As well as the guns which de Boigne held behind the front face, there were the kelasis who had dragged them into action (possibly even the gun-bullocks), the *sais*'s or horse holders, the runners, the assistant surgeons, a water-carrier with his full goat-skin for each company, the corps of drums, and the reserves. All the officers, Indian and European, except de Boigne, stood in the fighting line on the right of their respective commands. De Boigne himself sat alone on his horse in the centre looking out over the hedge of bayonets. When he saw the Rathors preparing to charge he gave an order to the front face; which turned sharply, wheeled by subdivisions, fell back through the gun-intervals and reformed in the rear of the gun-line. This 'unmasked' the eight six-pounders, which were now free to fire to their front, the 'detachments' standing smartly to attention around them, and the European gunner in command of each with his match burning ready. It must be understood that this and all the subsequent movements described had to be performed with the utmost precision. At the slightest sign of muddle, or of a gap appearing in the ranks, an experienced enemy would dash into it, hacking and hewing at the infantry's backs, or even simply knocking them down with the shoulders of their horses in rows like ninepins. By this movement de Boigne had converted his square into a redoubt with the walls made of men instead of earth. In the British system the gunners were trained to fire rather slowly, a round every twenty seconds, so that the drill would be followed carefully and each round truly laid, and against a cavalry charge coming in from two miles off they hoped to fire two of shot, two of grape (that is if they had iron guns: the iron grape-shot tore out the bore of brass guns) and finally two or as many of the deadly case-shot as they could get off at point-blank. The moment the charge started the eight guns went off in a single crashing salvo, and from then on the salvos became more ragged as each detachment fell into its own rhythm of 'run up, sponge, load, ram, lay and fire'.

Eighteenth-century warfare was, of course, quite horrible. Modern soldiers are at least allowed to scatter to avoid fire and to take cover and to lie down, but in those days the flying lumps of metal simply pounded into packed, solid flesh. The final discharges of case can only be compared to firing six giant shot-guns into a crowd, or, in this case, into the field of the Grand National. The Rathors had never known gunnery like this, and they and their horses were butchered. They were not, however, the feeble troopers of poor Maphuz Khan of forty-one years before. They fought their way into the battery, wounded or dying, mounted or on foot, slashing away with their curved, razor-sharp sabres, the gunners defending themselves with handspike and rammer; and their infantry supports closing up to them with the bayonet: 'sticking to their guns' in the literal meaning of the familiar phrase.

In a few minutes it was impossible to see across the square for dust and powder-smoke. Everyone was shouting, the wounded and the horses screaming, and above all the wild yells of the Rathor war-cry: *'Jai Kali! Jai Bhowani!'*—'Victory to the Goddess of Death!' The most trying experience was for the men in the rear and unattacked face; forbidden to look round, and knowing that if their comrades did not stand firm the first inkling of it would be being knocked flat and trampled by a horse or a jab in the back from a lance-point. It was a relief, therefore, when the rest of the attackers lapped round the square, to be met first with smashing volleys from three hundred muskets at close range, and then the steel; the kneeling front-rank man with his butt on the ground, the crouching second-rank man at the 'on guard' position, and the standing rear-rank man holding his musket overhand, butt up, point down and jabbing at the attackers fixed by his comrades' points. The great tactical disadvantage cavalry suffer from is having to fight on horse-back. Horses are fragile and nervous, they will not face a *cheveux-de-frise* of steel points, and when they lose their riders they gallop about in panic, usually for home, breaking up the orderly ranks of the following squadrons. Soon, in a matter of minutes, between loose horses and the storm of fire, the Rathors had been driven off.

When the dust had settled and the clouds of white smoke had floated upwards in the hot Indian air, de Boigne took a view of the battlefield. His own square was intact, and except among the gunners he had suffered very few casualties. The path of the Rathor charge was marked by piles of dead men and horses to mark each salvo, culminating in an absolute rampart where the final burst of case had gone off in their faces at twenty yards. The plain was covered with loose horses and with dismounted or wounded men limping back. The leaders, however, were undaunted. They were holding up their swords and calling for their followers to rally again and form the ghol, the dense circle of horses jammed solidly together, and to make another attempt. De Boigne now took the step which distinguishes the true general from what Montgomery calls 'un bon chef ordinaire'. He had taken the measure of the Rajputs, and he had also finally tried the temper of the weapon he had created; but he was unsupported, and if he had to endure a long series of charges he would run out of ammunition and be inevitably ground down. He decided to attack, and to risk breaking his square.

First of all he had to 'take ground' to clear his front, and then, deploying as he went, marched up to within musket shot of the assembling Rathor cavalry. The guns were swung round and limbered up, and the sweating kelasis applied themselves to the drag ropes. The rear face of the square turned about, the companies in the left and right faces pivoted round until they were in open column. Then, to the steady beat of the side-drums and the hoarse barks of the non-commissioned officers warning men to keep in line and keep closed up, with measured step and shouldered arms, the brigade advanced on the astonished Rathors, who had never heard of infantry behaving like this.

As they watched, the approaching block of men appeared slowly to sprout wings, as the brigade began a most delicate and dangerous manoeuvre during the course of which it would for a few minutes be entirely vulnerable. The front face opened to form a flank to the batteries, and the companies inclining outwards marched up to 'form' on the left and the right: it will be seen that the rearmost had a long way to go and that the timing of the manoeuvre depended on them. Eventually de Boigne had his men drawn out in a long line, over three hundred yards, absolutely vulnerable to a determined push from the front, and even more so to anyone who had the presence of mind to ride at a flank. Before, however, the Rathor chiefs could divine what was happening, the whole line burst into flame, the guns once more with grape and case and the infantry with controlled, unhurried volleys by platoons, pausing from time to time to let the smoke clear and the target reappear again.

Flesh and blood could not stand it and in a few minutes the Rathors broke and fled for good.[2]

The scene was now an unusual one even for a battle of that period. Three of the major contestants had left the field. On one side the remainder of the Jodhpur and Jaipur forces wavered, and on the other the Imperial infantry stood sullen and inactive. De Boigne with his handful of sepoys stood triumphant and in possession of the ground. All that was now required was for the rest of Madhaji's army to advance, and the day was his, but they remained deaf to every order and appeal. De Boigne with great indignation was eventually forced to withdraw, and the battle was over. He spent an uneasy night at Lalsot with Madhaji while the cavalry filtered back from their 'battle of spurs' and Ismael's Moghul horse rejoined the enemy. Two days later the Imperial infantry, having had time to think matters over and, of course, listen to the blandishments of messengers from the other side, with insulting cries, with drums beating and colours flying marched off to join Ismael Beg. De Boigne was so angry that he asked for permission to charge them, but tough old Madhaji had lost heart. He realised that he had been a fool to rely on Ismael Beg, and also he was now far from home and in great danger. He decided to retreat. It took him eight days to reach Alwar, seventy miles to the north, pursued all the way by Ismael Beg. He then took stock of the situation, and saw he could not mend it with only de Boigne's men and his useless irregular cavalry, and very wisely took himself off to his own territory; where he patiently started to build up a force strong enough to make him independent of the unreliable Imperial troops.

The most obvious step was the one he did not take. De Boigne's brigade had proved successful beyond all his expectations. Before his Hindustan expedition it had behaved efficiently at some minor siege operations under one of his subsidiary chiefs called Appa Khandi Rao, and at Lalsot it had distinguished itself and demonstrated only too clearly how the handfuls of the Feringhi troops had enabled their accursed masters to steal a third of India. The retreat had proved the value of disciplined troops even more completely. For eight days it was de Boigne, not the cavalry, whose proper task it was, who held off Ismael Beg. Madhaji's best course was to expand this force, but this was the one thing he refused to do, in spite of de Boigne's earnest and repeated arguments. De Boigne had always been perfectly clear about this. It was not just a few reliable battalions who would turn the day: what was wanted was a reform of the whole system. When he had first entered the market as a mercenary he wanted a contract for five battalions, and had only agreed to Madhaji's terms because he needed the employment. Madhaji's refusal was based on the attention he had to pay to his own generals, who were firmly attached to their guerrilla system of warfare, and here in fact history may well prove them to have been right. Old Gopal Rao Bhao, arguing with Sindia's heir, wanted him to beware of the regular infantry and guns of which he was so proud, for they would be his downfall. 'We first,' he said, 'made our houses on the backs of horses, then in tents, now you are putting your soldiers into barracks build of mud. Take care they don't melt back into mud.'

Warren Hastings, allaying the fears felt in Calcutta about the Mahratta armies, oddly enough said much the same thing. 'The danger . . . in the progress the Mahrattas are making in the art of casting cannon, in the art and practice of artillery, and in the discipline of their armies is imaginary. The Mahrattas can never be formidable to us in the field on the principles of a European army . . . by doing so they detach themselves from their own plan of warfare, on which alone, if they acted wisely, they would place dependence.' This of course was perfectly true: it was exactly how Shivaji and his successors brought down the Emperor Aurungzeb, the last of the great Moghuls, in defeat and exhaustion to his grave, and it might well have worked against the British. There was also another reason. It was not merely a Mahratta but a universal practice in India not to trust too much power in the hands of one general. We frequently see armies sent off under the command of two, one to check on the other. It was to be sometime before Madhaji could bring himself completely to trust de Boigne.

In the meantime he looked around for reinforcements. From the Peshwa he received at first no help at all. Nana Farnavis the Prime Minister of the Peshwa was, if anything, happy to hear of Madhaji's reverse. What Madhaji needed however was something more solid than Mahrattas, and by a stroke of diplomacy he managed to secure the Rajah Ranjit Singh of Bharatpur (Bhurtpore) as an ally. Ranjit Singh was the ruler of the Jats, a solid, undemonstrative race of Hindu farmers who have provided India, and the British,

46

with some of their best soldiers. (It is the Jats who have the distinction of being the only Indian garrison to have successfully defended a fortress against a British force: their own Bhurtpore, against Lake in 1805.) Included in Ranjit Singh's army was a trained battalion of sepoys under a Frenchman called Lestineau or L'Estineau, whose origin is unknown, but who as a fighting man was better than the usual run of mercenaries. The Jat country is centred on Bhurtpore and Agra, so Madhaji had secured a firm base and an ally inside Hindustan, which altered the complexion of his strategy considerably. All this, however, took some time. Ranjit Singh had to be persuaded of Mahratta *bona fides* and Madhaji had to disgorge the great fortress of Dig and a large piece of Jat territory held by him before the Jat Raja was prepared to agree, and it was not until the April of 1788 that he felt strong enough to begin operations.

Meanwhile in Hindustan things had been going badly, and not only for Madhaji. To the east of Delhi and the north of Bareilly was a territory called Rohilkhand, inhabited by a race of immigrant Pathans, or Afghans, who were reputedly the detritus of an invading army who had decided to settle there. The Rohillas had kept many of the characteristics of that pugnacious, wicked, humorous and unreliable race. They were then commonly recruited in the army as assault troops. While Mohammed and Ismael Beg with most of the Imperial troops were away in Rajputana a Rohilla force invaded Hindustan from the north, captured Delhi, driving out the Mahratta garrison, and also the important stronghold of Aligahr. Only the intervention of Reinhardt's old brigade, now in the Imperial service under his widow Somru Begum gave the Emperor some temporary protection from these bandits. Their leader was Ghulam Kadir, a Rohilla adventurer.[3] He was a eunuch according to one account, and he was almost certainly unhinged. He once offered to marry the Somru Begum, who refused him but whether because of this unfortunate deficiency or merely because he was far too dangerous a man is not known. Ismael found that during his absence his claim, so to speak, had been jumped. He was now faced with a new rival in the struggle to control the Emperor and therefore the Empire. Ghulam Kadir was not a safe or desirable ally, but Ismael saw no other course open to him and he proposed, and the Rohilla agreed, that they should take over Hindustan together and share the spoils.

The spoils were the Jumna Doab, from which they easily evicted the new Mahratta jaghirdars. Then they went on to besiege Agra. This was more difficult. Its citadel is one of the great strongholds of India and a masterpiece of fortification. The defences consist of a double ring of curtain wall and bastions, one inside the other, and on three sides the River Jumna serves as a moat. Inside was one of the best of the Mahratta generals, a Brahman called Lakwa Dada. Ismael and Ghulam Kadir could neither storm nor starve him out, and he remained firmly in possession until the June of 1788 when de Boigne finally relieved him.

The first attempt was a failure, and the course of the battle resembled Lalsot. Madhaji, doubling his generals as was the custom, placed Appa Khandi Rao and a Jat called Rana Khan in command of a mixed army of irregular cavalry, Jat infantry and the three 'trained' battalions: two of de Boigne's, and Lestineau's.[4] Ismael and Ghulam Kadir raised the siege and went to meet them at Chaksana, not far from Bhurtpore, with an army of the usual Moghul pattern, mainly cavalry and guns. Ismael was by no means a bad soldier and he had the wit to see that de Boigne's brigade constituted the Mahratta strength and that the way to deal with it was to mass his artillery and cannonade it. This is the classical formula: to avoid the casualties the infantry have to open out, but if they open out they are defenceless against well-handled cavalry. Fortunately de Boigne did not have to endure his ordeal for long. Ghulam Kadir on his part charged without any preparatory fire and without much difficulty drove off the Mahratta cavalry—or rather they fled in their usual manner—and then drove back the Jat levies. Ismael, fancying that the battle was as good as over, charged de Boigne's brigade prematurely and received the same treatment the Rathors had had the year before. They were thrown back with great loss. Once again de Boigne was left in possession of the field, with the added advantage that this time Lestineau with his Jat battalion was standing solidly by him. All that was needed was for the Mahrattas to counter-attack, but once again they had gone. De Boigne and Lestineau had to withdraw and this proved the far more expensive part of the engagement, as it was eight miles to the safety of the walls of Bhurtpore where the rest of the army had preceded them.

In classical as in modern warfare, a retreat unassisted by cavalry, in daylight and in the face of a superior enemy is judged to be the most difficult of operations and is seldom carried out successfully. The temptation to go faster and faster to get out of danger becomes stronger and stronger as the withdrawal goes on; it is particularly trying for the rear-guard to stand and watch while others march back to the next position. Each position on the way back must be held for precisely the right period of time: to go too early leads to the withdrawal becoming a race between pursuers and pursued, but to stay too long may lead to being gripped and destroyed on the spot. Only the skilled commander with absolutely reliable troops can wait just long enough to give the pursuers a staggering blow and then break cleanly away while they are still dazed and repeat the process. Nor must it be imagined that the troops of northern India were contemptible. In 1804 Monson, a capable although not a brilliant British commander of a sepoy force, was utterly destroyed by the Mahrattas during a long retreat.

De Boigne had therefore passed the best practical test of command in the field there is. One of the most unusual things about him is that few generals are good trainers, good administrators and good fighting generals in the field as well. De Boigne was all three. Yet there is no record of him attending any military school, or of having any practical experience in operations, but he springs into action as if he were the veteran of a dozen fights. He was, like Clive, a 'heaven-born' general, but heaven-born generals still have to learn their profession. Nature had given him a cool head, quick perception and courage. For the rest he was self-taught. He felt that somehow he was destined to do something great and that this would have to do with the profession of arms. He had relieved his loneliness and frustration in Madras by learning his trade thoroughly. He was not a man to leave things to chance. He fought well, therefore, not instinctively but because he knew how. He had learnt how to manoeuvre in the same way as he had mastered every detail of the military organisation of the Company's army and so had it ready in his head when he wanted it: by practice and study.

Ghulam Kadir's base and capital was Saharanpur, and by a lucky stroke for Madhaji it was raided by the Sikhs in force while the redoubtable Ghulam was occupied at Agra. Madhaji sent some of his cavalry marching by circuitous routes to assist the Sikhs and this distracted Ghulam Kadir from the siege of Agra. He left hastily for his capital leaving Ismael Beg to face Madhaji's next offensive. On the 18th June, 1788, the two Hindu generals arrived outside Agra, and in a hard day's fighting de Boigne, virtually in tactical command, first withstood the shock of Ismael's attack, then attacked in turn, scattered his infantry, took his guns and burned and sacked his camp. Ismael swam his horse across the Jumna and fled, and eventually arrived at the camp of his Rohilla ally. There he learned what it was to be alone and defeated, without an army and without influence.

So far the old Emperor Shah Alam had been left unmolested in Delhi. After hearing of the battle of Agra he wrote to Madhaji, whom he still regarded as his only hope, to come back to Delhi and re-assert himself as his protector and Vakil-ul-Mutluq as before. Madhaji, however, was quite determined not to overreach himself again. He was still expecting a contingent of troops from the Peshwa, although characteristically these were being delayed by Farnavis until he was sure that Madhaji was in too strong a position to be refused, and his regular troops had to be rested and made up to strength. He was now firmly based in the country of his allies the Jats around Agra, and he was determined not to move until he could move in strength. Also he believed that Ismael Beg and Ghulam Kadir were ill-assorted. The Moghul amirs were not squeamish men or easily frightened, but Ghulam was a terrible creature. He was a brigand on a large scale, and a homicidal sadist to boot. Madhaji judged that it was only a matter of time before they fell out, and he saw no point in fighting if the dissensions of his enemies would do his work for him. He did not order a northward move, therefore, until about September. This was to prove an unpleasant three months for the unfortunate Emperor and for the capital.

Ghulam Kadir—after all he was only a *dacoit*, an armed gangrobber of the type which has infested India throughout its history, but on a large scale—had the lunatic idea of seizing the Empire for himself. He intercepted a letter from Shah Alam to Madhaji begging for help and fearing that he might be forestalled marched on Delhi, seized the fort and the palace, deposed Shah Alam, and set up some obscure youth from the Imperial family as his puppet Emperor. His real motives appear to have been the equally lunatic obsession that the Moghuls were still immensely rich. Not only the unsophisticated European mercenaries but the poor of India believed that their rulers had hidden in their castles cellars full of pearls and diamonds and rubies. (And to a certain extent this had been true. Indians were, and the poor still are, inveterate hoarders.) Delhi, however, and the Imperial treasures had been thoroughly sacked over forty years before by Nadir Shah, and Shah Alam had barely enough income to feed his household. Ghulam Kadir, disappointed in what he found, decided to drag the imagined secret of the hiding-place of the treasure from the deposed Emperor himself, and throwing the old man—he was about sixty-eight—on the ground sat on his chest and threatened to blind him. 'Spare these old eyes,' Shah Alam is reported to have said, 'already worn out by years of poring over the Koran,' but Ghulam picked them out with the point of his dagger. Disappointed, he searched the palace and the zenana where the harem lived. All that he succeeded in collecting was the jewellery of the princesses and the begums. Every Indian woman had her little treasure not only for adornment but also as a means of keeping her savings and securities: the poorer and simpler do to this day. Using such methods of persuasion as would occur to a man of his cast of mind the ladies were made to disgorge all these. His troops did the best they could with the shopkeepers and the merchants. Of the protests of Ismael Beg, now a defeated and discredited plotter, Ghulam Kadir took not the slightest notice. Ismael Beg, whatever his faults, has the distinction (if we do not count the rabble from the East India Company's cavalry who took over the palace in 1857) of being the last man to fight for the rights of the royal House of Timur the Lame, whose descendants had ruled in Delhi for two hundred years, and he was to continue to fight in this lost cause until his final defeat by one of de Boigne's battalion commanders. He now saw that of the two evils the Mahrattas were infinitely the more preferable, and he went over to them. When Rana Khan at last set off for Delhi accompanied by de Boigne and Lestineau, Ismael Beg arranged for such loyal Moghul troops who remained to open the gates of the city and they entered without firing a shot.

Ghulam Kadir fled, and his end was as disgusting as his life. He got as far as Meerut and one night, seeking to evade his pursuers, fell down a well, horse and all. (This is not as unlikely an accident as it sounds. The great wells of India are pieces of architecture, sometimes large enough to accommodate a modern swimming bath, with galleries, and flights of stairs leading down to the water.) He was badly injured and captured. His captors, acting on the Asian principle of justice that the more hideous the crime the more terrible the punishment deserved, truncated him and put his still-living torso into a basket to exhibit him in Delhi, but disappointingly for them, he died.

Lestineau, whose battalion had accompanied the pursuing force, found the spoils from the Imperial harem and various other trifles in Ghulam's baggage. It is a pity that we do not know more about this engaging scoundrel, for not only was he a tough and successful mercenary commander—his Jats had fought as hard as de Boigne's men at Chaksana and Agra—but he was a man who knew when to seize an opportunity. After all, he had come to India to look for the treasure of the Indies, or at least to make his fortune—what else was a mercenary's aim?—and here it was. It was for this he had come to this harsh, alien country from beloved France, slaved for unreliable princes, marched far and lain hard, and stood up to be shot at. However, he was not a man to act rashly or hastily. Pay-day for his battalion was due shortly. Lestineau waited until he could get his hands on the imprest-chest, and then, and only then, when he was assured of a supply of ready money as well as the less nego-tiable and recognisable jewels and bullion, left with the utmost promptness for the safety of British territory, and eventually, it is said, reached France safely and lived happily ever afterwards. At least, so one cannot help hoping. It would be pleasant to think of him sipping his wine on the pavement of some little French town, and astounding his *copains* with his stories of the Great Moghul. Alas, according to Young, he later became insane.

De Boigne, too, had made his fortune, but more honestly, and he was also tired of soldiering. He had had four years of incessant administration, almost all of which had been done by him personally, and three severe campaigns. He may have been slightly disgruntled, because all had turned on his two battalions, while he had had to put up with the futilities of Mahratta warfare, and had been twice abandoned to fight his own way out. He was 'good with money', never ostentatious or extravagant, and for four years he had drawn a 1000 rupees a month, most of which he had saved. He decided to resign, and on applying to his benefactor Claude Martine in Lucknow as to how best to make his money grow, on his advice set up with him as a merchant. This was sometime in 1789, after he had been garrisoning Delhi for some months. In 1790, when he had nearly established himself in the cloth and dye-stuffs business, he was visited by a vakil from Madhaji. Would he return, naming his own terms, and raise him an army of 10,000 men?

4 *The Army of Hindustan*

WHETHER the reason was that de Boigne was already bored with commerce, or whether he was tempted by Madhaji's offer, or whether it was thirst for glory and that his first essay in command had convinced him that he had the seeds of greatness in him, he wound up his affairs in a matter of days and travelled with Madhaji's vakil the 250 miles to Muttra to hear what he had to say. This was very much to the point. Madhaji had by then time to think things over. It was essential to his plans to have a military instrument that could fight and a man in whom he could trust in command of it. He had taken de Boigne's measure and he knew that he was that man. His enemies were now defeated and he felt strong enough to do as he pleased, even to over-ruling his own generals or making his rivals in the Confederacy jealous without fear of the consequences. Also, and this was the deciding factor, he was now the unchallenged ruler *de facto* of Hindustan with access to its riches. Before, he simply could not afford to pay for more than de Boigne's two battalions, especially as de Boigne would not be fobbed off with uncollected land revenue but demanded hard cash, paid regularly on the nail.

Now he could afford what he wanted he wasted no time in haggling, for he knew that de Boigne was not that sort of man. He had no ready cash, but he offered him an enormous and wealthy province centred on Aligarh worth 16 lakhs of rupees, say £200,000 a year, in the Doab as his jaghir. (This at least was its theoretical value, in terms of revenue, if it could be collected.) From the gross sum he could raise de Boigne was to keep two per cent for himself, and also his salary of 4000 rupees a month, say £15,000 a year. From the balance he was to finance and raise a force of ten battalions, with a view to increasing it later.

We can be sure that de Boigne, always careful over money matters, had already made some thorough calculations. He had been in India long enough to know just how efficient, or inefficient, the jaghir system was. He realised that once he took it on he would not be just a general but a great landowner and a magistrate as well, virtually the nawab, or prefect, of the province which would easily distract him from his main task. The jaghir could not run itself and its income would have to pay not only for himself and his brigade but also for its government and for the administrative costs of collecting the revenue. A force of the size he was contracting for could not cost less than £84,000 a year, a good deal more on active service. Nevertheless his boundless self-confidence told him that he could do all these things, and more; for if he could arrange for the revenue to be collected fairly and properly without his being swindled, and if he could bring some sort of order into his domain, then he believed that he could make it far more valuable by simply permitting it to prosper. He wasted no time in striking a bargain with Madhaji Sindia. Once again he displayed his extraordinary capacity for work and this time for civil as well as military administration. He began work some time in January 1790 and by May was ready for the first demand to be made on his new force.

No one knew better than de Boigne that while generals arrange battles and majors and captains win them the men who make the campaign possible at all are the paymaster and the quartermaster. The first thing he settled was the financial side. The revenue had first of all to be fixed village by village, fairly collected and then guarded from embezzlement. Remember that he was living in a world where it was the accepted thing for every official concerned to take his 'cut'. The very cook sent to the bazaar to buy a few seers of rice and a handful of peppers added his 'squeeze' to the bill as a matter of custom: *dastur*, the word for custom, is the slang for 'squeeze'. De Boigne's two per cent on the gross revenue was simply the official recognition of it; a promise not to overdo things, as it were. De Boigne got round this difficulty by employing two independent sets of accountants, knowing well that they would from jealousy check on each other. One kept their accounts in French, the other in the more usual Persian and de Boigne audited them one against the other. Next, he re-engaged Sangster and set him up as director of the arsenal in Agra. There Sangster cast excellent cannon, and made muskets as good as the European model for 10 rupees each; gunpowder from sulphur and saltpetre from Bikanir and cannon shot from Gwalior iron. Eventually he ran five arsenals, each under a superintendent. Then there was the question of uniforms. The infantry wore scarlet, black belts and cartridge boxes, and *pagris* (turbans) of blue cotton.

The small cavalry force he raised later on the scale of one regiment per brigade were to be dressed in green, with red *pagris* and cummerbunds (sashes). This in itself was a formidable operation. The cloth had to be brought from Calcutta and the tailors, who were a sort of cottage industry, gathered from everywhere. Then there was the transport. Each battalion required a hundred bullocks for its guns and their attendant ammunition wagons. De Boigne also believed very sensibly, and also originally, that infantry should march lightly equipped and arrive in action fresh. They could not do this if loaded down like pack animals; the ordinary infantryman had to stagger along under a load of sixty or seventy pounds. Accordingly every platoon had a camel plus one for battalion headquarters, to carry the men's 'packs', or knapsacks. De Boigne's battalions became so famous for their marching that the First Brigade was nicknamed the 'Flying Army'—the *Cheria Fauj* (literally The Army of Birds). Altogether, somewhere or somehow, there had to be collected for his first echelon seven hundred good quality bullocks and one hundred and twenty-six camels. The cavalry by the usual custom produced their own horses, a system good in that it made the trooper look after his horse; bad in that sometimes he was reluctant to risk it in battle.

The great difficulty was officers. De Boigne seems to have been hard put to recruit enough of the right quality, and this may account for the fact that he at first raised no more than seven regular battalions. To make up the numbers he recruited three battalions of the Muslim mercenaries, Pathans or Rohillas, known as najibs. These, militarily speaking, resembled our own Highlanders in their pre-Culloden style of fighting and equipment. They were armed with shields and the curved, cross-hilted swords called *tulwars* and with a long matchlock. This, of course, was a fire-arm ignited by a match which the matchlockman had to keep alight without blowing himself up or burning himself while he stuffed loose powder, bullet and wad down the barrel, aimed and fired. The difficulty was to know what to do with it in close combat, men not having three hands. The more impetuous Highlanders used simply to throw their muskets away and charge. It was, after all, only a one-shot weapon. These najibs were not capable of manoeuvre but they could launch a damaging attack and behind a wall or in a trench they were tough and useful soldiers. De Boigne wisely let them fight in their own way until he could re-equip them with musket and bayonet and train them properly. One of de Boigne's excellent ideas was to attach to each battalion fifty armed men of the warlike Mewati people who undertook all camp fatigues, baggage-guards, wood-cutting, foraging, thus relieving the fighting troops from these duties, and who could also fight at a pinch. Another was, following the advice of Marshal Saxe (whose military 'Reveries' he may well have studied) to give each battalion a name after the place where it was raised; such as the Delhi, the Agra, the Ujjain battalions. This encourages *esprit de corps* far better than a mere number or the ephemeral name of the commanding officer.

What we do not know, which is tantalising, is how he arranged his troops by caste, race and religion. The later British Indian army had to pay great attention to this, because apart from the fact that 'Indians' are an amalgam of races with strong clan and community loyalties there was the difference between the two main religions and also powerful inter-caste taboos about food and hygiene. How acute these could be is illustrated by Skinner's experience when he and an old Rajput officer were abandoned wounded on a battlefield some years later, and the Rajput refused water from the hand of a low caste woman; he would rather have died. De Boigne's recruiting ground was Oudh, Rohilkhand and the Jumna Doab, which seems to have been a general source of supply of infantry soldiers for all the various armies. (De Boigne mentions allowing the troops he captured and disbanded at Patun to go freely home and to cross the Jumna.) Races are easily confused with caste—'Rajput' loosely applies to either—and doubtless de Boigne followed the same practice as the Company's army and mixed them all together, which did not matter when the men bought and cooked their own food over the camp fire. The najib battalions of matchlock *cum* sword-and-buckler men were exclusively Muslim, as were the Hindustani or 'Moghuls'. It would also be natural for locally recruited battalions to contain a majority of local men: the Bhurtpore battalion, for instance, might have a predominance of Jats.

The organisation he finally adopted was of eight British type regular battalions and two strong battalions of najibs. Each had a battery of two 3-pounders, two 6-pounders and one howitzer attached. By conventional military terminology this was not really a 'brigade' but the powerful, self-contained miniature army called a 'division'. However, there is no need to be pedantic and de Boigne's usage will be followed. His 'Brigade' had one serious weakness, which was that it had no subordinate formations. No one can command ten battalions directly and 'divisions' are divided into 'brigades' for ease of control. The practice in the Army of Hindustan seems to have been to regard the full brigade as a sort of pool detaching what we would call 'brigades' in the modern sense, i.e. groups of battalions and guns about 1500–2000 strong under an officer chosen *ad hoc* for the operation. This was usual for the numerous minor operations the army carried out during its existence. Only occasionally did a whole brigade fight united and even then it had to be divided into *ad hoc* 'wings'. It was a thoroughly bad system, although it must be said that it was a common enough practice at the time in all armies.[1]

Another great weakness was the lack of officers good enough to fill the senior appointments. Later an ample supply of good junior officers, all British or British 'country-born', flocked to join the Brigades, but for colonels (the highest rank, commanding a whole brigade) and the majors de Boigne had to depend on the old mercenary hacks of the vintage of Madec and Reinhardt. For the First Brigade he found just sufficient to command his seven regular battalions. Fremont, he promoted to be his own second-in-command, and Sangster to control his ordnance factories. The battalion commanders were John Hessing (Dutch), Baours, Pedron and Rohan (French), Roberts (English) and Sutherland (Scots). Of these, Baours was shortly to be killed in action, and possibly Rohan as well, and Roberts was severely wounded and disappears from the officer lists. Sutherland is believed to have been an officer of a Highland regiment—possibly the 73rd, who were in India—who on being disgraced became a mercenary. According to Skinner, who hated him, he was a most deceitful character, but he proved to be a most able officer and won at least one major victory.

The seventh was Pierre Cuiller, or 'Perron' as he came to be known when his nickname was transformed into his surname. Perron was at this date about thirty-five years old. In 1774, when he was about nineteen his father, who was a merchant, failed and became bankrupt. Perron bravely set off to make his own way in life, and laid out his little stock of money to set up as a pedlar of hand-kerchiefs and trinkets. This was a miserable failure. He then took work in a cannon foundry in Nantes, then joined the army, and then the navy, arriving off the Malabar coast, possibly in about 1780, in the *Sardinia* frigate of Suffren's eastern fleet. He had 'India fever', like many others, and deserted. From the Malabar coast, the present state of Kerala, he tramped to upper India, where he took service under Sangster, who at that time was commanding the corps Madec had sold to Chettri Singh of Gohad. Sangster found him useful in his cannon-foundry, and a good man generally. Perron's next ten years are an epitome of the life of an Indian mercenary. Chettri Singh eventually disbanded his force, and Perron was recruited by Lestineau seeing service at Chaksana and Agra. Then, it will be remembered, Lestineau bolted with the pay and with jewels he had recovered from Ghulam Kadir. It never occurred, of course, to Ranjit Singh of Bhurtpore, their employer, that he might replace the money or that the poor sepoys might like to be paid, so they mutinied; the sole protest those ill-used men could ever make. They were accordingly disbanded. Perron next looked for employment in Somru Begum's corps, but that fine body of men was fifteen months in arrears with its pay, so Perron remained unemployed. He might at this moment have despaired. He had been ten years in India to rise only to the rank of sergeant and was now married, to a French-Indian half-caste, the sister of a mercenary called Derridon, and penniless. At best the life of a 'poor white' or 'Eurasian' in India was difficult; looked down on by the pros-perous Europeans and regarded as casteless by the natives: at its worst without money or work it was intolerable. Then, possibly through Sangster's influence, he was engaged by de Boigne. De Boigne may also have noted him in Lestineau's battalion as a stout fighter during the Agra campaign. There he had another stroke of luck. Although disbanded, Lestineau's sepoys had never dispersed. One can imagine them, poor fellows, hanging about with their endless Indian patience, begging for forgiveness, or service, or to work, or for anything; and presenting pathetic little screeds written for a few annas by the letter-writers of the bazaar beginning with a pious invocation and ending with promises to pray always for his Lordship, his Highness, the Protector of the Poor. . . . De Boigne snapped up the lot, and they became the

59

Bhurtpore Battalion. What was more sensible than to put a man who knew Jats and had served with them in command of them? So Sergeant Perron became Captain Perron, and soon impressed de Boigne, who supervised everything, with the business-like way he set about reconstructing and retraining his old unit. With the rest of the Brigade it was soon to be put to the test.

It will be remembered that Ismael Beg, the victor by chicane of Lalsot and later ally of Ghulam Kadir, had submitted to Madhaji in the previous year. It was not long before he started to plot again with his uncle's old allies Bijai Singh of Jodhpur and Pratap Singh of Jaipur, the two Rajput princes. He himself collected a force of Moghul cavalry and joined them in the Ajmir district, where they assembled a typical army of the old style, some 55,000 troops of every sort, mostly horsemen, and 129 guns. By May this mob had advanced as far towards Delhi as a town called Patun. As has been explained, these armies were incapable of manoeuvre and battles were literally 'pitched'; one side took up a position and defied the other to drive it from its ground. The combined chiefs took up an extremely strong position near Patun in a pass in the hills whose flanks were protected by both jungle and mountain. Moghul armies were good at field works and fortifications and there they dug in strongly and built redoubts for the artillery.

Madhaji acted at once. He ordered de Boigne to mobilise, and following the usual custom appointed two field commanders; de Boigne and Lakwa Dada, the Brahman who had successfully held Agra, who commanded the irregular Mahratta light horse. It was de Boigne, however, who directed the operations. He first carefully reconnoitred the position, in which according to custom the chiefs decided to stay ensconced but inactive. He decided that it was too strong for an immediate frontal assault and that the defenders must be manoeuvred out into the open where he could get at them. He tried to work round the flanks but the ground was too difficult, and trailing his coat across their front had no effect. These manoeuvres took up three weeks, and he became impatient. Then he learned from his spies that the combined chiefs had consulted the astrologers, who replied quite accurately that the 20th June was an auspicious day for a decisive battle. Indian astrologers are very good, and their military advice was probably no worse than some that emerges from the operational planning staffs of our day. De Boigne decided to take advantage of this by demonstrating in force in front of their position in the hope of enticing them out. Fortunately we have his own account of the battle in a letter to a friend, published later in a Calcutta journal.[2]

'Our various skirmishes since the severe cannonade of the 8th and 9th Ramzan are not, I hope, unknown to you. I have often tried to harass and surprise the enemy, but their naturally strong and almost impregnable situation added to their very great superiority in numbers both in troops and artillery, rendered my exertions fruitless. At last, tired out by vexation, I determined to march from our ground in three columns so as to form the line from the centre of each with ease and celerity. In that way I advanced to a little more than a cannon-shot from the enemy, where I formed my little army in two lines and a reserve with the Mahratta horse in the rear and on our flanks. After waiting the best part of the day with impatient hopes to see them marching against us as they had threatened at last, at about three o'clock, a few Mahratta horse began to skirmish with the enemy's right wing, consisting of horse which shortly increased to five or six thousand, but they were soon beaten off. I was now encouraged to try whether something better could not be done by our side, and in order to induce them to come out from their stronghold I ordered the line to advance after a warm cannonade of about an hour from both sides. The enemy not appearing to come out I still advanced until we were within reach with grape-shot, then halting, gave and received from each gun some forty rounds of grape, which made it a warm business, we being in the plain and they in their trenches. The evening was now far advanced, and seeing numerous bodies of the enemy cavalry in motion ready to fall on us if they could find an opening, I thought it prudent to move on rather quicker, which we did until the firing of platoons began. [I.e. he was now in musket shot of the trenches, say 100 yards at most.] We had already lost such numbers of people, principally clashies (*kelasis*) that those remaining could not drag the guns any further. I therefore gave orders to storm the lines, sword in hand, which was as soon executed. Upon which the enemy, not relishing at all the close fighting, gave way on all sides, infantry as well as cavalry, leaving us in possession of all their guns, baggage, bazaar, elephants and everything else. The day now being closed put an end to the slaughter of the enemy which must have been very considerable if we had an hour more daylight. However, it was a complete victory. Their cavalry, after losing about 2000 men and horses saved themselves by flight. The infantry, who could not run so fast, took refuge in the town of Patun, strongly fortified, but in the morning they thought it proper to give themselves up and surrendered to me all their arms, colours, etc. Nine battalions and irregular troops making above 12,000 men, are now prisoners of war. I have promised to allow them a safe conduct to the other side of the Jumna.

'The enemy's force consisted of 12,000 Rhattore (Rathor) cavalry, 6,000 from Jodhpur, 5,000 Moghuls under Ismael Beg and 2,000 under Allyhar Beg Khan. Of foot they had 12,000 men, and 100 pieces of artillery. With Ismael Beg, 5,000 tellengas and matchlockmen (*Telingas*: semi-regular infantry) with 21 pieces of artillery, 4,000 Rohillas, 5,000 fakirs called Attyles and Brackys (*Bairagis:* Hindu berserks) and Rajput sybundees (irregulars) and 4,000 Minahs (Ajmiri hill-folk), who were of great service to the enemy as the battle was given at the foot of the hills. My Brigade was 10,000 strong. The Mahratta cavalry stood on our flanks as spectators. They began the skirmish in which they had only six men killed and forty wounded. Had it not been for two battalions of mine who changed front when the enemy's cavalry were charging them the Mahrattas would have seen fine play. Our victory is astonishing! A complete victory gained by a handful of men over such a number in such a position. It may surprise you when I say that in less than three hours time 12,000 roundshot and 1,500 grapeshot were fired by us, and by the enemy much more, as they had two guns to our one.'

(This is an astonishing figure. It was physically possible provided the ammunition was there, and we know de Boigne's arrangements included a huge twelve-bullock 'tumbril' full of powder and shot for each gun. Nevertheless, 78 guns of the Royal Artillery in nine hours' fighting at Waterloo fired only 10,000 rounds. Without going into the arithmetic 7500 is probably nearer the truth.)

'During all the engagement I was on horseback encouraging my men. Thank God I have realised all the sanguine expectations of Sindia. My officers, in general, have behaved well; to them I am a great deal indebted for the fortunes of the day. We have had 129 men killed and 472 wounded. The enemy not more, perhaps not so much, as they were entrenched, but they have lost a vast number of cavalry.

'I have taken 107 pieces of artillery, 6,000 stands of arms, 252 colours, 15 elephants (among them 5 of Ismael Beg's), 200 camels, 513 horses, and above all 3,000 oxen. I intend to send the whole to Sindia as soon as it may be practicable. All their camp was burnt or destroyed; they have saved nothing but their lives. The terror of our arms alone put us in the possession of the town of Patan in which out troops found a great deal of plunder and near 2,000 horses. It would have required at any other time a month to take, its fortifications being very strong, and defended by three hills close to each other. The place was never taken before. . . .'

As soon as Madhaji heard the news he ordered the two generals advance and re-asserted his authority over the states of Jaipur and Jodhpur. Raja Pratap Singh surrendered at once. He must have had his regrets when he recalled that he had originally offered his conqueror a post back in 1784 and had then changed his mind. Next de Boigne marched to where the fortress of Ajmir guarded the gap in the Aruvalli hills on the road to Jodhpur and besieged it. He made no progress, however, having no heavy artillery, and on hearing that Raja Bijai Singh was collecting another army he left some of Lakwa Dada's cavalry to watch the garrison and marched westward into the Rajputana deserts to meet him. Now the Rajputs in general, the Rajputs of Marwar especially and the clan of Rathor in particular whose homeland it was have always made a fetish of bravery; so much so that it was remarked on even in India, the home of some of the most warlike peoples in the world. For them the practice of warfare and the display of courage were ends in themselves. They were intensely loyal; like the ancient English 'they would not know how to face the stout lads round Stourmere were they to journey lordless home'. To return defeated and alive was a deep, caste-losing disgrace. Their wives would not sleep with them, the old men would beat them and pull off their turbans—a deadly insult!—and there would be vulgar verses chanted after them in the bazaars. The Rathors had now broken twice under the terrible salvoes of de Boigne's guns, and to add insult to injury after Patun the despised Mahrattas had chased and slaughtered them as far as Jaipur. They were now the subject of insulting

songs and catchphrases.³ One suggested that they were fit only to
'guard the petticoats of Amber' (the great Rajput stronghold),
another that women had stolen their horses while another said that
they had lost all the trappings of manhood. Freely translated one
runs:

> 'Five of the things of Marwar
> Horse, shoe and turban
>   manly moustache and sword
> Five signs of manhood
> Left the Rathors at Patun.'

They were determined therefore to wash out this stain either in
the blood of de Boigne's brigade or their own. Bijai Singh when he
arrived in Jodhpur had called up every man who could ride a
horse or bear arms between the ages of fourteen and sixty.

For the next encounter Bijai Singh remained in Jodhpur
leaving the army to his general Gangaram Bandari, who followed
the usual and unenterprising policy of entrenching himself. He
chose a position on the road to Jodhpur under the walls of the town
of Mertah. De Boigne had a slow and difficult approach. There
were of course nothing in the way of metalled roads in those days,
and he first had to spend two whole days passing his cannon over a
ford in a large river and then to plod through a sandy desert,
picking his route from well to well so as to water his cattle. Gangaram
did nothing to oppose him, even missing a golden chance at the
ford of the Luni river when de Boigne's column was strung out and
divided.

The brigade came up to Mertah unmolested on the 10th September and de Boigne looked over the position with his customary
thoroughness. It was already after midday, and he put off his
attack until the morning of the 11th for the cold-blooded reason
that he wanted plenty of daylight for the pursuit so as to be sure of
destroying his enemy completely. Before dawn on the 11th he
marshalled his little force in absolute silence, and anyone familiar
with Asia will understand what a feat this was and the state of
discipline to which he had brought not only his sepoys but his
irregulars and his artillery bullock drivers. Before the sun had risen
or his unsuspecting opponents had woken up he had dropped the
trails of his guns within grape-shot range of the outer line of

Gangaram's defences and carried them after a brisk attack. Everything was going perfectly when to his annoyance and dismay he saw Rohan, to whom he had entrusted his left wing of three battalions, beginning to advance without waiting for his centre and right. There was the sudden thunder of hooves, the yell of the Rathor slogan and a ghol some four hundred strong emerged from the enemy camp, shot through its own second line as if it were the enemy's and fell on his infantry. In no time they were scattered and being sabred helplessly.

The Rathor chiefs had all gone to bed the night before, with the cavalryman's typical indifference to military precautions, stupefied with opium; eating or drinking the crude drug being the great Rajput vice.[4] It took some time in the early dawn for the excited messengers to shake them into consciousness and for them to grasp the news that the front was broken, the camp entered and all apparently lost. When they had taken this in they decided that they could not leave the field defeated a third time and resolved ceremonially to 'wash their hands of life'. They drugged themselves afresh, this time with the fear-removing bhang, called up their followers and asking them to 'remember Patan' led by the chief of Ahwa they formed the ghol and rode out to die. Their trajectory took them to the spot where Rohan, with his battalions in open column and echeloned out, his guns on the move and out of action, was beyond the reach of support from the rest of the brigade. They could not have been worse disposed to receive cavalry when the Rathors raced screaming up and hit them like a stampede. While the enemy cavalry was engaged in hacking and hewing at their victims the shocked de Boigne immediately formed his whole remaining force into a hollow square. In no time the ghol galloped up to it followed, like a comet, by a long streaming tail of horsemen which gained in numbers and enthusiasm when they perceived the disaster to Rohan. The square was soon surrounded by a milling mob, from which groups broke off to charge the line as the impulse took them and without any concerted plan of attack. Alas for them, this time the Rathors faced not a little clump of beleaguered infantry alone and unsupported as at Lalsot, but an army; presenting a wall of red coats and a triple row of bayonets on every side, studded at intervals by batteries loaded with case. The Rathors were, as was their wish, all killed.

One of de Boigne's officers describing the scene wrote: 'It is impossible for me to describe the feats of the "Jerd Kopperah Wallahs", or the enemy forlorn hope. I saw after their line was broken fifteen or twenty men return to charge a thousand infantry and advance within ten or fifteen paces (of our line) before all were shot.' At the bitter end, of the twenty-two chiefs who had taken the oath together that morning five remained. Their tired and frightened horses would no longer face the noise and flame of the musketry, so they dismounted and with eleven of their faithful squires walked deliberately up to the bayonet points to die.

The only survivor was the Thakur of Ahwa who commanded the whole Rathor cavalry force and who had led their charge. He was found on the battle-field with twenty-seven wounds. Lakwa Dada ordered his personal surgeon to attend to him, but the Thakur refused treatment until all his wounded troopers had been attended to first and died a few days after the battle.[5] Gangaram Bandari disguised himself as a servant and tried to sneak away but was ignominiously captured.

The same officer goes on to say that de Boigne went on to take Mertah by storm and that 'the pillage lasted three days, and to mention all the particulars attending it would make your teeth water. The ladies seemed displeased with our coming so abruptly into the town, but at length grew more kind, acknowledging with good grace that none but the brave deserve the fair.'

Mertah, by the custom of war, having defied the attackers and faced the 'storm' was lawfully given over to the sack, which was the right of the storming parties. The last sentence is interesting. One would have thought that the 'ladies' would have preferred death to revealing their faces, let alone being touched by a polluting Feringhi but, convinced possibly by Gallic and Scots charm, they decided that surrender was more agreeable than virtue.

De Boigne's casualties were light, all things considered. He lost some seven hundred killed and wounded in his left wing, one officer killed and one disabled by a shot from an 'organ', or multi-barrelled cannon. Rohan never appears in the officer lists again, so he too was killed as a penalty for his rashness, or perhaps he was sacked by de Boigne for his mistake. Bijai Singh had put some 30,000 cavalry and 100,000 infantry in the field. (In military history all these large figures ending in rows of 'noughts' should be viewed with suspicion, especially in Asian warfare. They are often a synonym for phrases such as 'as myriad as the locusts'. A good quarter were camp-followers and another quarter Falstaffian soldiers pressed from their villages to make up the musters. It is not a bad rule to halve the alleged strength.) The Rajputs suffered terribly in this disastrous affair, which following so soon after Patun, broke the Rajput reputation and power for ever. Soon after the battle the dauntless Ismael Beg turned up at Jodhpur and urged Bijai Singh to try again, but the Raja had lost heart and sent vakils to de Boigne and Lakwa Dada to sue for peace. It cost him six million rupees and the whole province of Ajmir. The business settled, de Boigne left a detachment behind to see the treaty observed and marched back north in great content, a hard and successful campaign behind him and the sepoys happy at going home and rich from the spoil of Mertah. Nothing is pleasanter than a peaceful march in the northern Indian winter, the days sunny and the nights sparkling and sometimes crisp with frost: deer, ducks and sand grouse to be shot *en route*; and a comfortable camp, a bonfire and bottles of wine in the evenings. He arrived at Muttra on New Year's Day 1791 to receive a salute of guns and a tremendous welcome from Madhaji, whom he had made the most powerful man in Moghul India. Madhaji gave Lakwa Dada the whole province of Ajmir in jaghir, a generous reward for watching de Boigne doing all the work, but de Boigne received something he valued far more. He was ordered to raise a Second and a Third Brigade at once. He was also given an even larger jaghir to support them; and in keeping with his new position his pay was raised from four to six thousand rupees a month.

There remained one small matter. Ismael Beg, a man unlucky but of great courage and pertinacity, had raised yet another army, of 20,000 men, and had turned up again in Hindustan. This was an achievement in itself, as he was a landless fugitive, and had to pay them with promises. He received some support from Tukaji Holkar, who conceived this as a round-about way of getting at his triumphant rival Madhaji: the houses of Sindia and Holkar always being at odds. One of his fellow amirs and one of his enemies in the days of the civil wars had been Najaf Kuli Khan (from whose attack at Gokalgarh George Thomas rescued the Emperor in 1788, thus starting his remarkable career, as will be told later). He had died, but his wife, one of those martial Indian ladies, had indignantly refused to hand over his jaghirs to the infidel Madhaji, and had shut herself up in one of his strongest fortresses, Kanaund, not far from Delhi. Ismael joined her in her resistance. It was important for Madhaji to scotch this rebellion, in his own territory and only eighty miles from the capital, at once; for it was essential that a man in his position should not even appear to be threatened or challenged. De Boigne himself was immersed in all the work of expanding the army, and if he was distracted from this it would defer the day of his master's absolute supremacy. He looked round for a subordinate and selected not Fremont, now the natural choice and in command of the First Brigade, but Perron. He sent him off with four battalions to settle the hash of Ismael once and for all and to bring the refractory Begum to heel. Perron did not disappoint him. He marched rapidly over to Kanaund, where he found Ismael Beg camped under the walls, beat him, captured all his guns and drove him and the survivors inside them grossly to over-crowd the garrison. The siege proved a slow business, as he had no proper siege artillery and Kanaund was very strong. However, it was brought to an end by a stroke of luck. The Begum, poor lady, was relieving the tedium of operations with a game of chess with one of her eunuchs when a chance shot sailed over the wall and through the window of her apartment in the women's quarters and killed her. Without her the defenders lost heart, and Ismael, seeing the game was up, asked for quarter and surrendered the place.

One cannot help wondering if the French non-commissioned officers of the eighteenth century were not of a special vintage. Consider Augereau, or Massena, or Sergeant Bernadotte, who was shortly to be captured by the British in southern India. There was Perron, eighteen months before a sergeant out of a post and almost on the point of begging his bread, first commanding a battalion as if he was born to it and now as a brigadier-general defeating an old and seasoned campaigner. He has been treated contemptuously by the British historians, but we shall be able to see if he was not as able and as daring and ambitious as any of those adventurous men, for he was alone while they were only the pupils and servants of Napoleon. He was robust, one of the first attributes of a general. At Kanaund he had a hand blown off when throwing a faulty grenade but an accident which would put a modern European in hospital for a month did not cause him to leave his post in command. Nor was he without honour. When Madhaji heard that Ismael was in his hands at last he decided to put him to death. No one who had made such a fool of the old Patel as Ismael and his uncle had at Lalsot was to be allowed to escape his revenge. Perron immediately complained that he had promised quarter, and he and de Boigne stood up to the furious old Mahratta together and saved Ismael's life. It says a great deal for Madhaji and for his affection for de Boigne that he gave way, for such a code of honour was to him inexplicable and ridiculous; and also that he refrained from any underhand little tricks with poison or a noose in a fortress cell. He locked Ismael up in Agra fort with a pension sufficient to ensure his dignity and comfort until he died in 1799. As for Perron, de Boigne was delighted with him on every count. He promoted him and gave him the Second Brigade.

5   *The Subahdar of Hindustan*

DE BOIGNE spent the next two years in the work of expanding his brigade into the Army of Hindustan undisturbed by campaigning. The First Brigade was reorganised, the Second made ready by the end of 1791 and the Third by 1793. The three brigade commanders were at first Fremont of the First, Perron of the Second and Sutherland of the Third. The Dutch John Hessing had left de Boigne after a disagreement and had obtained an independent command from Madhaji Sindia in the shape of his personal escort. He was in any case getting on in years and had a grown up son in one of the brigades. He eventually settled down in the comfortable post of the commander of the permanent garrison of Agra fort.

De Boigne, now that he had the resources, improved on his original model and made each brigade more flexible and more of a self-contained, all-round 'division' with its artillery, engineers and a strong regiment of cavalry, so that he did not have to rely for that arm on the Moghuls or the somewhat flighty Mahrattas.

Being French-trained he knew that good cavalry did not gallop about as if at a point-to-point but charged slowly in compact formation and rallied quickly: in short, were as disciplined as infantry. These horsemen were equipped with 'galloper' guns, the fore-runners of the horse artillery, for their close support: advanced thinking for India, for they were not introduced into the Company's cavalry until 1800. The infantry battalions were exactly on the British model, small and highly manoeuvrable: each of eight fighting companies fifty strong and an attached battery of three- and six-pounder guns and a howitzer. In addition he retained a najib battalion for skirmishing. The total strength of the army excluding the garrisons of the forts was some 27,000 and by de Boigne's wise provision of 'followers' to do all the camp chores and guards they were all fighters; there was no fat in the organisation. To house it in peace he built a 'cantonment' at Koil, or Aligarh as it is now commonly called after the great fort outside the city; with barracks, married quarters, hospitals, gun parks and magazines. Taking it all in all it was one of the most efficient and best found armies ever raised in the history of India, for no expense was spared; unlike the Company's armies which suffered dreadfully from government parsimony; as, indeed, did the fine British-Indian army until well after 1939.

This invincible force, commanded by a loyal and incorruptible general, made Madhaji Sindia in fact the absolute ruler of the rump of the Empire and lord paramount over all Rajputana, whatever title he chose to give himself. The blind old Emperor was virtually his prisoner in his own palace at Delhi. His senior general, Gopal Rao Bhao, was his Subhadar or governor over all Hindustan; one of his Sindia kinsman watched the Sikh marches from Saharanpur; Appa Khandi Rao was the deputy in Mewat; and Lakwa Dada, his able Brahman general, sat in Ajmir over the temporarily cowed Rajputs. Now at last he felt strong enough to proceed with the next stage of his grand design, which was to detach the Peshwa from his reliance on Nana Farnavis and assert himself as the leader of the Confederacy.

However, he found himself at this stage being subjected at first to irritation and then outright aggression from his old enemy and rival, Tukaji Holkar of Indore. Madhaji, in spite of all his triumphs, had, so as to secure the loyalty of the bulk of the ordinary Mahrattas, carefully kept up the fiction that he was still only the poor old *patel* of his native Mahratta village whose sole aspiration was to continue as the hereditary slipper-bearer, the most menial of offices, to the Peshwa. He maintained that it was the Peshwa who was really Vakil-ul-Mutluq, or Regent, and that he was merely discharging the duty on the Peshwa's behalf. It was a pretence that had its disadvantages. It is an amiable Indian tradition that fortune must be shared with all the family. A man suddenly raised to a high and lucrative office may expect to be remembered and descended upon by indigent cousins and aunts, and especially by place-seeking relatives. Nepotism was an Indian virtue, like generosity, and to deny it was in defiance of charity and even religion. This sound ethical principle was somewhat liberally interpreted by Tukaji Holkar. Lakwa Dada was happily and busily engaged collecting revenue in Jodhpur and Marwar, when some of Tukaji's men turned up to assist, on the grounds that this was now Mahratta territory, and they naturally expected a share. Lakwa was incensed that these fellows who had not helped to shake the bough should now come to pick up the fruit. Madhaji was more than incensed: he was alarmed. He had already noted that Tukaji had taken a leaf out of his book and had hired a French mercenary to raise a brigade of regular troops for him. This incursion, he saw at once, was more than the Mahratta instinct to gather like jackals when there was anything to loot: it was a deliberate challenge. The last thing he wanted at this delicate moment was a rupture, for his aim was to heal these incessant rivalries and disputes, and he avoided an armed clash until 1793. Then, in the July of that year, Tukaji appeared in arms west of the Chambal river in territory Madhaji regarded as peculiarly his own. He decided to fight.

Tukaji had with him his new mercenary brigade of four battalions raised in imitation of de Boigne's. Its commander was the Chevalier Dudrenac, the son of an officer of the old French Royal Navy who had arrived in India as a midshipman or a cadet in 1773.[1] Succumbing to the prevailing temptation he had deserted or resigned to seek his fortune as a soldier with one of the Indian princes. He was a veteran of Madec's old brigade of *condottieri* and had had a lot of experience, ending with the Reinhardt, or 'Somru' brigade under his wife the 'Begum'. This he had found too much for him, and had taken service under Holkar when the fashion of copying Sindia's regular infantry spread with de Boigne's victories. He was, by then, completely 'Indianised'. There is an account of him surrendering to Amir Khan and placing his turban at the Pathan's feet while he joins his hands in the traditional Hindu greeting. Of course, many Europeans—Feringhis—adopted Indian ways, food and dress, even keeping their native wives in seclusion. (The great change from the eighteenth to the nineteenth century was that the new conquerors kept themselves utterly aloof from the natives.) For all that he was, as might be expected of a French officer, a man of determination and courage. Unfortunately he was also extremely inept and unlucky; he hardly engaged in an action without suffering a disaster. He was to suffer one at the hands of de Boigne.

For the campaign against Tukaji, Madhaji ordered Gopal Rao Bhao to take command of Lakwa Dada and the force already with him in Ajmir, reinforced by de Boigne himself and the now veteran First Brigade. This was in July. August and part of September passed in a certain amount of marching and counter-marching before they caught the Indore army retreating through the pass of

Lakhairi; for in those days, of course, unless both sides were determined to meet in pitched battle, it was possible for rival armies to march about for weeks without news of each other. At Lakhairi Sindia's army finally met Tukaji and Dudrenac blocking the pass. Only a narrow track with jungle on either side led up to their position. De Boigne, on whom as usual the business of operational control and all the work had devolved once there was the prospect of a fight, sent up three of his regular battalions to try to clear the way, together with one of his Rohilla irregular corps to see if they could work through the scrub on the defender's flanks. He himself had ridden up to watch their progress when there was a tremendous series of explosions in his rear. What had happened was that the leading battalions had left twelve of their great twelve-bullock 'tumbrils', or ammunition wagons, behind on the road up to the pass where they had halted, all jammed together nose to tail-board. At the same time his rearward battalions had come crowding up on the line of march unaware of the check in front until the entire narrow way was crowded with one battalion overlapping another. It was extremely careless and inexcusable, but it is the sort of thing that sometimes happens in the best regulated armies. The target offered to the Indore gunners was too easy to miss. Loose gunpowder is inflammable stuff, and can easily be set off by the inertial heat or the shower of sparks made by a shot hitting the ground. One wagon was hit and this exploded the rest with hideous consequences for the crowded infantry. Gunpowder is not as severe as our modern explosives, but the flaming grains of loose powder are an excellent incendiary, and those soldiers who were not killed by the immediate blast or the flying debris were terribly scorched and their uniforms set on fire. There was a panic to get away from the vicinity of the flaming wagons. At this moment some of Tukaji's troops who had also been making their way through the jungle emerged from it in force and threw themselves on the disordered ranks of the main body of the First Brigade.

De Boigne saw this disaster over his shoulder and came galloping back. The sight of their tall, handsome general on his magnificent Persian barb, as calm as ever, issuing his orders in the most ordinary way immediately rallied his men. Good soldiers are like iron filings in a magnetic field; they automatically seek for order and arrangement. Re-assured by de Boigne they obeyed the shouts of their havildars and jemadars to pull themselves together and close up on the colours. Knots of men began to form and present their bayonets to the exulting Indore attackers. While this desperate struggle was going on de Boigne managed to reach his new cavalry regiment and led it himself up through the clutter and into the attack. They succeeded in pushing the enemy up the pass or into the jungle. There were now two battles going on, one behind the other. While the forward echelon of the brigade ignored the hubbub in its rear and got on with its work the main body, reforming as it went, drove up towards it. As so often happened the sight of any rearward movement proved too much for the defenders at the top of the pass and soon all the Indore army was flooding back in confusion, and the battle was over. Dudrenac with great gallantry attempted to form a rear-guard but his troops were no match for the veterans of Patun and Mertah. De Boigne killed or captured them all, and took 38 guns. Tukaji and his cavalry scampered off as fast as their little ponies could carry them leaving Dudrenac to his fate. Fortunately he survived. They revenged themselves by sacking Sindia's capital of Ujjain which they found undefended on the way home. This did not improve relations between the two houses, but Tukaji's teeth were drawn.

This was the last battle de Boigne was ever to fight. It was not exactly a masterpiece of the tactical art, but then battles seldom if ever are. We often forget that those neat maps covered with rectangles and smoothly curved arrows which decorate works of military history conceal dreadful scenes of confusion, bloodshed, panic and despair, sometimes only glimpsed by the generals through gaps in the clouds of dust and powder-smoke. Battles are not games of chess. Lakhairi was a 'soldier's battle', like all de Boigne's battles. He was the victor because the discipline of his men was too strong to be broken even by the most violent of shocks, and because he himself was imperturbable; 'unflappable', as it was called in a later age.

Sometime after Lakhairi Madhaji found that his enemy Nana Farnavis had been tampering with Gopal Rao Bhao, and he removed him from the position of Subahdar and put de Boigne in his place. It is a unique comment on de Boigne's reputation that Gopal Rao, finding that the vengeful Madhaji was planning to execute him, fled for protection to the very man who had supplanted him; and that de Boigne saved his life as he had saved Ismael's. De Boigne was now in an extraordinary position of power and influence. It was he in fact and none other who was the real master and the paymaster of the Imperial army whose guns no prince in Moghul India now dared to face; and it was to his person that it was loyal. His troops manned the key fortresses of Hindustan. He was immensely rich; indeed, in terms of ready cash he was certainly richer than his master, and on top of this the revenues of the wealthiest tracts of Imperial territory passed through his hands. To cap all this he was now the Subahdar, the Governor-General, of the Imperial heartland of Hindustan and to all intents and purposes the Viceroy of Madhaji; 'Madhaji *Shah*'—'emperor'—as de Boigne styled him. Madhaji believed implicitly that de Boigne's loyalty would restrain his ambition and relied on this alone. De Boigne has been much admired for this restraint, especially when compared with Perron and how that officer acted when he reached the same dangerous heights.

De Boigne's complex character insulated him from any temptation to set himself up as a king, or even a king-maker. Although he had been intensely ambitious he was at the same time a cold man, with a strong, peculiarly French sense of what was practical and possible. He was inordinately proud and jealous of his own position; but a man so reserved, so clever and so prudent must have been proof against any romantic extravagances. Perron, who succeeded de Boigne and was in his own way an outstanding man succumbed to the temptations of power and meddled disastrously in politics, but de Boigne was too fastidious for intrigue and had no ambition beyond the reputation as a soldier he had already gained. Like an honest workman all he wanted was to take his wages and go home. He politely refused fantastic offers of wealth and power if only he would turn his coat; one from the Emperor Shah Alam and even one from the distant Zaman Shah, the King of Afghanistan. He made an exception of Madhaji, whom he admired, but saw with clear eyes and without moral indignation that the Mahrattas were absolutely untrustworthy. 'Being forced against my wish (he wrote to an English correspondent) to enter in to all the details of government since the death of Madhaji Shah I have the opportunity to know them better than I have been able to learn in ten years before ... one who is not acquainted perfectly with the Mahratta character ... can have no idea of their avarice and insensibility and bad faith. . . .' He knew that there was not one who would not try to pull him down or even murder him if the opportunity offered. It was one thing to be a professional soldier but, as Perron was to find, to go further was to become enmeshed in a morass of intrigue and treachery. He had assessed his own abilities and his own aims exactly. He had wished to be famous, on the level with great men, wealthy and a successful soldier. This he has achieved, and for him it was enough.

If de Boigne had ever had any doubts or secret imaginings they were resolved early in 1794. In September, 1793 Madhaji had finally left for Poona to apply his great gifts to winning over the Peshwa. On 12 February, 1794 when engaged in these diplomatic manoeuvres he suddenly died of a fever near Poona. A gathering of Sindia chiefs and henchmen approved of the succession of his only relative, a spoiled boy of 15 called Daulat Rao. This lad was already securely in the mental grip of a Brahmin minister called Baloba Tantia, whom he appointed his chief minister, and de Boigne foresaw all the evil consequences that were likely to flow from this. He no doubt also foresaw the inevitable slide into aimless civil war and a hopeless war with the British which were to follow as a result of the loss of Madhaji Sindia. He therefore declared his loyalty to Daulat Rao Sindia, but asked his permission to resign as soon as he was prepared to release him. It took him some time and diplomacy to disengage himself, as the young prince left, or was dragged off by Baloba Tantia to Poona to carry on the un-finished business left by the death of Madhaji Sindia, and de Boigne had to continue to govern Hindustan for the rest of 1794 and most of 1795.

It cannot be claimed that he governed brilliantly, or in any way constructively. He was after all only the military governor of a conquered state, without a civil service or any machinery for carrying it on in an anarchy where 'government' was limited to the collection of revenue and the suppression of rebellion. His deputies were Mahratta magnates indistinguishable from bandit chiefs and nothing he could do could alter their habits. He made no attempt to do anything of the kind and, in his realistic way, appointed Lakwa Dada as his deputy on the principle that sometimes poachers make the best game-keepers. He busied himself with holding *durbars*, or audiences, where complaints and petitions from all are heard (it being the essence of Indian rule that the king was, so to speak, the 'Omsbudman' himself. The humblest could go into the Presence crying the Hindi equivalent of 'Haro, mon Prince! On m'a fait tort!') with embassies, with relations with the Honourable East India Company who wrote him anxious letters about the state of the Taj Mahal, which they feared was becoming a ruin and about the treatment of the Emperor. He, the poor, blind old man, according to stories reaching Calcutta, was being robbed of his allowances by his chief warder and was starving to death, which had a germ of truth. He was also able to do his English friends little favours; such as giving the difficult half-caste godson of Colonel Burns, a boy called James Skinner, a commission as a second lieutenant in a najib battalion in one of the brigades. De Boigne, in spite of the affair of the court of inquiry in Madras and the promised adjutancy, remained on the best of terms with the British. He liked them, and late in life his home at Chambery was open to men like Grant Duff and Tod who came to consult him over historical matters. He was also cold-blooded enough to see that his escape route ran through the Company's territory and, what was more important, so did the credit system by which through the agency of his business in Lucknow he siphoned his enormous wealth back to London banks.

His only serious worries were the sporadic rebellions which broke out from time to time, and which he had to put down. He must certainly have heard of a curious incident which took place in one of these minor campaigns. He had despatched four battalions of the Second Brigade under a Major Gardner to suppress an outbreak in the ever-troublesome Mewat.[2] There Gardner was held up for some time by an obstinately defended fort. He was reinforced by order of Appa Khandi Rao with troops led by a ruffian called George Thomas who had raised a quasi-regular corps for his private use. The obstacle to Gardner's progress was a large outwork which prevented the process of digging saps and trenches and batteries to attack the main curtain wall. Gardner called a council of war. (Something much frowned on in modern military practice, as they lead to divided counsel and indecision, not to say dispute. They are therefore now called 'conferences'.) Thomas remained silent, apparently overawed by the presence of so many officers, but afterwards he strolled off and had a close look at the troublesome redoubt. Next morning before dawn, without telling anyone, he formed up his ragged contingent of Pathans and Rohillas in column and carried it in a single rush, which so dismayed the commander of the main fort that he surrendered. This caused the Mahratta chiefs to look at him and also his master Appa Rao closely and rather uneasily. They had heard of this Irish sailor once or twice before, and he was somewhat too successful in military matters for their peace of mind.

Perron, unlike de Boigne, may not have heard this news of his future rival and deadly enemy; it is even unlikely that he knew of his existence, there being so many Indianised European vagabonds serving in the mercenary ranks at that time. He himself was much occupied. He had been transferred to command the First Brigade, Fremont being ill (in fact he died about this time), and he had been sent to Poona with it to supply a set of teeth for Daulat Rao Sindia's conferrings with his fellow chiefs there. During the long and tortuous course of these discussions the members of the confederacy for once discovered something upon which they could agree and, as might have been expected, it was a project to acquire someone else's money. They decided that Ali Khan, the Nizam of Hyderabad and ruler of the Deccan owed them 'Chauth', as the Mahratta danegeld or blackmail was called, to the tune of eight million rupees, and they sent him a demand for it. As it happened the Nizam had a European-trained regular army of his own, and considered himself the match for any Mahratta army, and indeed this might have proved the case but for Perron and the *Cheria Fauj*. It was commanded by a celebrated Gascon adventurer, formerly a French regular officer, called François de Raymond and consisted of some 11,000 infantry and artillery with French officers. It had a high, if unjustified, reputation. The British regarded its extreme French sympathies with disfavour and had persuaded the Nizam to enlist another less politically-orientated corps in order to balance it. The Nizam, who was nervous of British power and a firm believer in the balance of power himself, had obligingly raised two more independent corps. Each was about three battalions strong, one commanded by an ex-quartermaster of the 19th Light Dragoons of the King's service; and the other by Colonel Boyd, the only recorded American mercenary, whose lieutenant was William Henry Tone, the brother of the Irish patriot. With such a force at his back Ali Khan decided he was not going to wait to be invaded and suffer the Deccan to be looted by the Mahrattas but would march north and meet them on their own ground. Altogether he disposed of some sixteen battalions of regular troops, together with artillery and the usual mob of native horse and infantry levies; perhaps 110,000 men. He met the Mahrattas near a place called Kharda some 100 miles west of Poona.[3]

The Mahratta army was made up of contingents from the Peshwa himself, from Sindia, from Tukaji Holkar and from the Bhonsla Raja of Berar. There were altogether four brigades of European-led troops. The irrepressible Dudrenac had persuaded Tukaji to allow him to raise some fresh battalions; John Hessing brought his independent corps and there was another, also in Sindia's service, raised in Mahashtra by a Neapolitan ex-muleteer of doubtful military origin called Michael Filose. Except perhaps for Dudrenac's corps none of these were worth a halfpenny, then or later. The battle was virtually fought and won by Perron. He was, however, assisted by a great stroke of luck, not that this diminishes his achievement: Napoleon always asserted that even the best generals had to be lucky as well.

Nizam Ali Khan, with what Herbert Compton disapprovingly calls 'the imbecile infatuation of an Oriental Potentate' had brought a new and favourite young wife with him and, perhaps rashly, had allowed her to join him with her ladies at his actual command post so she could watch her lord vanquish the infidels. When, however, the battle opened with a tremendous cannonade and with cavalry charge and countercharge in the centre the poor Begum was terrified by the noise and horrifying spectacle. She decided that she did not like battles in the least and demanded to be taken home immediately. Ali Khan, she insisted, should also retire at once from so dangerous and exposed a position and leave the horrid business to the soldiers. This, Ali Khan pointed out, would be inconvenient at the moment, but to console his darling he would send for that nice general Raymond whose troops would stand all round her and protect her from any possible harm. This is an amusing story which some find hard to believe in view of the strict seclusion imposed on Muslim ladies, but Moghul princes did sometimes take a favourite wife or two along with their enormous baggage trains and it was a practice not unknown in European warfare. The Russian ladies, it is said, drove out in their carriages to watch the battle on the Alma in 1854. Whatever the cause, Nizam Ali Khan undoubtedly sent Raymond some panic-stricken orders to withdraw and form a protective front round his immediate position.

Now as it so happened, the plan of deployment of the rival commanders had placed Perron and the First Brigade on the extreme left and Raymond on the extreme right so that the two finest mercenary corps in India faced each other. Perron soon succeeded in flanking his Gascon opponent and also had discomfited him by placing a grand battery of thirty guns on a ridge commanding his line of advance. Raymond thus had his hands full when he began to receive a series of inexplicable messages ordering him to fall back; inexplicable because, as far as he could see, the battle had barely started and nothing adverse had happened. To his dismay some of these reached his battalions direct, and they began obediently to retire, only of course, to be once again indignantly called forward by him. It was no moment to disengage, still less was this the sort of manoeuvre to practise in front of Perron. He, perceiving something was wrong in Raymond's ranks, pounced on him in a flash and threw him back. This inevitably started a panic, and the Nizam's whole force began to retreat in increasing disorder. The Mahratta commander-in-chief ordered the pursuit to halt at dusk, but Perron had learnt from de Boigne's example that the two ruling principles of Asian warfare were determined attack and a sustained and relentless pursuit. He pressed on in the dark, firing guns at random to keep the flying troops on the move, and attacking them and stampeding them again when his patrols found where they had halted to bivouac. Next morning he found that the Nizam and some of his escort had crowded into a small fort for refuge. Perron 'summoned' them, and after a few rounds of gunfire and the threat to assault they hung out the white flag. The unfortunate Nizam had to agree to pay a vast sum and to cede a large slice of territory before he and his tearful Begum were allowed to go home to Hyderabad. It was a thoroughly satisfactory campaign, not least for Perron. The main body had been barely engaged and he had won the battle unaided and with very few casualties. Daulat Rao Sindia had been present at the battle and had greatly admired Perron's dashing conduct of operations. This was to ensure his future.

These stirring exploits took place, of course, some one thousand marching miles away to the south of Delhi. De Boigne undoubtedly heard the news with pride and satisfaction. His troops had now been in the field exclusive of sieges and minor campaigns for no fewer than seven great battles; Lalsot, Chaksana, Agra, Patun, Mertah, Lakhairi and now Kharda; had entirely dominated all of them and won the last five outright. Nevertheless, he was now exhausted and had only one idea, which was to leave. Only his loyalty to his dead master made him stay at all, and his departure was becoming increasingly difficult, for Daulat Rao, perhaps aware of the deceit and intrigue surrounding him, wished earnestly for him to stay. De Boigne eventually escaped by insisting that he must return to Europe to restore his health. He claimed that he was worn out by eleven years of hard work and campaigning and also had been recently very ill, which was true; and said that he intended to return, which was less candid. Even when he was safely in England, where he went first, he was to receive a pathetic command from Daulat Rao ordering him to return. After a splendid review at Aligarh when he took a final salute of his battalions he set off for Calcutta on Christmas Day, 1795. He was accompanied by the Indian lady who may have been his legal wife, and her two children by him; Ali Bux, later Charles, Comte de Boigne, and Bunnoo, later Alexandra. His convoy consisted of four elephants, 150 camels and a long train of bullock carts, the whole escorted by his personal bodyguard regiment, splendid in their green and scarlet and silver-fringed *pagris*. Economical to the last, he sold the whole unit to the East India Company before he sailed. With these he made a stately progress, first to Lucknow to wind up his affairs there and to say farewell to Martine, the founder of his fortunes and then to Calcutta, where he lived for some months in great dignity and affluence until there was a suitable ship to take him home. He never saw India or a battlefield again.

De Boigne remains an opaque character. All his qualities are external and observed. He is reserved, calm and courteous: a formal figure in an eighteenth-century canvas. There is a lack of human detail. A commander in the camp and the field is the subject of close and sometimes jealous, sometimes anxious scrutiny by the men he leads. We have a glimpse of Cromwell on the eve of Dunbar suffering from agonies of indecision and biting his lip until the blood runs down his chin, or even Wellington—at Seringapatam—writh-ing with mortification at the ridiculous accident of losing his way and all contact with his battalion in the confusion of a night attack. De Boigne seems to have had no lieutenants or intimates who preserved any of the anecdotes or turns of speech soldier's love to tell about their commanders. He did not even have a nickname. De Boigne is always inhumanly calm and competent, without fear or even any misgivings. He marches on to his first battlefield at Lalsot and off his last at Lakhairi as cool, as detached and as deadly as if he had no emotions at all.

The fact is that he had no subordinates who were admitted to intimacy. He trusted no one and would delegate nothing that affected his hold over the army or the administration of his huge mansabs in the Doab which provided its financial support. He attended to every detail himself, right down to the promotion of individual officers and the commissioning of subalterns. The two great weaknesses of the army were due to him: the absence of a proper chain of command and the failure to select promising officers and train them for the higher appointments.

Clearly he was on the best of terms with his great master. Madhaji Sindia trusted him implicitly, as he would have trusted no other European or Indian, let alone a fellow Mahratta. No one but de Boigne could have induced Madhaji to spare his deadly enemy Ismael Beg once he was in his power, or to forgive Gopal Rao Bhao for his treachery. They respected and were loyal to each other. De Boigne had lifted Madhaji up on his bayonets, but in turn Madhaji had made de Boigne. Such a relationship between a prince and his chief minister or general is rare in the annals of Asia. But here again all this is public and political: nothing is known of their differences or their intimacies. De Boigne wrote letters about battles and was prepared to talk to the English visitors he loved to entertain when he lived at Chambery about the organisation of the Brigades, but he wrote no reminiscences and seldom committed himself on personalities or public affairs.

What little that is known about his private life reinforces this picture of a cold, secretive and prudent man. As was the custom in India in those days he took a mistress. Typically he chose a well-born Muslim lady, according to one account the daughter of a cavalry officer of Persian origin. Contrary to the usual practice he took her to England, where he first lived on his return to Europe. There, in a mysterious transaction (for she had become a Christian but it is not clear whether they were ever married) he discarded her, like an old horse or a piece of domestic equipment he no longer required, and married the young daughter of the French ambassador in London. Heaven knows what agonies and tears there were behind the purdah screen when he abandoned the unfortunate woman, uprooted from every human contact she knew, in London. To add to the poor woman's distress he took the children with him to France, where the daughter died while still a girl.[4] However, he made her a generous pension and, no doubt, remained calm, rational and correct throughout the whole painful business. His new bride soon found him uncongenial and left him. De Boigne settled down to good works in Chambery, so ironically the money wrung from groaning Indian peasants was used in the end to help the sick and orphans of Savoy. It is rare for men who have once tasted power and responsibility to abandon them willingly, but de Boigne threw them off as if he was glad to be relieved of the burden and never took any part in public affairs again, living through the whole Napoleonic era in peaceful inactivity.

All the same, this cold, calculating man was perhaps after all a romantic. He first took to the profession of arms to escape from the smell of his father's hides or the dust of a notary's office, but romantic as the ideas of uniforms and glory and battles may have been to a young man his real ambition was to be an explorer. 'It was all like a dream,' he once said of his extraordinary career in India, but his real dream was not of the crumbling monuments of Delhi, or the long grind over accounts and tables of equipments which took up his days in Hindustan, or even of the roar of battle, where he seemed so much at home, and the drumming of thousands of hooves and the Rathor war-cry. It was, perhaps, of the unaccomplished journey along Alexander's road through Persia—'the golden road to Samarkand'—ever with the hope that in the next valley there would appear the city with shining domes and marble palaces on which European eyes had never yet rested.

6 *The Adventures of George Thomas*

WHILE Benoit de Boigne was still nursing his dreams in Madras a man of a very different sort landed there, and without wasting time walked off into the jungle-clad hills to the westward and disappeared. Nothing more for certain is known about George Thomas until he bursts on to the Indian stage eight years later and fifteen hundred miles away in a style that he was to make peculiarly his own; sword in hand at the head of a handful of men and leading a desperate counter-attack. He is supposed to have reached India in 1781 and to have been a deserter from the Royal Navy.[1] This is possibly true, as the fleet commanded by Admiral Hughes was operating in those waters in that year and was at Madras in 1782, but it is disputed, and one version is that he came to India in a merchant ship. He was certainly a sailor; his nickname among his sepoys of 'Jehazi Sahib'— 'Sir Sailor'—is sufficient evidence for that. It is known that he was for some time in Reinhardt's old brigade, that in a dashing action he saved the person of the Emperor himself from capture, that he was promoted, conducted a vigorous and successful campaign against the Sikh brigands who infested the north-western part of the Empire and was dismissed, for 'misbehaviour' says one account; and then began his violent career as a mercenary under the Mahrattas and as a land-pirate on his own. His Memoirs, dictated to a Captain Francklin, are a mere recital of battles, plots and marches and only begin when he is thirty-seven with the eight missing years and four more as a mercenary behind him. Francklin (surely one of the dullest and most pompous biographers who ever netted such a subject) either did not ask Thomas anything about his early life or suppressed the more lurid and disreputable facts, primly observing that 'perfect correctness of conduct cannot be expected from a character like the one under consideration, as seclusion from civilised life and a long absence from the exercise of those duties which constitute the chief enjoyment of social happiness, must necessarily have tinctured the manners of the man with some portion of the spirit of the barbarians with whom he was so long intimate'. This is a fair specimen of Francklin's style, although he

Lieutenant General the Count de Boigne in his honoured old age, wearing the
Saint-Louis

Obiit Aug: 1802. Ætat 40.

GENERAL GEORGE THOMAS.

does add with justice that among other qualities Thomas 'was on a level with the most distinguished officers of his day', and that his understanding of the Indian peoples, which was the secret of his leadership, was unsurpassed. 'Coarse and illiterate,' says Lewis Smith, which is untrue, as Francklin records that he spoke and wrote both Persian and 'Hindostanee' (he probably meant Urdu) fluently and correctly. He is said to have had boundless ambition with abilities to match, to have judgement and prudence, and at the same time energy and daring beyond the ordinary, but all these are abstract qualities. We know little of the real Thomas, except for a few vivid glimpses through the eyes of the young British mercenaries James Skinner and Lewis Smith, who met him, dined at his table and fought against him: the Thomas with easy, affable manners, entertaining the junior officers, carrying a proposal from a rival; the haughty and dignified Thomas negotiating with the Viceroy of Hindustan as an equal; Thomas roaring drunk at table; Thomas the berserk, his face contorted with fury and charging at the head of his troops: a sight so terrifying that it made the younger Skinner (Robert), who was no coward, fairly take to his heels. The later, Victorian image of Thomas was of a wild but 'romantic' being who seemed far removed from their peaceful and subdued India, already crossed by railways and administered by sober officers with Christian principles and a classical education. They admired him for his Britishness, his pluck and his daring, but shook their heads over his 'going native', to use that odious phrase, his drinking and keeping a harem. They pigeon-holed him as a lovable Irish scapegrace; being Irish of course serving then as an excuse for any eccentricity. This seems an inadequate verdict on a man who seized a principality and ruled it so justly that his name was still remembered with affection and respect in the twentieth century, and who as a soldier on the Indian scene, if not quite the equal of a Lake or a young Arthur Wellesley, was certainly in the class of Clive, or Forde, or Adams, or Munro; these now forgotten men whose flights of tactical daring put the East India Company in possession of half a sub-continent.

The accepted story of Thomas' early life is that he was born at Roscrea in County Tipperary in 1756, that he ran away to sea, and that he was when he deserted in Madras a cabin-boy (of twenty-five ?), an ordinary seaman, a gunner, or a quartermaster.

He is then supposed to have spent some years with the petty chiefs called 'Polygars' in southern India who were a by-word for lawlessness.[2] (In fact the word *palegar* or *palegadu* simply means a hereditary landowner, and their lawlessness arose from their understandable reluctance to pay their taxes. The Nizam of Hyderabad tried on one occasion at least to borrow some Company's battalions to help him collect them, a squad of infantry carrying more weight in the India of those days than a final demand note.) After this he enlisted in the Hyderabad army commanded by the Gascon mercenary François Raymond, but soon deserted, having formed a keen dislike for the French. He then tramped to Delhi and found employment in the ranks of Reinhardt's old brigade and from then on, with the exception of a few details, his history is well authenticated. While, of course, it would be absurd to suggest that a man of humble birth and no education could not rise to the heights he achieved, it is not altogether satisfactory.

It cannot be doubted that he was a sailor, but his stiff and upright carriage and his habit of holding his head up and pulled back is unmistakable evidence of the attentions of the drill-sergeant. One account says rather disparagingly that he drilled his men 'as well as he was able', and another says that they were indifferently disciplined, but his columns were once noted moving to the attack 'as if they were on parade': the highest praise a soldier of those days could give. Thomas' campaigns show that he was fully equipped with a sound practical knowledge of siege-craft and the use of field-fortifications, both of which were important for the commanders of that period and was part of the formal education of officers. At Fatehpur, for instance, he made good use of an abatis—a dense belt of felled trees with the upper branches lopped and sharpened and pointing towards the enemy—something unknown in northern India. A sailor, or a marine, might reasonably be expected to fight with a musket or a cutlass, or serve a field-piece, but the lower deck is not a place to learn to ride. Riding itself is not a difficult art, but Thomas had an eye for a horse—his own stable was famous—and he also showed that he could lead a squadron of cavalry; indeed, his earlier operations against the Sikhs were almost entirely mounted affairs, judging by such scraps of evidence as we have. These were his purely military qualities.

There are other inconsistencies between his alleged origin and later life. In southern India in those days the ruling upper classes conversed in Persian, the common people their own language such as Malayalam, Canarese or Tamil and the soldiers the military *lingua franca* called 'Urdu', which meant originally the language of the army or 'horde.' It is perfectly possible to learn a language colloquially and by ear, but to write the Persian script used for both languages and 'speak, write, and read in Hindustani and Persian languages with uncommon fluency and precision', which are his biographer's own words, without any previous experience in forming letters or of the laws of grammar or syntax either argues a man of extraordinary intelligence or one who was already educated to some degree. Then, on a certain occasion he says that to retire 'would be a dishonour to myself, and to my progenitors, who never turned their backs on an enemy'. Now, even allowing for Francklin's style, and for the fact that courage and patriotism were not then regarded as ludicrous, even in common men, this is an unusual phrase to find in the mouth of an illiterate man off an Irish bog who had spent allegedly all his formative years in the brutal and degrading slavery of an eighteenth-century British warship. Finally, and in this all his contemporaries are agreed, ruffian and land-pirate though he may have been, he was never guilty of any gross crime in an environment where torture, betrayal and assassination were commonplace, and he adhered strictly to the mercenary code, he never abandoned an unlucky or defeated master to whom he was contracted, and was almost naïvely honest in money matters.

If it is permissible to guess, then Thomas' real story may have been as follows. From his name he appears to have been the descendant of a recent Protestant immigrant in Ireland, possibly of Cromwellian times. He may have been of modest but respectable birth, and have received at least some dame-schooling. Being of an adventurous disposition he enlisted in the British army, where he would have been at home, for it was full of Irishmen. The Royal Horse Artillery could have accounted for both his skill in gunnery and his horsemanship, but it was not yet formed, so conceivably he may have been a dragoon. It is known that he was a rebellious subordinate, and one who resented the faintest slight, and that his mild and jovial manner could suddenly erupt into fits of homicidal rage. If some officer or sergeant had raised a cane or a foot to him, as was the bad custom of those times, Thomas may well have struck back and earned himself a hanging, or a flogging to death. He fled, deserted, and found his way on board ship. The King's ships were always short of men and their captains were always glad to obtain hands and ask no questions. He thus reached India, where he deserted once more at the first opportunity, and disappeared as promptly and as thoroughly as he could. It may or may not be significant, but long afterwards he said that he wished to serve the King of England, to the 'end of his days', 'which I can only do as a soldier *in this part of the world*'. There remains one other faint clue about Thomas. The cartouche below his portrait is decorated, perhaps only by chance, with the heraldic charge of a family which had already produced distinguished soldiers. Could George Thomas have been that stand-by of Victorian novels, the illegitimate offspring of a noble family?—but to pursue this is to go beyond guesswork into romance, and Thomas' career is quite remarkable enough as it is.

We can best begin therefore at the enlistment of Thomas, probably as one of the European gunners required in the artillery, in Reinhardt's former brigade. When he joined them they were probably the most useless, the most expensive and the most mutinous troops in all India. Reinhardt, after Patna and serving various masters, each farther away from the advancing British, had finally been taken into the Imperial service and had dug himself in snugly in his jaghir at a town called Sardhana, not far north of Meerut. Here he had built himself a palace and barracks for his troops. He understood the business of managing his jaghirs to a nicety, keeping his expenses low by employing the dregs of the Company's and the French deserters as 'officers', and by paying his sepoys as much in arrears as he dared, sometimes a year or more. From time to time the exasperated troops rioted and beat up their officers, and if they could catch Reinhardt would strip his trousers off and sit him astride a hot cannon until he paid them something on account. Reinhardt's real gift was for survival. He could endure any humiliation as long as he avoided dismissal or ejection from his jaghir, or fighting a battle. In return for being allowed to continue in command he never asked too much of his troops. According to Lewis Smith, who thought such conduct unprofessional and that it lowered the whole reputation of the mercenary corps, his tactics were, if he actually arrived on a battlefield 'to draw his brigade out into a line, fire a few shots, form square, and retreat . . . by which singular mode of warfare though they have acquired no laurels they have preserved their reputation.' Smith was writing after Reinhardt was dead, but the brigade stuck to his system, much to the anxiety and embarrassment of Reinhardt's wife, who had inherited the force.

Madame Reinhardt, or Mrs. Somers, or 'the Begum Somru' to give her the name by which she was commonly known to the British, was the daughter of an Arab trader and a Kashmiri woman, and when Reinhardt first came across her she was a dancing-girl. She was a tiny, attractive little thing, and Reinhardt, as men of his age often do, took a violent fancy to her. She, sensible creature, saw the opportunity of escaping from the dubious occupation of entertaining rich Hindu *banias* or itinerant Pathan horse-dealers in search of a night on the town, and insisted on marriage. Reinhardt was already married, or at least lived with an Indian woman who had produced him an heir, but the girl was insistent. The first wife was dismissed, and the dancer, to tie the bond with her Feringhi more firmly, became a Roman Catholic. She was christened Joanna but was never called anything else except the 'Begum Somru'—'begum' being the feminine of 'beg', or Lord, often used as a courtesy title for Muslim ladies, and Somru an Indianisation of Sombre, or Somers, Reinhardt's *alias*. Somru Begum would be more correct. Reinhardt's death in 1778 was a great blow to her, because, as has been explained, the possession of mansabs and jaghirs was not hereditary; but the little Begum went off to Delhi and somehow secured the reversion of the jaghirs to herself, so that her fortune was secure, and in turn guaranteed the military liability. (This was not an altogether unusual transaction. There are two or three examples of wives succeeding their husbands, and Haidar Ali, the ruler of Mysore, actually appointed the widow of one of his mercenaries in command of his force and gave her the rank of colonel. One or two commanded in the field. India has a long tradition of masterful women.) The Begum, however, soon found that in taking responsibility for the brigade she had bitten off more than she could chew. The crew of officers she had inherited from her husband had no intention of ever fighting, or being dismissed, or of allowing the number of their useless mouths to be reduced, or of being disciplined. Three sound mercenary officers resigned from the command in succession, confessing themselves unable to do anything with them, and they continued to live on the Begum, who was terrified of them, like the suitors of Penelope. For her the discovery of Thomas was a God-send.

This took place at a siege where two rival Moghul nobles were amusing themselves in the course of one of the struggles for power in the palace after Lalsot and Madhaji's retreat from Delhi. Ismael Beg was temporarily in the ascendent and therefore had with him the poor doddering old Emperor, Ali Johur Shah Alam II; possession of whose person, as the evidence and source of legal authority was the aim of most of these operations. He had called on the Imperial troops, which included Somru Begum's brigade to support him. Ismael's opponent had a long, strong position based on the 'fort', i.e. castle, of Gokalgarh, near Agra, and an extended system of entrenchments. The battle was not pressed very vigorously on either side. Early one morning, however, the defenders learned that part of Ismael's troops had been making a night of it. (As has been said, the Rajputs, who provided a strong component of the Imperial army, were particularly addicted to opium.) The defenders therefore in an unsporting fashion made a strong sortie directed on the Emperor's own camp, which was assailed by infantry from the front and bombarded from the rear by some batteries of artillery which had emerged from the fort and circled round Ismael's siege works. By dawn the confusion in the Imperialist lines was complete, except where the Begum's brigade stood under arms and in orderly ranks in its camp, which was some distance off from the point attacked. There it remained motionless as it had at Buxar under Reinhardt twenty-two years before when the fate of eastern India was being decided, deaf to all orders to move. The Begum commanded and implored, but her officers adhered to the sound principle they had learned from their dead master: that it was unwise to intervene until it was quite clear which way the currrent of a battle was flowing—whether the Emperor was in danger or not. At this point Thomas reported to her with a hundred volunteers and a six-pounder gun: a piece of artillery that was to become almost his personal weapon. At the crises of all his battles he can be seen trundling up a gun and emptying it at point blank range in his opponents' faces.

The Begum led the counter-attack in her palanquin and between her screams of encouragement for Thomas and her abuse of the enemy, and Thomas cheering on his men, and the banging of the six-pounder, those rebels who had not already succumbed to the temptation of looting the Imperial camp were soon dispersed, the Emperor was rescued and his blear-eyed officers were given time to kick their men out of their hang-overs and into a sense of their duty.[3] It was not a heroic action, but the Emperor was delighted. As soon as things had calmed down he held a durbar, or an audience. The Begum was congratulated on her devotion and he gave Thomas a handsome present. The Begum was even more delighted than the Emperor. She had found someone in her ramshackle army who could actually fight. Gokalgarh was the making of Thomas. Not long afterwards the Moghul authorities ordered the Begum to take over the responsibility of protecting the area north-west of Delhi from the raids of the Sikh bandits who were terrorising it, and allotted an extra jaghir to cover the cost of the operation. She gave both the jaghir and the task to Thomas.

The Sikhs, with whom Thomas was to be at war for most of his career, were a brotherhood of religious warriors. Sikhism was originally founded by a Punjabi called Nanak who, dissatisfied with both Hinduism and Islam, taught his followers to avoid the ascetism of one and the fanaticism of the other and literally to mind their own business—like Voltaire 'to cultivate their own gardens'—to practise tolerance and virtue, and to believe in one, invisible, unknowable God. There are still a few Nanaki Sikhs so called after their founder who follow this pure Unitarian creed. It is, of course, almost unnecessary to say that as happens with religious movements the Sikhs were immediately persecuted by the Moghuls, who saw the Sikhs as heretics of an odious kind and as rebels. Sikh and Muslim hate each other bitterly to this day. (The Hindus were more tolerant of Sikhism, which they saw merely as a variation of their own all-embracing creed, like Jainism. Also, the majority of Sikhs were Jats who continued to observe their Hindu caste rules.) The children of one of the Gurus, or teachers, who succeeded Nanak were murdered, another child saw his father executed, and the faithful were scattered. This boy, Govind, grew up and brought a new revelation. The Sikhs were to save themselves in this world by becoming warriors, and in the next by listening to his teaching.

Every male would add 'Singh' to his name, and observe five rules, the name of each beginning with the letter 'k' in the Punjabi language; they must never cut their hair or beards, they would comb it with an iron comb, they would always wear a pair of cotton drawers, an iron quoit or a bangle, and carry a sword; the symbols of holiness, poverty, modesty, eternity, and a soldier. The Punjabi people, Muslim or Sikh or Hindu, are among the most aggressive and warlike in the world, and the brethren received these laws with enthusiasm. Continuing the natural line of development of religions, the new Sikhs resembled the old Nanakis as the Scottish Covenanters the early Christians. In no time the oppressed turned into the oppressors, and by the end of the eighteenth century the whole Punjab had been lost to the Empire not by conquest, but by Sikh anarchy. The effective frontier to the north-west ran within a hundred miles of Delhi; and the smoke of burning villages, the sparkle of Sikh lance points and the long lines of the dust raised by their hard-riding *jathas*, or raiding parties came ever closer to the capital.

Thomas, like de Boigne, was one of those unusual men who arrives fully equipped to accept high responsibility without having served any apprenticeship. The career of his rival and enemy, Cuiller-Perron is far easier to understand. Perron, like Thomas, was a deserting sailor, but he worked his way up through the ranks of the Army of Hindustan to succeed de Boigne through sheer perseverance and fighting ability in every rank from sergeant to commander of a brigade. By contrast Thomas moves at one bound from the lowest of mercenary appointments to become what we would now term a director of operations, a commander in the field and the administrator of a large territory. It is important not to exaggerate his achievement and equally important to say that, except for one or two clues, there is no surviving account of this phase of his career, but we can extrapolate from his second and later Sikh campaign in which he played the same role in much the same conditions. Even if only the most cautious and grudging interpretation is made from what evidence there is his feat was a remarkable one, especially if the accepted view is taken, that he was an illiterate deserter from the lower deck.

He immediately displayed that he had as clear a grasp of what used to be called the 'principles of war' as any graduate of the

Staff College. Then, and throughout his life, speed, mobility, and offensive action were his watchwords. In his view the correct method of dealing with wasps was to burn the nest. He never wasted energy in pursuing raiders after the damage, or his troops by stringing them out in long cordons or in rows of forts. Being fortunately untroubled by public opinion, humane ideas or fear of 'escalation', he answered one raid with another, and his heavy hand was also felt by those who compromised with the raiders or paid them by blackmail; he was not above demanding a 'fine' or a 'contribution' himself. To carry out such a policy over the long frontier running roughly south-west from Saharanpur for two hundred miles required good cavalry, well-mounted and well-trained and capable of the long, fast marches with an action at the end which are the true test of horse-mastership. In action the test of cavalry is that they must never get excited or out of hand, charge solidly knee to knee and always obey the command to rally. Whether Thomas discovered these facts for himself or whether he was taught, he became famous for his marches and his fighting. The British Colonel Tod was of the opinion that 'with five hundred of his Rohilla cavalry he could at any time have disposed of thrice that number of Sikh horse'.

This is the only mention of Thomas ever disposing of a force of such strength. In his own little army he seldom had more than a hundred and fifty horsemen, and fifty is the more usual number mentioned, although it is clear that this was a *corps d'élite*. The factor limiting numbers was expense. In India cavalry was organised on the 'sillidar' system, by which the troopers were expected to provide their own horses and forage, and had to be paid accordingly, apart from the fact that mounted troops expected to be paid more than the infantry, being, as in the West, more often drawn from the yeoman class than the peasantry, and expected to have dash and initiative rather than robot-like obedience. A trooper in the Army of Hindustan, for instance, was paid 24 rupees a month as against a foot-soldier's five and a half, and even if his master provided his horse, as in de Boigne's own bodyguard, he still expected eight. (The sillidar cavalry continued into this century in the British-Indian army, when it was discontinued on grounds of efficiency.) If one allows 8 rupees to the pound sterling and considers the relative value of money it can be seen there was an effective upper limit on the numbers of good cavalry, and the poor performance of the vast masses of the Hindustani or Moghul horse and the Mahrattas and Rajputs, who are always numbered in 'tens of thousands', can be understood. Even for a regiment of five hundred sabres therefore Thomas would have had to find, if de Boigne's pay scales are taken as a guide, a figure of the order of 4000 rupees a month. The whole of his future kingdom of Hariana although admittedly in a run-down condition, only produced some twenty-two thousand, and it is certain that his jaghir produced nothing like this figure. It is said to have been worth 80,000 rupees per annum. This was not much to support even a small army when all the expenses of providing equipment, draught animals and expendable stores like ammunition were taken into account, to say nothing of Thomas' extravagant practice of paying gratuities to the disabled and pensions to widows. Thomas was all through his career in money trouble over his troops, resorting sometimes to brigandage or the spoils of battle to pay them. He never believed in stinting them and as a result his army was seldom more than two thousand infantry, a hundred or two hundred cavalry and two or three batteries of artillery. He made up for lack of numbers by the quality of his troops, the extraordinary rapidity of his marches and his tactical skill. However, this is to anticipate. What is said of him in this phase is that he doubled the revenues of his jaghir, and not merely by giving the screw one or two extra turns; but by good management, by imposing law and order, which had almost ceased to exist in the Empire, and above all by shielding his people from the depredations of others. All the revenue went to his border force, and only his pay into his own pocket. When he was suddenly dismissed he had only four hundred rupees to show after three years' opportunity for peculation.

Thomas failed through being too successful and his fall was sudden and complete. His weakness was his arrogance, and he was a man without tact and, at any rate at this stage in his career, with little political sense. It never seems to have occurred to him that his sudden elevation as the Begum's favourite was bound to arouse violent jealousy in the brigade, or if it did he regarded the officers over whose heads he had jumped with contempt, and did not believe that they could threaten him. He was secure in his own jaghir, where he had established himself in the fort of Tapal some distance away from Sardhana, he controlled what was virtually his own force; he had the confidence of the Begum, and indeed had married, or at least she had given him, one of the bevy of attractive young girls with whom she always surrounded herself. The Begum after the departure of her previous importations was chary of putting any one officer in full command of her brigade, but Thomas stood high in her counsels and she took his advice. All this was very galling for the others. It was bad enough that this British tramp had made them all lose face by showing them up at Gokalgarh, but it was monstrous that he should have been given the Tapal jaghir, which was simply an invitation to enrich himself. His prestige with the troops was dangerous to them. Indian sepoys, who were themselves mercenaries and professionals, like all other soldiers, admired men who lead them successfully in battle, and it would be the end of discipline in the brigade if Thomas' galloping about on the frontier undermined their loyalty to their appointed officers. Thoughts like these may have been going through their heads, but what alarmed them most was learning that Thomas, on being asked by the Begum how to improve her brigade, had advised her to throw out all her French officers. Thomas' chief rival was a man he calls 'Le Vassoo', possibly Levassoult or Le Vaisseaux, a man slightly superior to the rest and who was in command of the artillery.

Levassoult may not have been much of a soldier, but he was an able conspirator, and he worked hard to ingratiate himself with the Begum and began to insinuate that George Thomas was too successful and too ambitious and also, perhaps, disloyal. He brought off his coup when Thomas was away to the north and involved in one of his harrying operations against the Sikhs. It is always a mistake to be absent from the ruler's ear when a struggle for power is taking place. Levassoult led a group of senior officers into an audience with the Begum and pretended to reveal that Thomas was plotting not only to take over the brigade, but to oust her and become the jaghirdar or Sardhana as well. Her loyal officers had refused to listen to his blandishments, and that was why he was recommending to her that they should be dismissed. The Begum, added Levassoult, need have no anxiety, they were solidly loyal to her, and would deal with Thomas if she gave them leave. Now, there may have been at least a little truth in this. Thomas was notoriously insubordinate and he seems never to have grasped the idea that a jaghir allotted to support troops in mansab was not actually his. He may well have been getting too big for his boots, and there may have been disputes between him and the Begum; a possible cause being that the Begum was being refused her just share of the revenues from Tapal. At all events the Begum fell for the story, and took prompt action to bring Thomas back.

As it happened Thomas' wife was staying with her late mistress, and was therefore instantly available as a hostage. A message from her, or from the Begum, or both, reached Thomas, whose reaction was prompt and characteristic. The bare idea of opposition always roused him, and also the Begum's reputation was such that he would not leave his wife at her mercy. There is a well authenticated story of two of her young ladies, or slaves, or whatever they were, perhaps becoming tired of an all-feminine society, running away with two sepoys. They stole some of the Begum's jewellery when they left and set fire to the palace on leaving to cover their tracks. The two wretched girls were caught, and in the Begum's presence flogged almost to death and then buried alive. It is probably a reaction against the great authority women wield in Indian family life and the respect they enjoy that they are sometimes treated with obscene cruelty. Terrible things were done inside the secrecy of the zenana, apart from the use of poison or the noose. On one occasion a Sikh princess was put to death by her own waiting women, who were ordered to beat her to death with their slippers, and did so. To be struck by a shoe was particularly degrading. Thomas took no risks and wasted no time. He made one of his lightning marches, burst into the palace, rescued his wife, and was ensconced in his small fort at Tapal before the conspirators had realised what had happened. His goose, however, was cooked. His own troops, or his portion of the troops from the brigade who might have backed him were all on the border and a couple of hundred miles away. He had only the fifty odd sabres who had accompanied him and this was not enough to hold Tapal even against the Somru brigade. Thomas accepted his dismissal under the threat of its cannon. He was lucky to be alive, but it seems that one or more of the officers drew the line at killing him, and the Begum allowed him and his wife to leave unmolested. She may also have been influenced by the fact that Thomas' wife was one of her girls. The Begum is said to have adopted one or two of her favourites, who thus by Indian custom became fully and legally her daughters. It is an intriguing thought that Thomas may therefore have been her adoptive son-in-law, and it is noteworthy that after Thomas' death in 1802 Mrs. Thomas and her children were given a home for the rest of their lives by the Begum. She may have therefore had some scruples about executing him. Whatever the reasons the outcome was for her providential, for she soon took the one false step in a long life spent in the practice of survival among a complexity of dangers.

She believed that she had in Levassoult found her saviour from her terrible brigade, and she first promoted him to the long vacant command, and not long afterwards married him. The second step is the more perplexing. To marry was to commit herself to a certain amount of subordination, whereas until then she had seen, like other feminine rulers, that her position was best secured by playing one rival off against another. As for men, while there was gossip about her and one of her former officers, the fact that she never had any children and the existence of her zenana full of charming girls, which was still in existence and remarked upon, particularly by the young British officers twenty years later, raises some doubt about her feelings in the matter. Perhaps she felt at forty-five and after a storm-tossed life that marriage would be respectable and secure her against the attentions of other suitors. At all events she was married to Levassoult in the presence of two of her senior officers and according to the rites of the Roman Catholic Church by a Carmelite missionary.

Her choice is another example of the great difficulty one race had in forming an opinion on a member of the other. As it happens, the names of both the witnesses to her marriage are known, and show that she had at least two capable and honest mercenaries; one being Bernier who was to fight George Thomas himself to a standstill, and the other a Swiss called Saleur who eventually she promoted to command her brigade. Either was far superior to Levassoult, who was a conceited idiot. His promotion soon went to his head. Instead of seeing what the sepoys' grievances were, and paying them honestly, he clamped down on discipline; and instead of dismissing the ruffian element among the officers he banned them from his mess table, as being socially beneath him. (In those days a commander was expected to keep open house for his officers, and was paid 'table money' for the purpose.) Levassoult was, in short, one of those officers whom one sees from time to time, who is able, without in the least understanding what he is doing, to reduce even a good unit to simmering discontent, and can invariably be found as the irritant in any mutiny. Things in the brigade went from bad to worse. On one occasion the troops refused to march, and finally they really rose in mutiny and Levassoult who had completely lost his nerve suggested to the Begum that they should escape to Chandernagore in French territory.

The survivor of a suicide pact can never be quite free of suspicion, and there were those unkind enough to say that the Begum chose this uncertain and oblique way of getting rid of her unfortunate choice. They had agreed, who first made the suggestion is not recorded, that they would kill themselves rather than fall into the hands of the mutineers, and what happened was that when a troop of her cavalry caught up with them the Begum stabbed herself in the breast and sank back into the arms of one or more of her girls, who began to scream their heads off. She was travelling in a purdah bullock cart, that is to say, one with curtains to ensure privacy, and Levassoult, who was riding, came up in the flurry and asked what had happened. 'She is dead,' screamed the girls, 'she has stabbed herself.' Levassoult never thought to look inside, or to resist his pursuers, or even to gallop away. A second enquiry brought more screams that the Begum was dead where upon Levassoult drew a pistol, put it in his mouth and blew the top of his head off.[4] The disappointed mutineers hacked his corpse about and then looked for the Begum. She had in fact inflicted a wound on herself no more severe than the scratch Lady Caroline Lamb made in her bosom to frighten Byron. They took her back to Sardhana and chained her to a gun. That she was not immediately murdered in some unpleasant way is credited to Saleur, who advised the mutinous officers against doing anything rash. Mutiny was one thing, he pointed out, but they had discovered the son of Reinhardt by his first wife, Balthazar Sombre or Jafar Yab Khan, and installed him in the Begum's place. This was an act of rebellion, and none of their business, as Sardhana was an Imperial fief and the Begum was an Imperial vassal. They wavered, and while they hesitated the Begum thought of the erring George Thomas, now a successful brigadier with the Mahrattas and once more busy on the Sikh border and fortunately only some forty-five miles away, preparing to 'chastise', to use one of his expressions, a town which had been co-operating with the raiders.

Whether it was the Begum's pathetic situation, or the promise of a large reward, or pressure from his wife, Thomas acted promptly and with no little skill. He persuaded the Governor of Saharanpur, his master of the moment, to move some troops towards Sardhana, ordered one of his own battalions to march at their best pace to it at once, and taking his own cavalry bodyguard set off himself. He realised that it was important not to frighten the mutineers into any desperate action, so he paused outside the town, camped and sent word that he represented the Imperial authority, and that if the Begum was freed and reinstated all would be forgiven, but if not, they would answer for it. The mutineers had no desire to face the Jehazi Sahib in battle and then be tied to the mouths of their own guns and blown to pieces if they survived, so Balthazar was turned out and the Begum released and restored to her place.[5]

Next morning George rode into the lines, but when the hard core of the mutineers saw that his escort was only fifty horsemen they changed their minds, and for a moment Thomas was wondering whether to fight, or fly or to brazen it out when the van-guard of his battalion appeared in the town. Though this still left Thomas facing odds of four to one it was enough to tip the balance. The mutineers, who were not fighting stuff, backed down, the Begum was restored, poor Balthazar was packed off to a cell in Agra fort where he died, no one was punished, and all the officers were made to sign a declaration of loyalty. The only objection made to this was on theological grounds. Pious Muslims usually begin important documents with the invocation 'In the name of God, the merciful and compassionate,' adding sometimes 'and of the holy apostle of God, Mohammed.' The Christians required the addition of the name of his Son, but the Muslim 'munshi' rebelled at putting his hand to a heresy so revolting that it implied the Almighty was capable of descending to paternity, and compromised by writing: 'and His Majesty King Jesus Christ'. To this all the European officers put their marks, except Saleur, who was able to sign his name. He was promoted and placed in command, and the troubles in the Somru brigade were over. It continued its pacific career, and even when ordered in 1803 to Assaye avoided the main engagement. After the defeat Saleur, evading Wellesley's pursuit, marched it rapidly back to Sardhana where the Begum had wasted no time in declaring for the British.

It would be pleasant to record that Thomas and the Begum were reconciled, but they never were. He marched off immediately to his unfinished business in the north, covering the forty-five miles in twenty-four hours, to the discomfiture of the disaffected garrison commander who thought that he was still safely in Sardhana, beat him inside his defences and stormed his fort before nightfall. Thomas was not one to let military grass grow under his feet. He never saw the Begum again.

The Sardhana revolt is out of chronological sequence, but it completes the story of Thomas and the Begum. It is now necessary to take up the thread again from the moment of Thomas' dismissal at Tapal. He turned brigand: and the promptness with which he became a brigand on each occasion when he was out of mercenary employment, and his familiarity with the technique, do seem to indicate that there may have been something in the rumours that in his early days he had been a bandit, or the accomplice of bandits, when with the Palegars. He wasted no time in assembling a band of desperate men. Some of these may have been his own loyal troopers, but a fighter of his reputation would have had no difficulty in collecting as many more as he wanted of the floating population of unemployed soldiers. Finally he had a force of about two hundred mounted men. To pay them something on account and to provide funds to live on he sacked and put to ransom a large village; confiscating for his own share of the spoil all the brass *lotas* or brass jars which are an essential part of the domestic furniture of every Indian family, to melt them down and cast a small cannon. Such a leader and such a band of war-hardened men, all mounted, could have lived off the proceeds of *dacoity* indefinitely, but robbery was for Thomas not a way of life but simply a means of supply. His aim was to hire himself and his force out to a suitable employer, and eventually he found one.

Dates are a little uncertain, but Thomas recalled that shortly after hearing of the death of Madhaji Sindia, which took place in February, 1794, his new master sent for him to escort him to Delhi where a durbar of Mahratta chiefs was being held to discuss the question of a successor. The siege of Gokalgahr and the rescue of the Emperor were sometime in 1788, and Thomas'

A Sikh Akhali or 'Immortal', the type of Sikh raider Thomas fought so often

A Mohammedan irregular horseman, here a Multani, of the type recruited by Thomas

appointment as warden of the Sikh marches is supposed to have lasted about three years, or three and a half, ending in 1792; so he may have lived on casual banditry for about a year. His immediate future was not to be noticeably different.

Appa Khandi Rao was a Mahratta of the Mahrattas; brave, cunning, devious, capable of assassinating his own brother, and grasping and avaricious to a degree. He was one of Sindia's generals who had been rewarded with a large and totally unmanageable jaghir in Mewat. The Mewatis had been plundered and taxed unbearably by each successive victor in the perpetual civil war in Hindustan and they were now refusing to yield a penny. Appa had been much impressed by what he had seen of the two battalions de Boigne had raised for his master in their first action under his own command, and with the usual difficulty Indians had in assessing the quality of Europeans and believing that one was as good as another, he engaged Thomas to raise a similar force of a thousand men, a squadron of cavalry and some artillery. His discreditable role was to be Appa's debt-collector and bully, and the first task he was given was to take over a completely lawless district in Mewat which had paid no revenues for years, and extract enough money from it to pay his soldiers. It is this phase of his career which led to the assumption that Thomas was unable to train or discipline troops. He collected some eight hundred ruffians of sorts, but to keep them had to pay them, and to pay them had to use them at once in Mewat to 'levy a contribution', as Thomas used to call it. This was a proposal his new subjects treated with derision. They started by stealing Thomas' own horse from the picket-line in his camp, and then attacked him and chased him out of the district. But for his bodyguard he would have been killed. It was from this disorderly and ignoble beginning that Thomas started his second climb to fame.

The Jehazi Sahib and the Rao Sahib

GEORGE THOMAS was to serve Appa Khandi Rao for some three years, possibly from March or April in 1794 to Appa's death in the early part of 1797. His new master was one of the great Mahratta notables, a cousin of Madhaji Sindia, who had followed the fortunes of his house from Panipat onwards. His fellows, and inevitable rivals, were men like Ghopal Rao Bhao, Bapu Sindia, Ambaji Angria and Lakwa Dada, who was not a Mahratta but a man of the highest, or Brahmin, caste; one of those whose intelligence and ability so often led them to high office in both Hindu and Muslim courts. 'Rao' is a title, roughly equivalent to 'baron', but there were no fixed grades of nobility in India. 'Rao', like 'Beg' or 'Sahib' is simply assumed, or proffered. Appa's patent was the oldest one, which was to command a following among the Mahrattas and successfully to lead it in war. In the carve-up of the jaghirs of the Moghul amirs which followed Madhaji Sindia's final conquest of Delhi, a large territory, virtually a sub-province lying to the south and west of Delhi comprising the district of Mewat and what was later the state of Alwar, was given to Appa as his share. As has been explained earlier this position was feudal: Appa's duty was to govern the territory for the Emperor—actually for Sindia, to collect the land revenue, pay over a fixed proportion to the Mahratta authorities, reward himself, and also, as mansabdar, meet his feudal obligation of maintaining a body of troops for Sindia's service—the 'Army of Hindustan' being, of course, Madhaji's and after him Daulat Rao Sindia's personal force. In addition each of the Mahratta chieftains had to keep up his share of Mahratta irregular horse and possibly some najibs and infantry levies as well. By the end of 1793 Appa had failed on all three of these counts. His trouble was age and illness. He had in his day been a good fighting man, by Mahratta standards, but now that he was old and ailing he lacked the energy and grip required to subdue his new domains, whose people did not exactly welcome the Mahratta rule which to them was synonymous with robbery, or to keep his own troops in order.

The whole countryside had been wasted by banditry in the civil wars. The population, and in particular the Mewatis, were a truculent and ungovernable race, and he found it hard to raise any revenue. He owed the central government no less than two lacs of rupees which he ought to have collected and paid over. His troops were in arrears with their pay. He had made a mess of a small but tiresome campaign Madhaji had entrusted to him in Bundelkhand where his troops had mutinied. Madhaji, highly dissatisfied, had dismissed him. Strictly speaking, therefore, he now had no legal title to his jaghirs; but what with Madhaji suddenly dying and the confusion ensuing on the reign of a minor and the general looseness of Mahratta administration he had not yet been physically dispossessed. Nevertheless, defenceless as he was, he feared that it was only a matter of time before his rapacious colleagues decided that his lands be better shared among themselves. When therefore he heard that the formidable Jehazi Sahib, George Thomas, had been disgraced by the Begum and was going cheap, he pricked up his ears and took heart. As has been said, de Boigne's first engagements had been under Appa's command, and he had been most impressed by his performance. He thought he might do well to have a Feringhi of his own. Thomas already had a nucleus of troops or of bandits. Appa as an old soldier and a Mahratta was a good judge of both. Thomas, he decided, was his man. So he was, but he did not foresee what a tiger he had by the tail.

After some difficulties about ready money, of which Appa was infernally short but without which Thomas could not begin to recruit, they came to an agreement. Thomas received an advance payment of 40,000 rupees in cash and the right to collect the revenues of three tax-districts in Mewat, and in return he was to maintain a force of 1000 men with a quota of cavalry and artillery. The cavalry were no problem. Thomas throughout his career had retained a little mounted *corps d'elite* devoted to his person who formed his escort—his 'household troops'. Their casualties were severe, and the troopers may well have been changed two or three times over, but they had a continuous existence from Thomas' early campaigns against the Sikhs until they disbanded after his fall. At the moment they were outlaws and bandits under Thomas' leadership, but to

reconvert to regular cavalry required no effort. The greater proportion of the cash advance probably went on cannon which were
expensive but without which Thomas never operated, and on
engaging the half-castes or European deserters who were required
to command each gun and also the fighting castes suitable for the
actual gunners. This left little to pay for good infantry, and accounts
for the rabble Thomas picked up, doubtless in the hope of training
them later. With this dubious force he marched on a town called
Tijara, the largest in the district allotted to him. His route lay
through an outlying jaghir belonging to his late mistress the Begum,
and partly by way of revenge—Thomas never forgot or forgave
an injury until he had levelled the score—partly to replenish his
war-chest and partly to whet the appetite of his troops he sacked it
thoroughly and collected a large 'contribution'.

The system of collecting revenue from recalcitrant peasants or
villagers was brutal in the extreme: indeed, according to reliable
British sources there was no practical difference between the
collection of chauth and plain brigandage. It was accomplished by
massacre, torture, murder, rape and abduction. Thomas himself is
not believed to have descended to the grosser cruelties, although
this is hard to believe completely in view of the type of troops he
recruited. A wretched woman dragged from hiding to amuse the
troopers, the edge of a sabre offered to the throat of the headman's
son or a torch run along the thatch of his roof were doubtless
effective persuaders. He does admit rather airily that on one
occasion the town whose ransom he was negotiating caught fire
'by accident', thus most unfortunately destroying much of the loot
and reducing the value of his haul. The Mewatis and the inhabitants of Tijara had long since lost patience with this sort of thing.
What they had they intended to keep and they firmly believed in
the proverb that 'the man who held the bigger stick owned the
buffalo'. Like the peasants of most of northern India they could
assemble a 'home guard', on which their lives and safety depended,
armed variously with swords, spears, bows, matchlocks and that by
no means despicable weapon, the iron-bound Indian quarterstaff, or
lathi. As irregular soldiers they were as good as any to be found in
the feudal Indian array. Tijara was fortified and the surrounding
country—covered with scrub jungle and cut up by ravines—was
ideal for ambuscade. Indeed, the last visitation they had had by

troops in search of revenue had been from Somru Begum's brigade and they had seen those reluctant warriors off their premises in fine style. The approach of Thomas' column had been closely watched, and the men of Tijara awaited him in no passive mood.[1]

George Thomas was to prove himself an excellent general but on this occasion he made one of the worst of mistakes possible to a commander in the field, which is to underestimate the enemy. His rage when he found that his sentries had allowed his camp to be entered by thieves, and that these had actually stolen one of his own prized chargers from the picket line, led him to make a precipitate attack and into a well-laid ambush. His recruits to a man broke and fled: many he never saw again. He himself had to run too, hotly pursued, until he came upon one of his cannon stuck in the bottom of a nullah. A few of his devoted cavalry kept the Mewatis at bay with swordstrokes for a few desperate minutes while their commander, always happier with a six-pounder at hand, helped drag it into action and blasted off a few rounds of grape at point-blank. The men of Tijara thought this enough, having made their point, and drew back behind their walls or into their jungles. Thus Thomas escaped with his life.

He was not, however, defeated. After a day or two he managed to round up some 300 of his stragglers and advanced on Tijara again. This was an unexpected and embarrassing move, for its successful defenders had dispersed in the euphoria of victory or had somewhat necessarily returned to their fields and their businesses. The headmen offered to treat, and Thomas, who unless he was thwarted was capable of being the most reasonable of men, settled the whole affair with considerable diplomacy, obtaining the submission to Appa's authority not only of Tijara but the other two districts as well. Thus he was provided with a base and a source of money to pay his troops. He was also provided with recruits, as Thomas was much impressed with the martial qualities of the Mewatis and recruited sufficient to replace the men who had deserted him, anticipating a sound military policy followed by the more sober British administrators who followed him in India in the years to come. Having given his officers a little time to knock the new recruits into some sort of shape he set about reducing the rest of Mewat and Alwar to a proper state of subjection. His methods were uncompromising. At the slightest sign of defiance from town or village he stormed and sacked it until the mere terror of his name was enough to open the gates and bring submission.

A terrible example of his methods is his capture of Bairi, a strong place of a pattern common enough in India; the town protected by a wall and bastions with an inner stronghold, or 'fort'. The headman of Bairi, who justly considered that Appa Rao's rule was illegal, had resolved to resist and had hired three hundred Jat and Rajput mercenaries to help garrison the town and the fort. Normally such a place stoutly defended would require a formal siege. Thomas was perfectly familiar with the science of advancing parallels, building batteries and so on, but often he had neither enough troops to 'invest' a place—to encircle and blockade it completely—nor the big guns required to batter a breach in the walls. Above all he lacked time: his whole military philosophy rested on speed in marching and an immediate, ferocious assault. His methods were desperate but, as the more orthodox British who were great stormers of forts repeatedly demonstrated, once over the wall and inside the discipline of regular troops could prevail over the uncoordinated valour of the defenders. This is what happened at Bairi. A brief bombardment set the town on fire and then Thomas, who had only a strong battalion, rushed at the walls and made 'lodgement' inside the town. He then found himself in serious trouble, trapped in a street of burning buildings, attacked and under fire from front and flank. He was forced to withdraw and in the confusion no one noticed that one of his Indian officers had been wounded and had dropped behind. Thomas' troops, powerless to help, watched the defenders capture him and thrust him living into the flames. Then, to quote Thomas, or rather, Francklin and his unlikely version of Thomas' idiom: 'Equally animated and enraged by the spectacle, my troops rushed forward to the attack with an ardour that was irresistible. Having gained entire possession of the fort the soldiers with clamorous expressions of revenge insisted on the death of everyone of the garrison that remained and I was not inclined to refuse . . . but it cost us dear, the enemy to a man making a brave resistance. . . .' Thomas goes on to describe how after the death of the Rajputs and Jats in the fort itself the defenders of the town tried to escape, how he pursued them with his cavalry, and how 'after a desperate conflict they gave way on all sides and most of them were cut to pieces'. In short, the entire defending force was refused quarter and slaughtered for having the temerity to defend their own, and their town burned. Although such incidents were common enough in the warfare of that place and age it was a bloody and brutal affair.[2] It made the name of Thomas a word of terror, and in the next two years no *kiladar* (commandant) was hardy enough to resist him to the point of facing a storm. By such methods, always marching at a most un-Indian speed, seldom pausing to argue or bargain but hurling his ferocious and loot-hungry troops on to town and village at the first hint of defiance, did Thomas establish the rule of his master firmly through all Alwar and Mewat.

However, his success began to alarm the Mahratta authorities. This was the middle of the year 1794: judging by the weather it was about June, which is when the monsoon rains are at their height. De Boigne, it will be remembered, prudently wishing not to involve himself in purely Mahratta infighting, had appointed Lakwa Dada as his deputy governor of Hindustan. Lakwa, who was a highly intelligent and capable man, did not wish to turn Appa out although he was technically a rebel, because in Mahratta politics the shifts in power were so violent and so rapid that there was no point in making a man irrevocably an enemy who might well be needed later as an ally. He merely wished to bring Appa to heel and for this indirect methods were better. It may therefore have been Lakwa who was behind a conspiracy of Appa's own officers—of his own Mahratta irregulars, that is, as distinct from Thomas'—to arrest him together with his family. Appa somehow had wind of this and had taken refuge in a small fort, but was surrounded by his rebellious troops who camped outside it. He was thus trapped but he managed to send a message for help to Thomas, who was in camp some forty miles away. It reached Thomas late one afternoon. The monsoon was in full blast, the country was flooded and the roads, such as they were, deep in mud. By the standards of native armies he would have done well to be ready to move the following morning, to make two days march of it, and arrive towards the end of the second day. Some indication of the pitch of discipline to which Thomas had brought his little force is that he was able to start then and there and keep it marching all the first night. After a short rest next day he resumed and, typically, disconcerted Appa's treacherous levies by his arrival in their camp in the dark hours of the second night twenty odd hours before it was thought possible. He secured his master's person and enabled him to bestow his family who were with him in safety without coming to blows with the mutineers; but trouble began when he started to withdraw; as it so often does on such occasions and in the face of such troops.

Appa had decided that his best course was to make a bolt for his stronghold at Kanaund whose garrison was still loyal and from which it would require a regular siege by Lakwa to extract him, so he ordered Thomas to escort him there. The column started to plod back through the mud, but soon the mutineers plucked up courage, first following and sniping and then becoming bolder and bolder in their attacks. A long column on the march is desperately vulnerable to this sort of thing; there is continual halting, the rear guard has to face about and deploy, the troops begin to fidget and fire without orders and it can be altogether trying. It is always a problem for a commander who has not succeeded in breaking clear of the pursuers to know what to do at nightfall. If he halts and forms a defensive perimeter he may find at dawn that he is surrounded, whereas if he plods on in the dark and the enemy is active and enterprising they may infiltrate into his column and throw it into complete disorder. Fortunately for Thomas and Appa the mutineers had not sense enough to continue with their harassing tactics but cut across their line of retreat and blocked the road. Thomas gratefully formed his battalion for the assault and invited Appa to honour and encourage the troops by mounting his elephant and leading the charge. To this soldierly suggestion the old Mahratta warrior agreed with great spirit, and with Thomas hurrahing, the elephant trumpeting, and the sepoys shouting their respective war-cries, to which Appa added (we hope) the dreaded 'Hur, Hur, Mahadeo!' of the Mahratta slogan, they burst through the rebel ranks, scattered them, and completed the long march to Kanaund without further interference.

Appa was delighted. He gave Thomas a present of solid cash, always a rare commodity with Mahrattas and also with Thomas (and so much more *useful*, one cannot help feeling, than a DSO or a CMG), an elephant and a palanquin; the last, the privilege of an amir, so that he could keep up his position of the *Sahib Bahadur* commanding the victorious troops of the Rao Sahib. As for the elephant, Thomas may well have anticipated the great Mr. Jorrocks with his 'Confound all presents wot eat'; and he was not really a palanquin man, preferring the saddle. But Appa's gifts did not stop at elephants and palanquins. He presented Thomas with another large jaghir and one much more valuable than Tijara as a gift, based on the town of Jhajjar, about fifty miles west of Delhi. He also ordered him to increase his force to a full brigade. The order to expand his little force was more to Thomas' liking than presents, even of money. The master of three battalions of drilled, regular troops together with batteries of guns and his cavalry bodyguard would be a man of some consequence; one who could fairly call himself a general. (In fact, following the usage of the time rank was not invariably used as a mode of address among the mercenary officers. It was 'Monsieur de Boigne' or 'Monsieur Perron' or 'Mr. Thomas'. Similarly 'brigade', itself a loose term, alternated with 'corps' or 'Mr. Thomas' party'. The strength of Thomas' force at any moment varied with casualties, desertion and difficulties over pay, but from this point on it can be called a brigade following the ordinary military usage, not to be confused with the ten-battalion brigades in the Army of Hindustan.) Jhajjar he held on to throughout the rest of his career, as a base for himself. He built his own 'fort' in the district. A small town grew up around it which exists to this day under the name of Jehazgarh—'Sailor's Castle'.[3]

Lakwa Dada, however, had not finished with Appa; indeed he had barely started. In due course he entered Mewat on a tour of inspection. Appa believed that it was now politically possible to improve his relations with the Mahratta authorities. Madhaji was dead; Ghopal Rao, an enemy of his, was in disgrace, there was the new, young Sindia who perhaps could be placated. He felt himself, reinforced by the Jehazi Sahib and his invincible brigade, to be in a strong position from which he could negotiate. He had a further incentive. He knew that he had not much longer to live, and he was seriously concerned to secure his inheritance for his nephew and adoptive son, Vaman Rao. Accordingly he repaired to Lakwa's camp to make his peace; without Thomas, whose person and brigade he kept well out of sight as a token of his loyalty and his readiness to come to terms. Lakwa did not choose to dispossess Appa, who after all was an old and respected Mahratta chief and had been a follower of the house of Sindia in bad times as well as good, but he drove a hard bargain. He reminded Appa that he owed the treasury 200,000 rupees. The terms he offered him were that he was to get rid of Thomas, that Thomas' three districts in Mewat were to be surrendered to the Mahratta authorities and that the collection of the land revenue over the whole of Appa's domain would be made directly by his own agents until his financial affairs had been straightened up. Lakwa Dada was a Brahmin, and this was the sort of businesslike arrangement a Brahmin would make. He had not reckoned with Thomas.

At this juncture Thomas was free to leave, and there could have been nothing dishonourable in his doing so. He had been deprived of the means to pay his troops, Appa had fallen and clearly his contract was now void. Thomas' ideas of loyalty were, however, peculiarly his own, and on this occasion highly embarrassing to its object. Appa was engaged in a delicate piece of diplomacy, and clearly felt that left to himself he would placate the powerful commander-in-chief and deputy governor and eventually all would be well. Thomas, like one of those dogs of which Konrad Lorenz tells us, who assume that the family they have adopted are members of a pack of which they are the leader, regarded Appa as his own personal property. He was indignant that anyone had dared tamper with him, and, regardless of what his master had agreed, denounced the arrangements. He did not complain about Tijara and his own tax-districts, probably considering that it would take better men than Lakwa's to squeeze any money out of the obstreperous Mewatis; but the rest of Appa's domain he held with a hand of iron, promptly and ferociously attacking any town or district he suspected of disaffection. (In fact, it was in this period that he stormed Bairi and massacred its defenders.) When Appa attempted to dismiss him, rather feebly, in a letter ordering to disband his troops, he refused to obey. His troops, he said, were owed a large arrears of pay, and any attempt to disband them without full payment in cash would be dangerous. As Appa's funds and credit were now attached this proved an insuperable obstacle. Having made this clear Thomas, realising the source of the order for his dismissal, characteristically stormed off to beard the great Lakwa Dada himself whom he accused to his face of trying to bring about his downfall. The Brahmin mildly professed to be surprised at this accusation. He had heard nothing of it, he said, but he added, not without humour, if Thomas was thinking of leaving Appa he would be glad to employ him himself.

This broad hint Thomas disregarded. Always defiant at the slightest show of opposition he had decided to hold Appa to his contract and to stiffen his spine against Lakwa Dada. That intelligent man saw little point in trying to suppress Thomas, which would be a bloody and expensive business. Besides, Thomas might yet prove useful to him. He saw that what was required was some task to divert his enormous and dangerous energy to some useful object outside Appa's country, even if only temporarily. As commander-in-chief he was fully entitled to order Appa to make his troops available for general service, and it happened conveniently that there was a suitable operation taking place at the moment.

Major Gardner and four battalions of the Army of Hindustan were besieging a place called Sowalgarh but making little progress, so Thomas was instructed to take his people there and reinforce him. Thomas had no choice but to obey, nor was he disinclined to do so. He was always ready for a fight, particularly if there was money to be made out of it. As regards money, however, there was the little problem of his unpaid troops, who struck on hearing the orders; but he persuaded them to march, selling up his property so as to give them something on account. At Sowalgarh, as has been related, he 'wiped the eye' of the regulars by capturing the key redoubt without orders and unassisted. With his share of the ransom that the defenders had to pay to escape a storm he was able to pay his troops their arrears, so that difficulty was surmounted. Thus all ended fairly happily, but there was the beginning of a rift between Thomas and his master, who, he may have felt, had been disloyal to *him*, and who had too tamely accepted the orders from Lakwa for his dismissal. This, in his overbearing and haughty way, he would have considered a piece of impudence. It was not long before he had another and more serious clash with Appa over the disposal of a prisoner. Not long after Lakwa Dada had removed himself from Mewat, Appa, egged on by his fiery commander, ordered or permitted Thomas to eject all the troops and official tax-collectors Lakwa had put in as receivers.

We can only conjecture why this fresh rebellion was tolerated and why Appa and Thomas were not immediately suppressed by a detachment of the Army of Hindustan who were the only troops good enough to deal with Thomas. A possible answer is that, in the first place, apart from the general anarchy resulting from the decay of the Imperial system, the Mahrattas were incapable of administration or of maintaining order. Insurrection was their normal condition of life. De Boigne, so briefly governor of Hindustan, was slowly disengaging himself from his appointment and had no desire to meddle in purely Mahratta squabbles. In the second place, all the attention of Sindia and his followers was now attracted to the struggle for power in the south, with the intrigues over the Peshwa and the campaign against the Nizam. De Boigne's brigades were scattered in various tasks and there was no direction or purpose behind their use. Lakwa Dada himself, was about to fall out with Sindia, and he had his own political affairs to attend to, of which Appa's formed only a small part. Therefore it was perfectly natural once Lakwa had turned his back for Appa and Thomas to disregard the whole agreement. No Mahratta, certainly not one with Thomas to help him, would sit tamely by watching his own territories being ransacked by any tax-gatherers other than his own. They set upon Lakwa's people without conference or delay.

Appa and Thomas were, in the course of these operations, engaged in reducing the town of Nurnool which was stoutly defended by one of Lakwa's officers, a Brahmin and a man of considerable wealth. He privately offered to surrender the town to Thomas in exchange for a personal safe-conduct, which Thomas agreed. Appa had not been consulted by his commander in the field and with good reason was most offended. He thought it a wicked waste not to 'shake down' the Brahmin and extract a large ransom from him. He told Thomas to hand him over: the prisoner was his, not Thomas', who was merely his subordinate and not free to make his own terms. Thomas refused. For him it was not only a matter of honour but of good military sense. He and his troops had faced great dangers and suffered many casualties to establish their reputations, and were now reaping the benefits. They were men terrible in battle, but whose offer of quarter could be trusted. If now he was seen to play false, then no one would ever rely upon his word again. Garrisons in future would as a result elect to take their chance if 'summoned', and defy him to the bitter end—which would be as wasteful for him as it would be costly for them. This argument did not move Appa. He was not going to kill the Brahmin, only to squeeze him; but the fate of the Brahmin now became the smaller issue. What was much more offensive was Thomas' open defiance of his orders. It is impossible to keep a secret in India, everyone knew what was happening, and therefore as long as the Brahmin remained in the safety of Thomas' camp Appa's face was 'blackened'.[4]

Thomas understood all this perfectly well. For over twenty years he had been living as an Indian among Indians—with the poorer classes he had met on the long road from Madras to Delhi and with the great Mahratta and Moghul officials. It was not that he merely 'understood' Indians—a somehow slightly offensive phrase implying that they are a different species of humanity—but that by acclimatisation he had virtually become one. Thomas was a man of superior intelligence and when he chose could be charming and diplomatic, qualities which if he had kept his temper would have served him best on this occasion. His trouble was that like so many men of dominating character he believed himself to be invariably in the right. His was an unusual character, but one, it must be said, by no means unknown in military life. He was entirely self-confident. He was a man of almost manic energy and irritability who found it intolerable to be at rest. Faced with any sort of opposition he invariably adopted the same solution: in the field he attacked, in debate or negotiation he held his view defiantly and without the slightest compromise. He was quite incapable of dissimulation, or of throwing away a small point in order to gain a greater one. He could never understand that even in a strong position it does not pay to press an opponent too hard. As is often the case in a man of such character he coupled extreme solicitude for his men with a total disrespect for his superiors, whom he disobeyed and hectored in a most outrageous manner. Indians have an almost feminine sensitivity. They fear humiliation far more than physical danger. In all human relationships they prefer subtlety, insinuation and flexibility to Western bluntness which they consider a sign of stupidity and lack of breeding. To be shouted at or hectored is for an Indian a deadly insult: enought to sting him even to the point of murder. Thomas knew all this and when he was calm could be as diplomatic as any Brahmin. His trouble was that once he was crossed he became irrational and ungovernable.

The result of his arrogance and obstinacy was that Appa tried to arrest him; and also, possibly, bearing in mind that he was a Mahratta, to murder him. After the fall of Nurnool Appa had established his court in a large house in the town. Thomas for the best of reasons always lived in camp among his troops and protected by his guards. A few days after the dispute Appa summoned Thomas in the ordinary way to give him his routine instructions. On arrival Thomas was told that the Rao Sahib was unwell, and that he was to go up to his room. Accordingly he left his escort without which no man of his standing would go about in the courtyard, and, suspecting nothing, went on upstairs. There he found Appa dressed and, apparently, perfectly fit. The reason for the visit was to reopen the question of the prisoner. Thomas once more abruptly refused to hand the man over. At this final defiance Appa left by one door for his inner appartments while, through the other, or outer, door filed a party of armed men. They may have been assassins, or they may have been merely what are called in modern criminal circles 'frighteners' and were in all probability the Pathan bullies who were commonly used for this sort of work. Thomas saw he was trapped. He had the sense, however, to remain seated and absolutely calm, making no move which might startle his touchy and highly aggressive company. At this point a letter from Appa was put into his hand demanding the prisoner forthwith, on pain of arrest and dismissal. Thomas read this slowly and with great attention and then, to the discomfiture of the would-be assassins around him who might have expected him to make a bolt for the door or for the window, so that he could shout for his escort, he rose and strode through the inner door to confront the quailing Appa. Thomas' loud and disrespectful tone and his even more disrespectful gesture of placing his hand on his sword-hilt, made it clear that if there was to be any violence the first victim would be the Rao Sahib himself. The upshot of a deadly game of bluff was that Thomas was able safely to return to his camp. From there he sent a senior officer with a message of resignation which, of course, he had no intention of allowing to be accepted; knowing well that Appa could not afford to lose him. Poor old man, all that he desired was that this noisy and violent Feringhi would try to treat him with the respect due to his rank and occasionally to see his point of view; but there was no help for it. He was forced to give in, being finally put to the humiliating necessity of going personally to Thomas in his camp, abandoning his claim to the prisoner and begging him not to resign. No Indian, certainly no Mahratta, could ever have forgiven that.

It is as useless to placate men like Thomas as it is to resist them half-heartedly. The consequence is even more disobedience and more demands. Not long after this Thomas in the course of a small operation captured a number of cannon. He and the Rao again fell out violently over their disposal, for guns were valuable booty in terms of cash. Appa claimed them as his own. Not so, said Thomas, they were by custom the property of the troops who actually captured them and he refused to hand them over; he wanted them to sell and so give his chronically underpaid sepoys something on account. Appa now saw that Thomas was becoming a menace, though when he excused himself after this next attempt to do away with Thomas he said that it was the work of his servants who had acted without telling him. He may well have been speaking the truth. His nephew and heir-designate was certainly implacable in his determination to rid himself of Thomas as it was becoming increasingly clear to him and to Appa's entourage that it was Thomas, not they, who was running Appa's affairs and that the Rao was completely in Thomas' power. To the Indian way of thinking it seemed to them, as it had seemed to Somru Begum and her advisers, that his next step would inevitably be to supplant Appa and take over his territory himself. Conveniently for the plotters it happened that there was a band of Ghosais on their way through Appa's territory, to Hardwar or to Benares, and a deal to eliminate Thomas was made with them. According to Thomas, 10,000 rupees was to have been the price of his head.

The Goshais and Bairagis have long since disappeared from the Indian scene, at any rate as armed bands. Nevertheless, it is still possible today occasionally to see among the peaceful tribes of wandering *saddhus* and *sannyasis* a nude, ash-smeared being with an expression of almost satanic malevolence that ill accords with true Hinduism and is altogether disturbing and alarming even to the least superstitious and most superior Western foreigner. Such creatures incline towards the destructive, or Shivite, side of the Hindu trinity. The Goshais consisted of whole bands of such men, dedicated not to poverty and to contemplation of the Deity but to violence and death; preferably by suicide under the wheels of the festival cars of the Jaganath who is an aspect of Shiv the Destroyer. When not engaged in self-immolation they wandered through the country in troops as destructive and as thieving as the rhesus monkeys who are such a pest and who are equally protected by religion. Goshais could also gain merit by death in battle, and were thus much in demand as mercenaries for any particularly desperate or dangerous affair.[5] Like the ancient Norse berserkers a few genuine *saddhus* may have been actual psychopaths whose numbers were increased by ordinary criminals who had adopted the religious life as disguise and protection for robbery and murder. Whatever they were in theory, they were in practice a repulsive and dangerous breed, hated and feared by all, especially the peaceful villagers and peasants on whom they chiefly preyed. Thomas wasted no time or pity in dealing with this particular band. He probably would not have tolerated their presence in his bailiwick in any case. He got wind of the plot from a friend in Appa's confidence or perhaps a spy he had inserted into his entourage, for Thomas was by then an experienced intriguer and not the naïve trooper who had been outmanoeuvred by Levassoult in Sardhana years before. He fell upon the Goshais without warning and slaughtered a large number of them. This led to another quarrel with Appa, and another spurious reconciliation. Appa claimed that he was ill, in fact dying, which was true; pleaded that the plot had been made without his knowledge; and ended pathetically by beseeching Thomas to become the guardian of his heir Vaman Rao and to serve him as he had served himself and defend his rights after Appa had gone.

All this was somewhat embarrassing for Thomas. He was certainly loyal to Appa after his fashion; although nowhere in his memoirs does he reveal the faintest affection or liking for him, or indeed anyone except possibly one of his English officers. Apart from any honourable feelings he may have had his fortunes and Appa's were entwined, and prudence as well as loyalty demanded that Thomas should stick to him as long as he lived. Vaman Rao was a different matter. It was clear to Thomas that the young man was firmly in the hands of his own enemies in Appa's entourage and that his relationship with him was likely to be difficult to say the least of it. At this point, however, the whole problem of his increasingly uneasy position as Appa's mercenary commander was shelved.

There were new and sinister developments in the Punjab. In normal times the Sikhs and the Afghans, who are of course Pathans by race and Muslim by religion, were hereditary enemies, but now Zaman Shah, the grandson of the victor of Panipat and the King of Afghanistan, had designs to invade India and had begun to meddle in Sikh affairs, courting them and encouraging them in their raids, behind which there was felt a new weight and determination.[6] Both Lakwa Dada and Bapu Sindia, who as the governor of Saharanpur was responsible for the defence of the frontier, were much perturbed. The Sikhs were a manageable nuisance, but ever since the fatal day of Panipat the name of Afghan had had a terrible sound in Mahratta ears. They had no reserves on which they could call, no one to take charge of affairs. The army was depleted, and the new Sindia, Daulat Rao, was far away in the south with part of the regulars with him. At this particular moment, in late 1795 or early 1796, there was no one to take a grip of affairs in Hindustan. De Boigne had gone and Perron, his successor designate was with Daulat Rao in Poona. Sutherland was occupied in the troublesome campaign against the Bundelkhandi Rajputs in which Appa had failed. Fremont was dead. None of the other officers was capable of taking the initiative. The only other regular troops available in the Imperial service was Somru Begum's Sardhana brigade, but this was still under the command of the futile Levassoult and was in more than its usual state of chaotic indiscipline. (It was shortly after this that his suicide and Thomas' dashing rescue of the Begum took place.) Lakwa Dada decided that the answer was to put George Thomas' energy and aggression to permanent good use against the Sikhs. This would also have the result of completely detaching him from Appa, which was from his point of view an added political advantage as it would make that slippery chieftain more amenable. Thomas had already expanded his force to some three battalions, he was a proved commander of great ability and had fought the Sikhs before. Lakwa Dada therefore offered him control of three large and important territories from whose revenues he was to support his force, whose size was now fixed at 2000 infantry, 200 cavalry and 16 guns, with the task of guarding the whole Sikh frontier under the general direction of Bapu Sindia.

This was a splendid offer; a general's command. Thomas very naturally accepted. His future with Appa was uncertain for Appa was a dying man, and Thomas badly needed fresh financial support for his troops. The new post gave him wealth and a recognised

9   117

regular position among the Mahrattas: he would in fact have a larger establishment and greater responsibility than even de Boigne himself when he was first employed by Madhaji. What was as significant, however, as his rank or the size of his force was the extent and position of his new domain. He retained, being still nominally also in Appa's employment, Jhajjar and his own Jehazgahr, both secured by garrisons under his own command, and loyal to him only. His new territories adjoined Jhajjar and stretched northward in the order Sonpat, Panipat and Kurnool, a total of a hundred miles. Thus he controlled, as a glance at the map will show, all the strategic approaches to Delhi from the west and the north. Panipat itself lies on the classic invasion route into India from Asia and had been the scene of three of the decisive battles of Indian history. (In 1526 and 1556, when first Babur and then Akbar established the Moghul rule, and in 1761.) As a mercenary general his reputation was by now second only to de Boigne's as far as fighting was concerned. He had so far fought no great battles and his opponents had been irregular levies on the old untrained Indian pattern but, if his initial fiasco at Tijara is excepted, he had never been defeated in the field and he had never summoned a fortress without taking it. Nor was there any question of he himself being merely an unpolished irregular or guerrilla, like his contemporary the great Pathan mercenary Amir Khan. The only irregular or unexpected aspect of his military behaviour was his speed of movement and his penchant for head-long attack; but his headlong attacks were made very scientifically. He was also as skilled in the use of engineers and artillery and in siegecraft as he was in the open field. He may not have been an educated man like de Boigne or the devious and unreliable Sutherland, but he was fully the equal of Sergeant Perron. There was no reason at this stage in his career why it should not have been he who finally rose to the highest position among the mercenaries. As things turned out it would not have been an impossible outcome for him to have ousted Perron and to have succeeded him in command of the Army of Hindustan. All he needed to do now he had reached this important and powerful position was to exercise a little tact and a little political judgement. Being Thomas, what he actually achieved was a quarrel with both his masters ending in outright war; being dismissed, stripped of his territories and driven once more into outlawry.

His quarrel with Bapu Sindia is mysterious in so far that it was absolutely pointless. Neither Lakwa Dada nor Bapu Sindia had the slightest cause for complaint as far as Thomas' operations were concerned. He attacked the Sikhs with the greatest dash without sparing his own troops and gave them a series of savage beatings. By mid-1796 they had all fled north to the safety of Patiala. We can only assume that Thomas was more disobedient and overbearing than usual and that Bapu Sindia, unlike the ailing Appa, was a man of high stomach who did not for one instant intend to put up with Thomas' tantrums: in his view Thomas was a subordinate and was there to obey orders. According to Thomas what happened was that at the precise moment when Zaman Shah was approaching the Sutlej and affairs were at their most alarming Thomas' brigade felt it necessary to strike again for their arrears of pay. Thomas was always sympathetic to such demands. Apart from the fact that he had served in the ranks himself and saw the soldiers' point of view, they were not the sort of men who would tamely submit to unfair treatment or to rigid discipline. They had fought hard and had suffered heavy casualties in the Sikh campaign and being, like their commander, mercenaries they expected to be paid for their trouble. The evil of the mansab system was that it required the presence of the troops themselves to collect the revenue from which they were paid and they obviously could not be in two places at once.

It is of course not entirely impossible that Thomas like many other mercenary commanders in India had embezzled or withheld the funds he should have used to pay his troops, but this would have been quite out of character. What he proposed to do was to go off on a fund-raising expedition to Panipat and Kurnool. This Bapu refused to allow, in view of the situation. High words were exchanged as a result of which Thomas flew into one of his rages, declined to serve under Bapu any further and marched his troops away. Bapu was equally furious and gave orders that the withdrawal of Thomas' brigade was to be stopped even if it meant firing on them. This somewhat drastic step was taken, with the result that Bapu's troops were very roughly handled and driven off and their commander wounded. The indignant Bapu, all thought of the Sikh threat and Zaman Shah abandoned, took command in the field himself. There ensued the absurd spectacle of the governor of Saharanpur and his principal field commander hotly engaged with each other in the presence of their common enemy. Thomas' line of withdrawal from Saharanpur involved crossing the Jumna. Bapu cut in ahead of him and faced him at the ford, only for Thomas to shoot his way through. Then Bapu, who seems to have showed far more spirit against Thomas than ever he did against the Sikhs, turned out every unit he could muster; local levies, infantry from the Delhi garrison—he even managed to induce some of the Somru Begum's battalions to take the field—and once more cut in front of Thomas who was by now pushing hard for Jhajjar and safety. A full-scale battle took place. Bapu's tactics were old-fashioned but sound. He put his infantry in the centre so as to force Thomas to deploy in line and then used his cavalry to attack both the vulnerable flanks so exposed. Thomas, and this refutes any suggestions that his men were not properly trained or were incapable of manoeuvre, 'refused' his flanks, i.e. drew his flank battalions back so that they faced outwards. Their disciplined volleys held off the Mahratta horse—never very eager to charge home—while he pressed hard on the infantry in the centre. Eventually they broke and Thomas marched straight through the middle of Bapu's army unpursued, so severe were the losses that he had inflicted. Thus Thomas came safely back to Jhajjar, but he was ruined. There was no hope of retaining Kurnool or Panipat or Sonpat; he would have had to fight the entire Mahratta army for them and the population as well. To make matters worse Appa Khandi Rao had at last died, and while Thomas had been engaged with Bapu Sindia Vaman Rao had forcibly occupied some of the territory allotted to him by Appa.

Appa's end had been sombre. His disease was progressive and agonising, and he had finally decided to end his life by ritual suicide by drowning in the Ganges. Suicide was not forbidden to Hindus, although unusual except among fanatics and, of course, high-caste widows. He had sent for Thomas to come and bid him farewell and to urge him again to stand by young Vaman Rao, but Thomas had been too involved to leave his frontier operations at once and then it was too late, for poor Appa, unable to endure his sufferings until he reached the Ganges, had drowned himself in the Jumna.

Thomas on his return to Jhajjar was at first, for him, surprisingly restrained. To be sure, he refused to tolerate Vaman's seizure of parts of the districts of Jhajjar. He flung out his intruding troops

and, with that curious military knowledge he had acquired somewhere, forced the garrison of a small town to surrender hastily by
firing red-hot shot into it. To Vaman himself he behaved mildly,
offering a large quit-rent to be allowed to retain his jaghirs. Vaman
refused. Thomas suggested a peace-conference, but Vaman refused
again, saying that he did not trust Thomas, and shut himself up in
his uncle's old stronghold in Kanaund. He invited a conference
within, but this Thomas prudently declined in his turn. Vaman was
powerless to evict Thomas, who continued to hold Jhajjar by force
of arms but it did not help him in his present impasse. He now had
attached to his person some 2000 or 2500 veteran fighting men who
had followed all his fortunes, who were still unpaid and whom he
had persuaded to engage in a fighting retreat on the pretext of
giving them their dues and a well-earned rest when they reached
home. Neither the rent-roll of Jhajjar nor his own fortune would
provide enough to pay them off, but in any case he did not want to
disband them even if they agreed to go. They were his only security
against the mounting number of his enemies: the Somru Begum,
Vaman Rao, Lakwa Dada and Bapu Sindia. They were also his
sole real asset. To keep them he required 15,000 rupees a month at
the very least; this figure is exclusive of the cost of powder, shot,
new equipment, gratuities to the wounded and widows, remounts
and forage; and also excludes the expenses of his own household
and personal bodyguard, which were high. There was nothing for it.
His troops must pay themselves until he thought of some expedient,
and to this end he led them on a series of brutal expeditions whose
sole aim was to extort blackmail by offering towns and whole
districts the choice of paying up or being plundered. It was during
one of these, 120 miles off to the west of Bikanir, that his troops so
carelessly and expensively burnt down a town during the course
of negotiations. It parted with 52,000 rupees. This was enough to
keep the brigade going for a time. Thomas' soldiers were quite accustomed to being paid something on account and to hope for
something from the next raid, but it was a hand to mouth existence.
Sooner or later, Thomas knew, his force would gradually dissolve
and the enemies each raid created would eventually combine
against him.

At this point had he been an ordinary adventurer, like Madec or
Lestineau or Dudrenac, he could have taken what cash and portable

wealth he had and bolted for British territory, or he could have offered his services to the Rajputs, for Pratap Singh of Jaipur was still smarting over his defeat by the Mahrattas and ready to go to war again, or there was Jaswant Rao, who had succeeded Tukaji as Holkar in Indore and had inherited his feud with the Sindias; or there was the Peshwa himself, or his minister, Nana Farnavis. Thomas, however, had had enough of native masters. He was dreaming dreams, and his dreams were of kingship and conquest. Why not? Neither militarily nor in any other sense had he so far met his equal. The Mahrattas could not run their own affairs properly; while he, given a little peace and elbow room, had shown at Tapal and Tijara and now at Jhajjar that he could order things much better. He had at least the sense to feed the sheep before they were shorn and under his rough rule the peasants even thrived. The Mahrattas could not even effectively use their own admirable soldiers. Why, thought Thomas, could he not do what Sindia had done in Gwalior, or Haidar Ali in Mysore; or for that matter, what the English were doing everywhere? In 1797 he marched his little army off like a migrating tribe into the country called Hariana which lies west of Panipat and to the north of the Thar, or Great Indian Desert. Wasted by civil war and Sikh banditry it had been abandoned by Moghul rule. It seemed to him what no one else wanted he might as well take.

8 *King Thomas*

GEORGE THOMAS had now arrived at the most celebrated phase of his career. He was to invade and conquer a large territory, rule it as an independent sovereign, restore it from a wilderness to prosperity, and from its revenues sustain the army he had created with the intention of conquering the whole lost Moghul province of the Punjab. Like every other circumstance about Thomas it is difficult to arrive at the exact details, even the basic truth of this story. Thomas has inevitably attracted a certain amount of myth, for there was indeed something heroic about him. He provides a classic example of the man fighting against odds: of the handicaps of his humble origin, of the contradictions of his character and of the numbers and powers ranged against him. The ideas of conquest by the sword, of a 'white rajah', are also 'romantic', even to us, today; provided, of course, we do not look too closely at the process of conquest or the lineaments of the conqueror. Thomas himself when he recounted his adventures to Francklin was a dying man, his enormous self-confidence broken by the disaster which had suddenly overtaken him, and he was drinking heavily. By then he was prone to exaggeration. Astonishing as his successes in battle indeed were it is possible that in his memoirs he was confusing his hopes and his intentions with what he actually achieved. He undoubtedly did achieve a great deal in his brief reign, but it was truly brief. It extended only from 1797 to the end of 1801, and during this period he was continually at war and absent for four arduous campaigns. Perhaps all that happened was that under the iron hand of his protection, which permitted no other depredations but his own, there was an increase in the prosperity of Hariana from which he demanded sufficient blackmail money to support his troops in further bare-faced raids and robbery. We can, if we like, dismiss Thomas as simply a land-pirate, or a guerrilla, who from his desert base raided his neighbours until, to the great satisfaction of all the Indian peoples living within his reach (and also—who knows ?—of the British, who coldly rejected his overtures) he was put down by the Mahrattas; or in fact by Perron, which came to the same thing.

This is to take too extreme a view. The people of Rohtak remembered his rule with gratitude a century and more later and many undoubtedly welcomed it.[1] Colonel Tod believed that if things had gone better for Thomas he could have won the throne of Lahore. In 1801 Perron was himself in great political danger having angered Daulat Rao Sindia and aroused the jealousy of his chiefs. Had Thomas not been so irretrievably aggressive, had he had but one good adviser, had he but made the final move required to secure the defeat of the Third Brigade at Jehazgahr in 1801, had he avoided a confrontation with Perron until 1803 when the British were ready to move—then it is not too fantastic to believe that the descendants of Thomas might have been among the princes who attended the Durbar of George V in 1911. After all, why not? Thomas' Pathan contemporary, the great mercenary and freebooter Amir Khan who submitted to Lord Hardinge in 1817, was settled as Nawab of Tonk where his descendants are to this day.

Thomas himself says, and there is no reason to disbelieve him, that his reason for invading Hariana was purely to secure a military base for his great design. In his own words (or rather Francklin's version of them): 'As from the commencement of my career in Jhujjur I had resolved to establish an independency, I employed workmen and artificers of all kinds, and I now judged that nothing but force of arms could maintain me in my authority. I therefore increased their numbers (sic), cast my own artillery, commenced making muskets, matchlocks and powder and in short made the best preparations for carrying on an offensive and defensive war, till, at length, having gained a capital and a country bordering the Sikh territories, I wished to put myself in a capacity, when a favourable opportunity should offer, of attempting the conquest of the Punjab and aspired to the honour of planting the British standard on the banks of the Attock!' All his ambitions, all his plans, therefore, turned on his army. It is acccordingly worth while before going on with his story to discuss what sort of force this was. Unfortunately, and most irritatingly, all the details which a military student would most dearly like to know have been omitted by the egregious Francklin to whom apparently it never occurred to ask the simplest question in elucidation; or if he did he failed to record the answer. It is therefore necessary to emphasise that what follows is conjecture and depends on deductions from circumstantial evidence; some of it only slight.

There are, broadly speaking, two schools of thought about the old pre-Mutiny, unreformed armies of India; and both are probably correct. One, already discussed, is that the troops in, say a battalion, were recruited and mixed together regardless of caste and creed, always assuming that the lower castes and the 'untouchables' were excluded. This is not unreasonable. We know that the Muslim Moghuls employed Hindus and that the caste-conscious Hindus employed both Muslim troops and Muslim officers in exactly the same way. Amir Khan and his Pathan cavalry were long employed, for instance, by Jaswant Rao Holkar. The accepted Indian code of manners ensured that men of different beliefs could enjoy social intercourse although this might exclude marriage or eating in company or even bodily contact. From the practical point of view in the armies of those days there were no arrangements for messes or for central cooking or even any regular rations for the men, who bought their own food and prepared it. There was therefore no bother about the complex taboos affecting food and drink. Many Indians today consider that the British, by their exaggerated attention to these things and by classifying Indians into 'martial' and 'non-martial' races and by separating tribe and creed created divisions where none existed before. Some add that this was deliberate and with sinister intention. As against this, Indians are clannish with a strong sense of family—nepotism is an Indian virtue—and the Indian sirdars, as the officers were then called, tended to recruit their own kind. There may have been no strict recruiting by class or exclusion on the grounds of class, but it would be natural for units to be made up of likes. The najib battalions were exclusively Muslim, de Boigne's Bhurtpore Battalion Jats and the celebrated Rathor cavalry all Rajputs from Marwar. In the Mahratta army the infantry may have been drawn from any caste or class, but their national arm, the irregular cavalry, were all Mahrattas. The bulk of the mercenary soldiers in India, however, were Muslims, or 'Mussalmans' as they were sometimes called; from the Punjab, from Hindustan where they were still called 'Moghuls' and the ever adventurous soldiers of fortune from across the Indus of Afghan or Pathan origin, some of these long settled in the country, like the Rohillas. The Sikhs were Thomas' selected opponents and naturally he recruited the Mohammedans who were their traditional enemies. By the middle of 1801 he had expanded his army to a total of possibly 10,000 including his field army and his garrisons and his most likely source of trained or semi-trained men would have been the floating population of mercenaries, some probably organised in bands or battalions under their leaders and ready to enlist under the banner of a successful and open-handed commander.

Thomas' army may therefore have been made up as follows, taking them in the traditional British order of priority. It is always Thomas' cavalry whom he mentions as standing by him at times of danger or of crisis; at Tijara, when rescuing the Begum from a grisly fate, and during the only mutiny he had to face and in the dark days of his defeat. They were his guards, in both connotations of the term; his bodyguard and his *corps d'élite*. Thomas with his reputation as a victorious, daring leader could command the services of all the most dashing blades in northern India and take his pick of them. It seems likely that they were mixed, Thomas being too shrewd to allow a group of all one kind to be so close to him. Next the artillery, which in the native armies was also by way of being a *corps d'élite*. Thomas was a great believer in artillery and an adept in gunnery. He paid great attention to his guns, both field and siege, possessing finally about fifty field pieces alone. The artillery arm was commanded, by custom, by Europeans and Eurasians, often deserters from the French or the British royal armies or the Company's army. They provided the gun-captains, those whom the Royal Artillery term the 'Number One'. The 'golandauz', the gunners proper, were from the fighting classes, while the bullock drivers and the kelasis who pulled the guns with dragropes were from appropriate castes. About his regular infantry we cannot be sure, but a slight clue is that all the Indian officers who are mentioned by Skinner and others have Muslim names. The regular infantry therefore probably had a solid 'Mussulman' core. For most of Thomas' career he had only a small force, perhaps three battalions or so. They were therefore made up of the best fighting men from the ample supply of recruits always available. Some may have been veterans of other regular corps, already able to drill and skilled in the use of arms. Skinner, with his regular background, considered that their discipline was not strict. This is probably true. As professionals, mercenaries and volunteers they probably had a free and easy relationship with their officers. They were certainly capable of the drill which was the 'battle-drill' of those times, and provided that could deploy into column and line, handle their arms and then fight like demons, which they did, Thomas was satisfied. There is hardly a mention of wearing uniforms, and Thomas had little time for long parade-ground training, for he was always in the field. In short, his infantry depended more for their success on their prowess and courage than on forming a robot-like machine responding automatically to every order: they resembled our modern commandos or Chindits rather than the Brigade of Guards. Finally, Thomas supplemented his excellent artillery and regular infantry with the serviceable irregulars he could enlist locally; Mewatis in Mewat and Hindus of Rajput stock from Hariana and also the bands of Rohillas who formed part of all the native armies.

Such a force demanded a special and intensely personal kind of leadership; indeed, it can be said that its size and character was determined by Thomas' methods of command. It is worth noting that until the end of his career he had no European subordinates and then only a few junior British officers. It is true that European officers were free of caste and race pressures, and that they were more energetic, more reliable and more attentive to the administrative detail on which the efficiency of all armies rests than their equally skilled and brave Indian colleagues. To appoint them to all the positions in command, however, as was the practice in both de Boigne's and the Company's units, cut off the general from the vital direct contact with Indian feeling and opinion. It also blocked the promotion of Indians and often subordinated the veterans of a dozen battles to some Feringhi boy who had obtained his commission by purchase and influence and could hardly speak Urdu or drill a platoon. This was a great source of discontent. Thomas' sirdars by contrast could rise to the level of their ability, they dealt with him face to face and they could speak to him daily of all the problems which arise in a multi-racial army. As a result, although they were mercenaries themselves and war was their livelihood, they were devoted to Thomas' person. We can be certain that Thomas frequently and earnestly consulted them on every matter, and that he did not march his force off into the desert west of

Jhajjar without discussing his plans, however guardedly, with them and making sure they were all behind him. The commanding officers of the old British-Indian Army, the finest multi-racial, mercenary force in history, always employed this principle; holding regular durbars to discuss at great oriental length every complaint and every aspect of the unit's life.

Thomas himself had the great advantage over other European mercenaries of being to all intents and purposes himself an Indian. He was not like de Boigne, who was always, in spite of his Persian mistress, the aloof, European expatriate; or Perron, who had belonged to that uneasy half-world of the Eurasian and the 'poor white'. Thomas' solitary wanderings in India lasting six years or so had given him an excellent insight in every nuance of caste, religion and tribe. He spoke all the necessary languages fluently and correctly. He lived like an Indian, he ate Indian food and probably dressed like an Indian for much of the time. He kept his women in purdah like a gentleman, unlike the Feringhis. Indians of both creeds were deeply shocked by European women who were allowed to go abroad unveiled, to meet other men, to eat in mixed company half-naked and even, it was said with horror, to *dance in public*. He knew all there was to know about his men with whom in his early days he had served in the ranks. For a violent and over-bearing man it is remarkable how patient and sympathetic he was when they committed the most heinous of military crimes: mutiny, refusing duty until they were paid and often at a critical moment. It was not that he was frightened of the pack of wolves he had recruited. He knew how close to starvation they lived and that if unpaid the soldiers would have to borrow money at extortionate rates to buy the very rations they had to live on while fighting, and also food for their families. He was solicitous on their behalf, in a manner unheard of in our own army half a century and more later. He would sell his own horses to give them something on account. If there were no tents the wounded had his while he slept in the open. He gave the disabled gratuities and, when he had any funds, a pension to widows. To be sure, he marched them off their legs, led many to their deaths, and expected them all to be as reckless of their lives as he was himself. This soldiers have always been able to tolerate, even wryly admire, provided they feel that there is some human bond between them and their commander. Thomas' flamboyance, his personal prowess in battle, even his frightful rages and his drinking, are the sort of eccentricities soldiers in their perverse way prefer to the more sober virtues. Above all, however, he was the one thing which soldiers respect: he was a commander who won battles: to his face he was 'Sahib Bahadur'—'your excellency', 'your Lordship'—but one of his nicknames was *Jahaj Jung*—'Ever Victorious George'. They believed in his *iqbal*—his good destiny, his 'star'—so they followed him to Hariana.

Thomas' kingdom, and it is no exaggeration to call it that, any more than it is to rate him as a general—many have had grander titles and done less—lay more or less in the south-western portion of the modern state of Hariana. Its boundaries were elastic, depending on whether Thomas was at home or away, or whether one of its outlying portions were in rebellion against him or not. At its greatest, at the end of his final Sikh campaign in 1800–1801, it extended from the fringe of the western or 'Thar' desert to the Jumna in the east and to the Sutlej in the north, but that only briefly and he was never able to consolidate it. What he held firmly throughout were the towns and districts of Sirsar, Hissar, Rohtak and Hansi together with his original adjoining possession of Jhajjar. These comprised an area extending north west from Jhajjar some 120 miles in length and 50 across. Hariana is reputedly so-called because of its greenness and fertility, but at the end of the century except where the deep wells made it possible for flocks to be watered, and along the banks of the seasonal rivers where the monsoon floods deposited silt and filled the tanks and wells it was a dry, barren country, much of it scrub and sandy desert. Once in the distant past it had been well-forested and prosperous, the hunting ground of the ancient kings. Now, however, its population had shrunk by three-quarters, many of its towns and villages were deserted and its revenues shrunk from a million and a quarter rupees in the high Moghul period of Akbar and Shahjehan to a mere two lacs. Its decline may have been due to the wars of the later Moghul period and the consequent neglect and ruin of the irrigation canals: equally probably it was due to those twin destroyers and desiccators, the goat and the felling-axe.[1]

Thomas had reconnoitred Hariana thoroughly during his command of the frontier force. He had established a garrison and a base there, in Hansi, from which cavalry patrols could observe any

Sikh incursions across the western end of his line. His experienced military eye had noted its present weakness and the advantages its position would offer him. His 'appreciation of the situation' therefore was based on sound reasoning. The people, mostly of Rajput stock, were warlike and refractory, but this as far as Thomas was concerned was an asset rather than otherwise. There was no central government, or even a shadow of it, Delhi having long relaxed its hold, and he believed rightly that it could be his without any great military effort. It was very poor. Thomas guessed rightly that no one would consider that it would be 'cost-effective', as we say today, to attempt the dangerous task of evicting him for a mere two lacs per annum. He, however, believed that he could do on a large scale in Hariana what he had done on a small one in Tapal years before under the Begum. He could, by restoring order and protecting the people against Sikh and other raiders create conditions in which the natural resilience and industry of the Hindu population would restore its prosperity and so, of course, support his expensive little army. Stategically it was a sound choice. It gave him access to the north and the cis-Sutlej Sikh states, while any army which attempted to invade him would have to plod across many miles of loose, sandy desert and be restricted in both size and approach by the location of the few wells. He himself had elected to move in during the monsoon season of 1797, when there was plenty of water, but only madmen like Thomas campaigned in the rainy season. (In this connexion it is worth noting that when in 1944 Admiral Mountbatten decided to continue operations in the rains it was considered an exceptionally bold stroke.)

Hansi, the site of his former outpost, was ideally sited in the heart of desert country. It was an ancient fortress city deserted and partly in ruins, with an inner fort and a perennial water supply within its walls. According to an Indian legend when Thomas' column marched in its population was a fakir and two lions. (The lions may well have shared the accommodation. Now a rarity, at that date they were widespread. Even as late as 1860, when British sportsmen were helping in their elimination, they were found as far east as Allahabad and south of the Chambal river.) At all events it had been deserted, but at no very distant date for its mud-brick walls and houses were still standing. Thomas set his men to work roofing the houses, clearing out the wells and repairing the gaps in the perimeter walls, mounting artillery, and preparing barracks and stables for themselves. It must be understood that armies of those days had nothing in the way of rations or 'services' of any kind. In the field the soldiers carried their own meagre ration of flour, and in camp or at home in their lines they depended on the civil traders of the 'Bazaar'. Thomas had with him in the middle of an inhospitable wilderness an army of some 2500 or 3000 men together with their animals and also their camp-followers; for however austere and mobile Thomas' flying columns may have been in war the demands of caste in normal living demanded cooks, grooms, barbers, transport-drivers and also those untouchable, unfortunate beings who attended to the hygiene of the camp and the barrack. In addition, as this was by way of being a migration, many of the officers and soldiers would have been followed by their wives and families. All these people had to be fed and provided with the ordinary means of living. Thomas had first of all to persuade traders of all kinds that they would cross the desert without being murdered or robbed, and that in Hansi they could be confident of fair treatment and regular payment. He also wanted carpenters, builders, smiths, wheel-wrights, armourers, foundry-men and, of course, because government and finance are inseparable, merchant-bankers and *shroffs* to handle his money matters, to arrange for credits, produce cash for paying the troops and bank the revenues. In one way or another Thomas succeeded in repopulating and revitalising Hansi, and it so remained and continued when the British arrived. However, many of the stories of Thomas' ephemeral rule may be considered to be exaggerated. For instance, he may indeed, as he said, have established a mint and issued his own rupee coinage, although we may wonder how a ruler so perpetually short of money obtained the precious metal. Nevertheless it must be admitted that in Hansi alone he achieved a feat of administration which commands our admiration.

All this occupied him from the rainy season of 1797, say June, to the end of 1798, interrupted by the war-like operations necessary to establish himself. As he had appreciated, the occupation of Hariana presented no great military difficulty. The only serious resistance he met was at the siege of a fort in the north, the country of the Bhattis, who defied Thomas and strongly defended it. There Thomas had one of his hand-to-hand encounters with the enemy; suitably heroic and quite typical, but most inappropriate for a general in command and the head of an emergent state. The rains and the consequent mud had interfered with the regular process of digging saps, advancing parallels and building batteries; so he had established an enclosing ring of redoubts round the place and waited for the weather to clear. We can well imagine his sepoys, wet and sulky, huddling under what shelter they could find with possibly a morsel of crude opium under a tongue here or there. The defenders had proved both aggressive and active and Thomas was very properly on a round of inspection to see if his troops were alert, and was actually in one of the redoubts when the defenders made a sudden sortie. The garrison of the redoubt panicked and ran away, leaving their commander to face the enemy single-handed: although perhaps this is not exactly the correct phrase. He had with him a number of his orderlies whose task it was—rather like loaders at a pheasant or a grouse shoot, except there were more of them—to carry Thomas' personal fire-arms and to hand him a succession of pistols, or blunderbusses filled with shot, or muskets with ball as deemed suitable for the target. His fusillade checked the enemy long enough for his faithful cavalry escort to cut their way to his aid and so to provide time for the infantry to be rallied and brought back to their posts and to drive back the sortie with loss. This and possibly the terrifying view at close quarters of the Jehazi Sahib in his berserk mood, rather discouraged the defence, and when Thomas eventually mounted a battery within breaching range and brought down a piece of their curtain wall they did not elect to face a storm. With this operation completed, and after a few sharp counter-raids to remind the Sikhs whose territory lay to his north-east that he was once more with them, Thomas settled his boundary for the moment in that quarter so that it ran more or less along the line of the Ghaggar river.

As for his southern boundary he managed at last to arrive at a friendly settlement with Vaman Rao, and convince him that he had no intention of robbing him of his patrimony. He insisted, however, on keeping Jhajjar on the grounds that this had been his uncle's personal gift to him for rescuing him from the mutineers in 1794. He claimed therefore that he was not a temporary mansabdar, holding it in exchange for military service, but the *zamindar*, or the land-holder. Vaman's original attempt to dispossess Thomas had coincided with a moment of extreme difficulty for him when his army was unpaid and Bapu Sindia out for his blood. Vaman's own troops had attacked Jhajjar, although unsuccessfully, when he was involved on the frontier and occupied part of his jaghirs, and there had been some sharp fighting when he returned. Thomas however was not a man to bear a grudge. He understood very well how a young heir would be pandered and pimped and toadied to by the courtiers in the hope of, ideally, debauching him so completely that all the running of affairs, with unlimited opportunities for embezzlement, would fall into their hands. All heirs and heir-apparents were exposed to the treatment: it was the chronic disease of Indian courts, as many later British 'residents' were to find. Vaman, after Thomas inflicted one or two sharp rebuffs on his Mahratta troops, had the sense to see for himself that he was too dangerous a man to have as an enemy, but that alternatively he could be most useful as a friend, or at least an ally. Vaman had soon found himself in the same difficulties as his uncle over keeping order and collecting revenue from his turbulent domain. He invited Thomas to help him and Thomas, always perfectly prepared to acquire some hard cash by hiring his troops on contract, agreed: provided that his claim to Jhajjar was recognised. This was satis-factorily settled and so he found himself on the best of terms with Vaman Rao after all, as his old master had so earnestly wished. This happy state of affairs was finally reached in 1797, or early in 1798. Thomas was thus able to devote himself to the affairs of his little kingdom.

He had only one great difficulty, always found in kingdoms great and small that maintain standing armies: he lacked money and what was even more important, for India has always been a great country for credit, he lacked cash to pay his troops. His bill for disablement and widows' pensions alone was 50,000 rupees a year. To continue to raid his neighbours was a mere expedient. It only enabled him to pay his troops something on account and suffered from the law of diminishing returns. He was too sensible to squeeze his own people, for it was essential that they should be attached to him, that they should prosper, and that he should demand only the revenues fixed by law. Yet he wanted money not only to keep his army contented and in being but to increase it and re-equip it for his great design of first reducing the Sikh states to the south of the Sutlej and then invading the Punjab. It now appeared as if this would not be possible until 1800. There was another consideration. An army like his did not thrive on idleness. Professional soldiers today must fashionably protest a thirst for peace, but Thomas' soldiers required a diet of blood as well as cash. Left in idleness they would begin to 'feel their oats' and become troublesome, and the more adventurous would begin to drift away to scenes of greater action. It was an anxious period for Thomas. Then, towards the end of 1798, a solution was offered from an unexpected quarter. His new relationship with Vaman Rao bore fruit.

It has already been mentioned, and will in due course be described in greater detail, how Mahratta politics and Daulat Rao Sindia's affairs were sinking into increasing turmoil. Even that stand-by of Sindia's house, the great Lakwa Dada, was being driven into rebellion over the affair of Madhaji Sindia's widows: what was to be known as the 'war of the Bais'. Pratap Singh of Jaipur, it will be remembered, was one of the two Rajput chieftains who had been brought under the Mahratta yoke by de Boigne. He now had taken advantage of their slackening grip to break loose and signified his independence in the usual way of refusing to pay his tribute, which was the original *casus belli*. No regular troops were available. The Mahratta authorities then suddenly thought of the heir of Appa, idly enjoying his jaghirs, and called upon him to take action against the Raja of Jaipur, bring him to heel and to collect his unpaid taxes.

It throws an interesting light on the fiscal system of the Mahrattas that their instructions to Vaman were to collect what he could and reward himself at the rate of ten annas per rupee, no less than 60 per cent of the take. It was an attractive proposition, but young Vaman saw that there were two insuperable obstacles. The first was that neither he nor his advisers had any military experience, at least not any that would be of value against the army of Pratap Singh. The second was he had no troops, except for the usual irregulars, and only a few of these. Like his uncle he had not found it easy to collect his own revenues and also, according to the hallowed custom, he had economised on the troops he was obliged to keep up to meet his feudal obligations, such as this. Vaman was therefore somewhat apprehensive, for if he failed or was found out he would be threatened with eviction, as his uncle had been before him after his failure in Bundelkhand in 1794. Like his uncle, he turned to Thomas. Thomas, too, thought it was an attractive business proposition. Jaipur was rich, and if his share was to be 30 per cent he might well gross a lac or even more. To keep a brigade in the field (which strictly speaking would have to be paid whether in the field or not, but Thomas' troops were accustomed to living on promises when in barracks, and only insisted on an advance before marching, or if they had absolutely empty pockets) would cost in round figures 15,000 rupees a month. This on a three months' campaign would show a handsome profit, apart from which there would be pickings. As against this, his programme to invade the Punjab would be put back and there would be the risk, as omelettes could not be made without breaking eggs, of his army being severely mauled by the formidable Rajputs and of his having to build it up again. He might do better to adopt a policy of small profits and quick returns, by blackmailing his Rajput neighbours on his own account for 'protection' against his raids. However, war with Jaipur would have Mahratta and therefore Imperial sanction, and he would be acting legally, for a change. The risk was great, but so was the hope of gain. Thomas accepted.

9   *General Thomas takes the Field*

GEORGE THOMAS' Jaipur campaign was a truly remarkable affair. It cannot be said that it was a masterpiece of orthodox strategy and it was carried out at fearful administrative risk and with reckless disregard of odds. If, however, the choice and unwavering pursuit of the object is, as all the best military theorists assert, the key to successful generalship, then Thomas was completely successful. His aim was to collect a large sum of money, which he did. In his memoirs Thomas has described it in full tactical detail, and quite simply and truthfully.[1] If his reputation as a commander of troops as opposed to a mere guerrilla and freebooter rested on nothing but his desert campaign and the battle of Fatehpur it would be secure. Thomas' and Vaman Rao's forces together totalled some 1000 horse, 3000 foot and 18 guns. Of these Vaman's contribution was 900 Mahratta and therefore perfectly useless cavalry, a semi-regular battalion of sorts, some 600 local levies and four cannon. Thomas, having made the necessary detachments required to police Hariana and garrison Hansi, Jhajjar and Jehazgahr mobilised a small but highly battle worthy brigade consisting of 90 cavalry of his select bodyguard, three regular battalions on the standard pattern with four guns available for each, two spare guns, 300 Rohilla najibs and 200 newly recruited Hariana irregulars. Thomas also had with him, the first time one is ever mentioned, an English officer, John Morris.

He joined forces with Vaman probably somewhere in the area of Kanaund and struck south-west into Jaipur territory following a route which would take them from town to town, and so near water for horses, gun-cattle and men. They entertained no conventional ideas of seeking out the Raja of Jaipur's main army and defeating it or anything of that nature. They hoped to keep out of the way of that ponderous but formidable horde. They simply marched into Jaipur territory, made themselves known, and with their bayonets and sabres as credentials, collected two lacs of rupees in no time with more coming merrily in as they zig-zagged southwards from one quarry to the next. It was some time before the outraged

General Thomas takes the Field

Pratap Singh learned what was happening, mobilised, if so technical a term can be used for the business of summoning his feudal array, and marched north to see, as it were, what was happening and put a stop to it.

It is necessary to say again that not only these Asian skirmishes but all the wars of the classical age into which strategists pretend to read so much artistry and skill, were conducted largely without roads, without maps, with no communications faster than a mounted man, and were between armies whose speed was about two and a half miles an hour. To credit the commanders of those days therefore with wonderful strategic insight or with extraordinary crassness is equally unreal. They and their armies wandered around in a slow, frustrating version of blind-man's buff, occasionally blundering into each other by chance. Battles were often 'pitched'—revealing term—so that they could take place at all. While Raja Pratap Singh and his field commander Raja Roraji Khavis with 40,000 horse and foot were circling around inquiring from the plundered towns where Thomas and Vaman had gone, they in their turn travelled even deeper into the desert unaware of their danger. Gradually they became uneasily aware that the Jaipur army was on their trail and, moreover, was between them and home. Vaman Rao argued that the jig was over. His Mahratta instinct told him that with their escape route cut and outnumbered by ten to one the correct plan was to slip away with the booty by a circuitous route and let Pratap Singh wear himself out chasing them. That was the way their respected ancestors had defeated even the Rajputs in the past. Thomas demurred. His was an infantry force, and while the Mahratta cavalry could scatter and scamper away, he himself was tied to the pace of the infantry, and of gun-bullocks unless he abandoned his guns which was out of the question. In any case, he for his own part said, memorably, that to retreat now 'would be a dishonour to myself and to my progenitors who never turned their backs on an enemy'. He added rather craftily that evasive Mahratta tactics were all very well in the old days, but if Daulat Rao Sindia heard that Vaman had abandoned his mission without firing a shot he might well dismiss him and confiscate all his estates. This impressed Vaman, but it was also perfectly clear that they were in a desperate position.

As was the custom of the times, they were living off the country

137

and had no reserves of food and no water. However, in a desperate position it is a good military maxim to choose the most dangerous and imaginative course even if it is the most hazardous. Thomas therefore proposed that instead of retiring they should advance even more deeply into the desert. They were within a couple of marches of the town of Fatehpur which like all the towns of the desert stood in its own oasis with wells full of water and plenty of supplies. His plan was to march there at once, refresh the troops, build up a stock of food and then see how matters turned out. Whatever happened it was better to fight with the soldiers rested and with full bellies than to be caught strung out in the burning and waterless desert by Pratap Singh's cavalry and camelry. After much anxious discussion this was the course agreed upon.

In the northern Indian winter the temperature ranges from 70 to 100 degrees Fahrenheit by day and in the desert the climate is, of course, intensely dry. It is delightful and invigorating for a shooting expedition or for a Christmas camp, but for a marching infantryman bowed down under a heavy pack and a musket and for the gunners straining at the drag-ropes and wheel-spokes to help the bullocks haul the guns through the loose sand, it was very different. The army had a long and thirsty march to Fatehpur and when it ended late one afternoon Thomas saw that Pratap Singh had deduced his intentions. The gates were shut, the walls of the town were lined with armed men, while outside a battalion of infantry stood guard over gangs of workmen who were engaged in breaking the gear for drawing water from the town wells and filling in the wells themselves so as to deny them to the invaders. Thomas, placing himself at the head of his squadron, immediately charged the covering force and after some hectic galloping about and slashing chased it away and saved the vital water. Then, with great impudence, for both sides knew that the Raja and his army were bearing down on them, Thomas and Vaman summoned Fatehpur to ransom itself or face a storm. The headman of the town, alarmed by what they had just seen and the fierce faces of Thomas' troopers assembling under the walls, immediately offered a lac of rupees to be spared. Vaman countered with a demand for ten million rupees, which was absurd—and bargaining was broken off. Thomas felt that it was a foolish moment to start a long haggle, important as it was not to appear to be alarmed or in a hurry. In the early hours of the next morning he formed up a storming party, escaladed the walls and quickly made a lodgment in the town. It surrendered at once on the promise of being spared a sack. This was a great relief to him, as to have been trapped between the walls of Fatehpur and the Jaipur army would have been most inconvenient. He then without delay began his preparations to meet Pratap Singh in battle.

He first of all put 400 men into the town; 100 of the Rohillas who specialised in defensive fighting and his 300 Hariana irregulars. He then cleared the wells out, and around them set the town's labourers to digging a three-sided redoubt, so sited that its open or rear face was closed and covered by the walls of Fatehpur, and emplacements for his guns so that when they were in camp they could sweep all the approaches to the vital wells. The entire perimeter of the redoubt he protected by an abatis. There were growing in quantity conveniently close to Fatehpur groves of *babul* trees, furnished with huge, grey, intensely sharp thorns like miniature bayonets. These were felled and piled in rows, several trees on top of one another with the tops outward and the butts roped together. As an obstacle it was as effective as a modern barbed-wire entanglement. (Indians were highly proficient in all kinds of field works and there is no reason why Thomas should not have learned his practical fortification from his experienced sirdars as he went along. Like red-hot shot, though, the abatis was not part of the Indian technique. It was a Canadian or an American practice, where one held up Abercrombie's attack in the terrible disaster the British suffered at Ticonderoga in 1755. Thomas may have heard stories of the American wars, or he may just have had an original mind; but it is details like this which whet our curiosity about his military past, as indeed does the whole of the Fatehpur operation.) Thus he provided himself with what in military jargon is called a 'firm base' in which his main fighting force could rest when not in action and where his transport, his reserve ammunition and his stocks of food and forage could be safely left. He sent out parties of men to fill up the more distant wells on the enemy line of advance.

All this took two days, during which he was fortunately not interferred with by the Rajput army. That advanced with the utmost deliberation, clearing out the wells as they went until finally it halted and camped six miles away from Fatehpur. There it stayed in a 'position in observation' without hurrying into battle.

139

The observing was, in fact, all on the side of Thomas' patrols. These told him that the camp was ill-guarded, a peace-time affair, with all the guns lumped together in one large park and not deployed in action to defend the camp. Thomas' first bold and imaginative plan was to approach the Jaipur camp at night and attack it at dawn, to spike all the guns and then see how the affair developed. Surprise was essential, so he told no one, not even Vaman Rao. Thomas, of course, had too few troops to 'invest', or surround the town. In consequence there was no bar to movement between his camp and Fatehpur, and Fatehpur and the Jaipur army, and he could be certain that any plans he made public or betrayed by preparations would soon be known to Roraji's spies. He also may have had in mind the possibility of Vaman himself betraying him so to purchase his own safety. Thomas was a wanted man in Jaipur because of his former raids, and such a betrayal was perfectly in keeping with the Mahratta character and with the morals of the time and place. Whatever the reason Thomas and his troops stole out of the redoubt before dawn without awakening a soul, leaving a message for Vaman to follow him with his Mahratta cavalry when the sun was up. This operation unfortunately miscarried. The march was slow and much delayed by the guns which stuck in the sand. Daylight found them in the open, far from the main enemy camp and with the enemy alarmed and alert. It could have been an awkward situation, but since Patun and Mertah the Rajputs had become cautious about attacking European-trained infantry. Roraji remained, under arms but ingloriously inactive, in his camp. Thomas instead of attacking his main body turned aside and rooted around the neighbouring wells, from which he chased the well-guards before having them filled in again. He also rounded up a large number of horses and cattle that had been sent out for that morning's watering, so that the projected night-attack turned profitably but absurdly into a cattle-rustling expedition. On his way back with his delighted troops whooping and herding the spoil—northern Indians are great horse- and cattle-fanciers—he met the angry and suspicious Mahrattas. Vaman Rao had to exercise all his tact, and eventually soothed his own people down by presenting both them and Thomas and his officers with *khiluts*, or robes of honour.

The next day Pratap Singh and his field commander Roraji decided at last to attack. Altogether they disposed of some 40,000 horse and foot and a large number of guns, some as heavy as 24-pounders. These are Thomas' figures, estimated by eye probably and not far out: they are much more convincing than the usual ones in six figures given in other accounts of Indian battles. Soon after sunrise the Jaipur army bore down on the city and the fortified camp in three huge, dense columns, the centre one held back so that the whole resembled the classic Asian battle-formation of a crescent with its enfolding horns advanced. On the right there was a mass of cavalry, who advanced on the redoubt, quite undeterred by the sight of the abatis and yelling scornfully that it would take more than a few thorn-bushes to stop men like them. The left-hand horn was directed on Fatehpur itself with orders to escalade the walls. It consisted of 4000 Rohillas, 6000 Jaipur levies and a force of no less than 300 Goshais. The Jaipur 'main battle', to use a not inappropriate mediaeval term, was of ten battalions of regular or semi-regular troops together with Pratap Singh's élite bodyguard of 1600 matchlock-men and sword-and-buckler-men. When he and Roraji saw Thomas march out from his camp against them with barely 2000 men they thought that the Lord, or rather Bhowani, had delivered him into their hands.

Thomas had no intention whatever of being trapped in his redoubt or of resting immobile under the walls of Fatehpur. He was about to demonstrate one of the classical moves of tactics: a mobile force acting around a pivot of manoeuvre. In Fatehpur he had already placed his garrison of irregulars. They, he was confident, protected by the walls, could hold off any threat long enough for him to intervene from outside. In the redoubt, guarding the baggage, the transport and the vital water he left Vaman Rao and his infantry levies, stiffened by a whole battalion of Thomas' own regulars supported by a battery of four guns. The town garrison and the redoubt thus provided the pivot. The next essential was to engage the Jaipur main body in the open and somehow to distract it and separate it from its wings. Thomas had reconnoitred the ground very carefully in the past two days. On the direct route between the Jaipur camp and the town was a ridge giving good command and a good field of fire for his excellent artillery. On this he posted eleven infantry companies of his two remaining battalions and two batteries, i.e. eight guns, all under the command of his English officer. Thomas considered Morris to be a brave officer but stupid and untrained—'better fitted to lead a forlorn hope than to direct troops in the field'—but he was confident that if ordered to stand and fight he would hold off Roraji to the bitter end. The 900 Mahratta horse of which he expected, and received, very little he put behind this position. From there, in whichever direction they fled it would be towards the enemy. Finally, he retained under his personal command five companies subtracted from the two battalions under Morris, comprising the grenadier, or special assault company from each, and three of the line companies; together with three guns and, inevitably, his cavalry bodyguard. This tiny force, 250 infantry, 90 cavalry and 20 or 30 gunners, was to be his 'mass of manoeuvre'! Nothing could be more revealing of Thomas' nerve and self-confidence.

These preparations completed, Thomas mounted his horse, doubtless one of the expensive Persian thoroughbreds he fancied, and rode on to the ridge with Morris to watch the long crescent of the Jaipur host roll slowly forward over the desert until he was enveloped by it in a huge half circle extending across the desert from flank to flank.

To say that Roraji's conduct of the battle was inept is an understatement. It is the hall-mark of a bad commander to allow himself to be defeated in detail. However, to be fair to him, his superiority in numbers was so great that he could reasonably have expected any of his three wings to have defeated Thomas without assistance from the others. His extraordinary and inexplicable delay in bringing his full strength at once against Morris may have been due to the time it took to drag his heavy guns all the way from his camp across the loose sand. He had no reason to believe that Thomas was much better than a freebooter or a brigand on a large scale and so there was no point in hurrying. Whatever the reason, he allowed himself with ten battalions to be held up by Morris' eleven companies, and watched supinely while Thomas bit off and spat out the two horns of the crescent.

The Rajput cavalry who formed the right wing, as might be expected, arrived on their objective before the rest, only to be met by a hot fire from the redoubt and to be baffled by the abatis. When they had lost what formation they had, and were reduced to milling around the obstacle shouting their war-cries, Thomas put his reserve into motion, and without interference or apparently even being noticed brought his three guns into action in close range of them, catching them in a damaging cross-fire between him and his guns in the redoubt. This drew a violent reaction. Thomas' little bodyguard squadron was attacked and soon overborne by the mass of Rajput horsemen, losing their Indian commander and a number of troopers. Then the two grenadier companies went to their assistance, forming into line and firing volley after volley into the Rajputs which they followed with a bayonet charge: an unusual way of dealing with cavalry. It was effective, because the Rajput cavalry believing as it did that it could ride over every obstacle and with its memories of Lalsot and Mertah growing dim, was shocked and chagrined by its repulse by 'a row of bushes' and was wincing under the disciplined musketry and the terrible effects of close-range gun-fire. Under the attack of the grenadiers and the incessant hail of grape and case, it dissolved into little groups and into single horsemen, scattered and streamed back across the plain.

Then Thomas was able to turn his attention to his right, where with loud and warlike cries the disorderly mob of Ghoseinis and Rohillas were attempting to swarm up the walls of Fatehpur. Fortunately for Thomas' garrison the townspeople had gone to ground, or rather had locked themselves and their wives and valuables firmly into their houses. They certainly made no attempt to assist their Raja's army. As far as they were concerned being occupied by Thomas was infinitely preferable to the prospect of liberation by several thousand excited Pathans and the blood-thirsty and maniacal Goshais. Thomas' irregulars were able to hold the walls without any great effort, throwing down any ladders that the escaladers set up and piking down their Rohilla compatriots or discharging matchlocks in their faces with great spirit. Now, however, things wore a less rosy complexion, for some of Roraji's guns had arrived and a six-gun battery was battering the tall houses overlooking the walls in which Thomas' matchlock-men were so firmly ensconced. Thomas now took his tiny striking force across the battlefield behind his own main position and the Mahratta cavalry, who stood distraught and incapable of action, and falling upon the inner flank of the Rajput left wing sent it flying. The artillery hastily limbered up and escaped him, except for a couple of huge 24-pounders. He then felt able to bring out four of

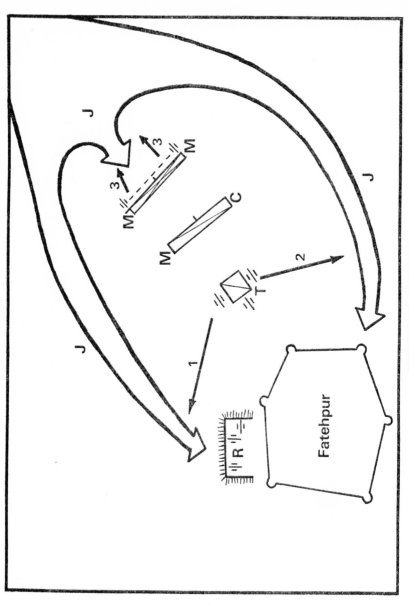

THOMAS AT FATEHPUR

J, Jaipur Army; MM, John Morris; MC, Mahratta Cavalry; T, Thomas; R, Redoubt, 1, 2, 3, Thomas'

his regular companies from the garrison of the redoubt into the main part of the battle. This settled the two flanks, and he went up to see how Morris was faring in front against Roraji's centre.

The Jaipur troops there had been able to observe, with the usual disastrous effect on the nerves of an undisciplined native army, first their right and then their left wing streaming back past them in defeat. Roraji called repeatedly on his battalions to advance, but when at last they half-heartedly responded they felt the murderous close-range fire from Thomas' infantry and guns on the ridge above them. They broke before they could cross bayonets, and set off in disorder for their own camp beyond any hope of rally. Thomas now perceived that this was the moment to launch without delay every man he had who could still walk or ride in the merciless pursuit that is the final act of victory. He called upon the Mahratta cavalry to charge the flying enemy, while he set his infantry in motion and sent back for his gun-bullocks which had been retired some distance for safety, so that he could bring up his artillery and smash any attempt by Roraji to make a stand.

No such effort was made, but Roraji was saved from complete destruction by a group of Rathor cavalry. This was a force commanded by the Thakur of Chummu in Marwar, Jodhpur. This chieftain felt disgraced by the way the battle had gone; it was not at all in the Rathor style. Halting his men and sternly ordering them to face the enemy, he formed them up into the ghol, the living cannon-ball of horsemen, and galloped at the luckless Mahratta cavalry who, without waiting for the shock, spun their ponies round and rode back through Thomas' infantry, completely breaking their ranks and scattering most of them. Disordered as they were, however, the sepoys stood their ground like men, meeting lance and sabre with musket and bayonet; even seizing the reins of the Rathor horsemen and attempting to pluck them from the saddle. They gave Thomas, now in his almost habitual position of extreme danger and left with only a handful of his men and personally commanding a six-pounder a moment's grace to form up and un-limber the gun. A lucky shot brought down the brave chief of Chummu. His equally brave but highly volatile clansmen, dismayed at his fall, withdrew carrying the body of their wounded master as rapidly as they had advanced. Roraji was unable to take any advantage of the Rathor counter-attack, his troops having no desire to face Thomas' volleys and salvoes again that day, but Thomas saw his bolt was shot. Morris was wounded, he had by now lost one man in four killed or wounded, and the rest were exhausted with the fighting, marching and counter-marching that had taken most of the morning and the baking afternoon. Collecting his shattered infantry and his wounded, he fell back on his camp.

There he learned with grim satisfaction of the fate of Vaman Rao's cavalry. Thomas had given orders that on no account, whatever the emergency, were the gaps in the prickly barrier around the perimeter of the redoubt to be opened, nor was anyone to be admitted except by his own personal permission. When the Mahratta horsemen arrived as if riding the hard finish of a race, pagris flying, whips busy, pale in the face, they begged earnestly to be admitted. Not so, said the sirdar Thomas had left in charge of the redoubt, in his literal Indian way; it was strictly forbidden by the express order of the Jehazi Sahib Bahadur himself. As it happened there were still a few disappointed Rathor cavaliers on their trail who arrived while this shouted dialogue was taking place across the abatis, and they spitted or sabred a large number of the luckless Mahrattas so as to relieve their feelings before turning their own horses' heads once again for home.

In speaking about generalship it is always necessary to avoid exaggeration. Brilliant tactics and brilliant successes are invariably made possible by the bad luck or ineptitude of the opposition. War is not a game of chess, and the outcome of battles, and this is still true today, depends largely on chance and on the operation of the brutal factors of numbers and weapons and the determination of the combatants. Nevertheless, it is impossible not to admire Thomas' conduct of the whole Fatehpur operation. It was highly professional, and professional soldiers will recognise that it was only an uncommonly able member of their craft who could have raised and trained the battalions who showed such cohesion and staying power for so long in the stress of heavy fighting and near-disaster.

Their discipline was to be tested further, because before long Thomas and Vaman Rao were forced to retreat. The morning after the battle Thomas in his lordly way sent vakils to Roraji saying that he was free to collect his wounded, and his more honourable dead for cremation. This courtesy had the favourable effect of encouraging Roraji to consider making terms—Pratap Singh seems to have disappeared after the battle—and after a certain amount of journeying to and from the rival camps by vakils Roraji came down with an offer of 50,000 rupees and an unmolested withdrawal from Jaipur territory if Vaman Rao and his partner would kindly go away. Thomas would have been glad to settle for this; Vaman, rightly but rashly, considered he was there as Sindia's agent and wanted to settle the whole question of tribute, to which Roraji replied that in the Raja's absence he could not improve on his offer. This, as Thomas feared, led to a dangerous delay and to his being bottled up under the walls of Fatehpur. Roraji was reinforced by a strong contingent from the Raja of Bikanir and settled down to a distant siege of Thomas, avoiding any action but harrying his foraging parties who had to go farther and farther afield as they ate up the supplies in Fatehpur.

Vaman Rao lost his bargaining position when he received a message from Daulat Rao Sindia *via* General Perron, who had by now been appointed Governor of Hindustan and had moved north from the Deccan, to break off the whole operation and leave Jaipur alone. The weather was becoming steadily hotter, Thomas' numbers were depleted and he could not face a second battle. Roraji would not repeat his original offer: on the contrary, he seemed determined to prevent the invaders leaving in peace. Thomas saw that he would have to fight his way out and the sooner the better. He broke camp and started his march in the middle of the night.

When day broke the Jaipur army, feeling the irresistible attraction of the sight of their enemy's back, began to swarm round his column in their mobs, but Thomas deployed into battle formation and they sheered off. By now, for him to bare his teeth was sufficient. A pursuit was kept up for two days, but at a respectful distance, mainly by artillery and rockets. (These rocketeers were a peculiar feature of ancient Indian warfare, already obsolete but still persisting.[2] Their weapons were not the scientific Congreve rocket used later by the Royal Horse Artillery but more the 'November 5th' type: iron pipes filled with a charge of powder and fired attached to a stick. They had a range of about half a mile and were unreliable and inaccurate. There were whole battalions of *jezail-burdars*, or rocketeers, in native armies, each man carrying two or three of these lethal fireworks. They could be effective when bursting in the dense and deep columns of a native army: against the more open order of regular troops, less so. They were, however, a great nuisance, and most alarming.) Thomas put a couple of field guns at the tail of his rear-guard with orders to drop into action from time to time to keep these rocket-men at a respectful distance. In this manner he was followed rather than pursued. He got his whole force off safely but it was none the less a trying retreat: 'The service was most severe,' Thomas said to Francklin. The hot weather was 'stoking up', as they used to say in India, the going was bad and the nearest water twenty or more miles off. Altogether they were on the march for fifteen hours. To encourage his exhausted men, Thomas dismounted and marched along on foot himself. Among the irregulars discipline, such as it was, broke down and when they finally reached an oasis they rushed at the wells, some falling in and one man being drowned. Thomas had to mount a regular guard over the well-heads to ensure orderly watering for the cattle and water supplies for the men. They finally settled down for an uneasy night faced by another gruelling march the next day. Their only consolation was that with their guns controlling the approaches the wretched Jaipur troops were in an even worse case and had a thirsty night. Their pursuit was already half-hearted and they turned back on the following day. Towards the evening Thomas arrived at a fair-sized town with five good wells and a good market. There he and Vaman decided to make a long halt, rest the troops, feed them up, attend to the wounded and decide on their next move.

After a week's rest the spirits of the soldiers had so far revived that Thomas and Vaman began, in spite of Sindia's instructions, to harry Jaipur again: it is difficult whether to admire their impudence or their tenacity the more. Pratap Singh now despaired. Apparently neither Sindia nor his great General Perron could control their agents: so Pratap Singh made another, final offer of 50,000 rupees to be quit of the pair of them. This they accepted gratefully and the two tax-gatherers having shared out their loot Vaman Rao marched off home.

Thomas is always vague about money matters in his memoirs. He never explains how much of the gross sums he mentions was made up in cash, kind or paper promises, and there is his habit—a general one—of referring grandly to 'lacs' of rupees, literally 100,000, but which is also a metaphor for a great deal of money.

Lieutenant-Colonel James Skinner, C.B.

Resaidar   Resaidar   Summud Khan   Jemadar   Jemadar   Beg
Sheik Jumah Hoosein.   Gholam Hoosein.   (Officer Brevdar)   Abdul Rahman.   Mirza Behterman

Some of Skinner's officers, all Mohammedans and probably all Pathans

Altogether the sums he mentions add up to something like four and a half to five lacs. Vaman Rao's share of this was ten annas in the rupee and assuming that they shared alike this could have given Thomas 150,000 rupees. His war-chest for his projected invasion of the Punjab was therefore building up satisfactorily, but his appetite for plunder was by no means satiated. He would have done much better at this stage in his career to have gone home to Hansi and devoted himself to some serious domestic administration; but he reflected that he had a long march home, an army in the field whose morale was high and which was only too ready to fight provided this brought the rupees clinking in, so he looked around for a convenient victim. He settled on the Raja of Bikanir, whose troops had in the most uncalled for and insulting manner reinforced Roraji and inconvenienced him; thus providing him with a *casus belli*. On his route home lay one of Bikanir's towns, 'Jeitpur' or Jitpura, and he put it to ransom. He then threatened Bikanir itself, but the Raja, one Surut Singh, although he was reputed to have some European mercenaries and good, trained troops of his own, was so terrified that he bought him off with an offer of two lacs of rupees. A half of this sum turned out to be in bills or promisory notes which were dishonoured when Thomas' bankers tried to negotiate them. This was to ensure Bikanir a second visit, in due course.

When Thomas returned to Hansi, however, he found other things to attract, or distract, him. First of all he heard that Lakwa Dada had been dismissed and had risen in armed rebellion. He also heard that the Mahratta authorities were preoccupied with a fresh and even more dangerous threat from Zaman Shah. Accordingly he tried to reassert his control over his old frontier districts of Panipat and Kurnool, but was warned off by General Perron, a warning he for once noticed and obeyed. Next, he embarked on an unprofitable raid on Patiala which turned out badly, as did an attempt to capture the city of Jhind just outside his borders and which would have made a valuable addition to his domain. Sahib Singh Phulkiani of Patiala was, for a Sikh, a spiritless creature; but his sister Kunur had the unusual distinction of 'seeing off' Thomas. She rallied the Sikh troops, forced him to raise the siege of Jhind, and encouraged the country folk to rise up all round him and harass him. Although Thomas when he met the Sikhs in the field gave them, as usual, a good beating or two, due to her efforts he ended up back in Hariana with nothing to show for his trouble except one or two empty victories and some casualties he could ill-afford. He bore Kunur no ill-will and in the next year was to rescue her from her brother's evil intentions, they having fallen out. (Perhaps he should have married her. It could have had the most intriguing political and genetic consequences.)

Then, in about April 1799, Thomas received an important offer. In the next chapter an attempt will be made to explain the tangled state into which Mahratta politics had collapsed by this time, some five years after the death of Madhaji Sindia. To explain Thomas' next campaign it is sufficient at this moment to say that Lakwa Dada had been dismissed from his post of commander-in-chief of Sindia's Mahratta army as he had opposed Daulat Rao over his harsh treatment of Madhaji's three widows; conduct which had caused a violent dispute among Daulat Rao's followers. Lakwa had retired to his jaghirs in Ajmir, which, it will be remembered, Madhaji had given him for his services against the Rajputs in the war of 1793, assembled his feudal troops and was under arms in Mewar, or Udaipur. (Marwar, the country of the Rathors, or Jodhpur, lies to the north-west of the Auravalli hills: Mewar to the south-east.) Lakwa Dada had been superseded as commander-in-chief of Sindia's Mahratta troops by Ambaji Angria, who had been ordered to mobilise and suppress Lakwa's rebellion. Lakwa being the most capable and determined of the Sindia's commanders, Ambaji was none too sure of being able to do so; and sure he wished to be, because he and Lakwa were bitter rivals and he wanted Lakwa's head on his own account. Accordingly he sent to George Thomas and asked for his assistance specifically demanding that Lakwa be ejected from Mewar, which he now completely occupied and dominated. For this Thomas would be paid 50,000 rupees a month until the task was completed. This was an offer he found impossible to refuse. Thomas had this urge always to be doing something, preferably something violent and dangerous. Whether the invitation was from Lakwa Dada or from Vaman Rao, or from Somru Begum or now from Ambaji, he found the temptation to take to the field irresistible. He had an old score with Lakwa dating from his interference in Appa's affairs and his attempt to dismiss him, and he welcomed the chance of settling it. On top of this a clear profit of 30,000 rupees a month plus any unconsidered trifles he might pick up on the side was not something he could afford to ignore considering the rate at which money slipped through his fingers.

The only objection to the expedition came from his troops and it was a more serious one than usual. They had now been fighting and marching hard for five, possibly six months. Naturally enough they wanted time to spend their money, see their wives and families and enjoy a rest and some leave. Now Thomas was proposing to march them off three hundred miles to Mewar, far from their own homes and country familiar to them, with the monsoon about to break when all sensible men stayed at home. This was the root cause of the trouble, although eventually the dispute centred on the question of *batta*: the special allowance paid for long absence from home in a distant theatre of war: something about which sepoys felt very strongly. It is possible that the flames of discontent were fanned by Lakwa Dada's agents, for Lakwa continued to try to upset Thomas' troops throughout the ensuing campaign. Whatever the cause, Thomas was now faced not with the usual firm but respectful suggestion from his troops put through their sirdars— that they found it impossible to march another step without some at least of their arrears of pay—but a genuine mutiny. Fortunately Thomas received timely warning of a plan to seize him and possibly to murder him. This was one of the great advantages of intimate contact with the officers and, let it not be forgotten, of an Indian wife! A commander always had to have an ear in the sepoys' lines. A great believer in taking all bulls immediately by the horns he called up his bodyguard and riding over to the lines of the dis-affected battalion he challenged the conspirators. The mutinous group were rash enough to greet him with a few ill-aimed shots, whereupon he rushed on them in one of his berserk rages and seized the ringleader with his own hands while his escort dealt with the remainder.

There could be only one punishment for a crime of this magnitude in the armies of India. The whole army was ordered to parade to 'witness punishment', the loyal battalions surrounding the one which had entertained the mutineers, and a six-pounder loaded with a blank charge of powder was brought up. The wretched ringleader was then dragged to the gun, his arms and legs wrenched back and tied to the wheels on either side so that his body was bent in an arc with the small of his back pressing against and blocking muzzle. When the nature of his offence had been explained to all the troops and they had been given time to appreciate the solemnity of the occasion the port-fire was applied to the vent and the mutineer's torso was blown away, leaving his limbs decorating the wheels. A peculiarly horrible feature of this form of execution was that the head always sailed vertically into the air and plopped down again between the feet, its expression of anguish and terror clearly visible to the spectators. One such victim and the exhibition of Thomas' wrath was sufficient to settle the affair. The men then marched south without further demur. They were discontented, and remained discontented for the duration of what was to be Thomas' most exacting campaign, but his authority was never challenged again.

The campaign in Mewar proved a disorderly affair and was conducted along peculiarly Mahratta lines. No sooner had Thomas completed the long march to join hands with Ambaji and with Sutherland and his Second Brigade, who had been sent to assist them, when Sindia ordered the whole operation to be cancelled as Lakwa Dada had made his peace and he was not to be interfered with. In spite of this Ambaji and Thomas decided to continue, Ambaji for his own good, or rather evil reasons, Thomas because he was under contract to Ambaji and needed the money and in any case he cared nothing for Sindia's orders or anyone else's. Ambaji was also Perron's enemy and rival; while Perron, having reached the summit position once held by de Boigne, in turn regarded both Lakwa and Ambaji as his enemies. Sutherland had been Perron's unsuccessful rival for the post of commander-in-chief of the Army of Hindustan. He, not anxious to see one of Perron's adversaries defeated, obeyed Sindia's orders and left. Thomas says that Sutherland at first remained and between them they planned a joint attack on Lakwa Dada but when their troops were actually concentrated for the battle, Sutherland suddenly and without a word of explanation marched away and disappeared. Reading between the lines he was undoubtedly bribed by Lakwa or invited a bribe from him. Sutherland was, according to James Skinner, brave and able but also a shifty and dishonest man. Lakwa Dada then turned his attention to Thomas, demanding that he should obey Sindia's orders and let him alone, plying him with information that Perron was planning to oust him from Jhajjar, inciting mutiny among his troops and finally suggesting that Thomas should turn his coat and join him. None of this made the slightest difference to Thomas, who fastened himself to Lakwa's trail like one of the slow-running but remorseless wild red-dogs of the Indian jungle until he eventually harried him out of Mewar.

This was not easily done. Lakwa was the ablest native general in the whole Mahratta Confederacy and he was only finally smashed by the combined efforts of Perron and his trained brigades and Ambaji some eighteen months later in 1801. His army consisted of 9000 cavalry, a large proportion of whom, judging by their form, were Rajputs recruited from Ajmir. Of infantry he had 2000 Rohillas and 6000 native levies of sorts and 6000 regulars. Some of these were almost certainly European-trained and led, for after Lakwa's defeat at Sounda Perron captured William Tone, who had migrated to Lakwa's service *via* that of the Peshwa; and also an Englishman—or a Welshman—called Evans of whom nothing is known. Lakwa's regular infantry fought with great determination in Mewar; on one occasion fording a neck-deep river, storming some field works garrisoned by three of Ambaji's battalions and a thousand Goshais; the latter refusing to surrender, they butchered them to the last man. These may well have been Tone's troops, but we cannot be certain. As well Lakwa had 90 pieces of artillery, but of course in native armies it was numbers and the size of the gun which was often esteemed more than efficiency. Thomas' few well-served field-guns were a far more effective weapon.

To meet this large force Thomas had brought south 150 cavalry, six battalions of trained infantry and 22 guns. He was therefore short of artillery if each battalion was to have had its four-gun battery. De Boigne, as has been mentioned, gave each battalion an artillery company and five guns as part of its regular establishment. At this date the habit of forming artillery into regular, established units had not been fully developed even in the British army. Thomas probably followed the old practice of keeping a 'park' of artillery, together with a corps of artillerymen and drivers to form temporary 'batteries' or to serve guns detached to battalions as needed. To assist, or to handicap him, Ambaji produced the usual mob of Mahratta horse and a certain number of trained infantry of sorts.

He, following the fashion, also had recruited two European officers. One was a real officer, Joseph Bellasis, of the Corps of Engineers in the East India Company's service and one of the new type of young professional soldier of British origin who were filtering into the Mahratta service: men like Hopkins, Skinner, the two Smiths, Hardinge and Dawes; educated men altogether superior to the French soldiers of fortune, who were mostly 'rankers', and to the deserters from the Company's army. Bellasis resigned his commission because of his debts, and attracted by the high pay and openings in the Mahratta service joined Ambaji in 1796. He raised a good brigade of four battalions for him. He later left as a result of a quarrel. Bellasis, with a humanity somewhat in advance of his time, had refused Ambaji's callous order to continue with a second operation before he had made arrangements for the numerous wounded resulting from a first, but rejoined Ambaji in 1799.[3] The other was a character called James Shepherd who arrived in India as a valet, an odd and unusual occupation for a European in India, who eventually became a colonel in the Company's service. He earned later the reputation of a brave and capable commander, but the brigade he raised for Ambaji were reckoned to be poor stuff, which is not surprising considering that he had no military knowledge and had to learn his new trade as he went along. It is not clear how great a part these two played in the Mewar compaign. If they were present it was their regular battalions that Lakwa Dada routed on two occasions. They achieved little whether their European commanders were present or not. The Mewar campaign was a duel between Lakwa Dada and Thomas.

Lakwa's plan of operations was well conceived. Lakwa was extremely *chalak*: that untranslatable word connoting 'up to every trick', and 'gamesman', a stretcher of the rules, '*slim*'. He was a great believer in what we call in our present-day military jargon '*psywar*'. He worked on Thomas' suspicions of Perron, who was nibbling off some of his outlying territory near Jhajjar; he sent agents to stir up mutiny among Thomas' men, or to induce them to desert and march home; he offered Thomas large bribes to change sides. He sent him letters purporting to come from Sindia not merely ordering the war to be discontinued but appointing Lakwa governor of the very territory he was defending. He agreed a truce, during which both sides were to leave the area and await a final ruling from Sindia; but when Lakwa entered his own Ajmir he merely picked up a large contingent of reinforcements and doubled back into Mewar again with the outwitted Thomas in angry pursuit. He shrewdly avoided contact with Thomas and concentrated on Ambaji's troops, whom he knocked about severely. He remained mobile and refrained from adopting one of the fortified defensive positions so beloved of Moghul tacticians and so exposing himself to the hammer-blows of Thomas' guns, and he tried from start to finish to wear out Thomas and his dogged army by endless marching along muddy roads over flooded nalas and through dripping jungles. Thomas for his part stuck to the sound Clausewitzian principle of trying to bring his enemy's main force to battle. Twice he baited Lakwa into an attack on him by offering an exposed detachment to attack; the second time leading him up to his main force and smashing him with his admirably served guns, only to be cheated of a decisive victory by darkness. On other occasions he ordered his men to dress like Ambaji's and to copy their ragged formations so as to entice Lakwa's troops within shot, but with only partial success, although on one occasion he nearly caught Lakwa himself. This went on through the rains without any real battle or a decision but in October when it became dry and cool Thomas was able to exploit the superior mobility of his force until the exasperated Lakwa was, for all his superior numbers, reduced to running away from him continually. He finally gave in and returned to Ajmir. He confessed that he had been completely baffled by Thomas' behaviour. What, he asked indignantly, was the purpose of making war for war's sake? Thomas had disregarded Sindia's orders, refused his most lavish bribes, disregarded his own interests and had engaged in a long and severe campaign, expensive for both of them, for no visible profit or reason! Lakwa gave as his opinion that what Thomas really wanted was to make himself king over them all. Here possibly he was not altogether wide of the mark.

Thomas, after Lakwa's defeat, found that his duties also included collecting the necessary sums to pay himself; Ambaji, of course, having nothing like the necessary 350,000 rupees in cash to fulfil his part of the bargain. Promising his troops that once this congenial task was complete he would march them home, he sacked or put to ransom four large towns, thus causing the wretched inhabitants of Mewar to pay for the inconvenience and anarchy an uncalled-for war had already inflicted on them. The British conquest of India may have been devoid of morality, but it at least gave the luckless *ryats* a break from this endless murder and pillage. He then started on his march home.

However, it was now felt by all concerned that Thomas, having served his purpose, and more than his purpose, should be eliminated. There had been a rapid rearrangement of the pieces on the Mahratta chess-board. Lakwa and Perron were reconciled, Ambaji dismissed from the post of Commander-in-Chief and Lakwa restored to it. Thomas and Ambaji were ordered to abandon Mewar. Ambaji first ordered Thomas to proceed to Datia in Bundelkhund, where there was always a festering rebellion, for further employment. Next, which was indeed spreading the net in sight of the bird, he was told to report to Lakwa Dada and place himself under his recent opponent's command. General Perron, who at this time had decided that Thomas was a potential enemy and an actual threat to his authority, instructed Pratap Singh to intercept Thomas and attack him if he disregarded his orders and tried to pass through Jaipur territory on his way back to Hariana. Thomas ignored all these orders and their originators. Lakwa Dada's own troops had dissolved in mutiny after their defeat. Pratap Singh had no ambition to try conclusions again with Thomas that year. Thomas marched home unscathed, rewarding his veterans with the sack of any promising town or village that lay in his path. They, in spite of their losses—from battle, sickness and desertion they were now possibly only half strength—were still full of fight. With his colossal impudence Thomas paused while in Pratap Singh's territory and attacked Sarajgarh, one of the Jaipur strongholds, extracted 50,000 rupees from the kiladar to spare the garrison and was on his way before he could be caught.

So Thomas, his pockets well lined, arrived in Hansi in about November. The weather now being cool he decided to round off the year with a raid on Bikanir to recover the lac or so he was still owed. With his former desert experience in mind he made arrangements for a supply of water on the march using *mussacks*, or complete goat skins. (He does not say how he carried them. Normally they were slung on the backs of the water-carrier caste or *bhistis*. De Boigne's battalions had eleven such men on establishment which works out at one per fifty men. *Bhistis* in armies lasted well into the next century and provided the original for that favourite of Victorian reciters, 'Gunga Din'.) Hearing of Thomas' plans, the Muslim Bhattis who lived to the north of Hariana and were at feud with the Raja of Bikanir offered him 40,000 rupees to reduce one of his forts. Thomas accepted the offer and carried out the operation in his usual dashing style. He made a night march across the desert, planted his siege batteries, opened fire at first light, breached the curtain wall in the course of the morning, and allowed the shaken garrison to march out with the honours of war at midday. He then handed the fort over to the Bhattis and proceeded with the pillage of Bikanir. He then returned to Hansi where, no doubt, he celebrated as good a Christmas as an Irishman could manage among his heathen subjects.

If we look at Thomas against the general canvas of Indian military history and compare him with the best of his contemporaries it must be admitted that he really was an astonishingly successful commander in the field. He was a sort of miniature Rommel: indeed, Rommel at the height of his fame handled forces no larger and in much the same manner. He anticipated Rommel's policy of instant action, rapid marches, and of attacking vigorously when in any danger or in doubt. Like Rommel, he led from in front. Like Rommel, he achieved striking successes against armies larger in numbers and equally brave, but sluggish to react and led by commanders unable to adjust to a new and baffling form of warfare. Thomas was a great taker of forts, one of the characteristics which enabled the British to dominate the Indian military scene in the eighteenth and nineteenth centuries. The Indian armies were skilled in defensive work, but in the attack they relied too much on close investment, starvation and subverting the kiladar or his garrison. Like the British, Thomas always saw the problem as one of breaking into the *enceinte* by artillery breach or escalade as soon as possible, so as to fight the garrison inside their own walls. At a rough guess, in 1799 he must have lost and replaced fifty per cent of his fighting troops. Even allowing for the possibility that his recruits were trained deserters from other forces, to keep his army in such a state of fighting efficiency for a whole year of heavy fighting —first scorched in the Thar desert, then soaked to their unaccustomed skins in Mewar, riddled with the fevers of the rains and the endemic dysentery of the camp, and worn out by at least a thousand miles of incessant marching—and still to retain its loyalty, was a professional *tour de force*. His defeat of Roraji Khavis in detail outside the walls of Fatehpur was a minor masterpiece in the old classical style. His long pursuit and defeat of Lakwa Dada, although not distinguished by any feats of tactical brilliance, is an equally good example of his tenacity.

Nevertheless, Lakwa Dada in his puzzled exasperation had detected Thomas' weakness. He had lost sight of his aim. His aggressiveness and his feverish need always to be active led him into wars fought for their own sake. His capital was the courage, the lives and the endurance of his élite troops which, if he seriously thought of conquering even part of the Punjab he could not afford to waste. He was also drawing too heavily on his own reserves of nervous energy. The tropics are hard on the man who works too hard. The incessant, wearing heat and humidity, the small nagging ailments that will not cure themselves—low fevers, prickly heat, the itch, sores that refuse to heal, loose bowels—sap the energy, wreck the temper and impair the judgement. Even today with modern medicine and hygiene Europeans require regular holidays in a cool climate. The natives simply slow down in preference to breaking down, which is the good reason for what appears to us to be their maddening slowness and lack of drive. By this time Thomas was forty-four years old and had been in the field for six years without rest. He spent whole days in the saddle, he marched like a sepoy and he led his own forlorn hopes like a grenadier. He carried on all his military administration and his civil affairs single-handed. He drank like a fish, which men of his cast of character do in occasional violent bouts as a relief from their tensions. By the end of 1799 Thomas was by no means a spent force, but he was burning himself out.

The Rise of General Perron

BEFORE de Boigne retired he warned Daulat Rao Sindia not to place any other officer in supreme command of the regular brigades as the temptations were so great. This Daulat Rao ignored, and rightly, as the strength of the Army of Hindustan lay in its excellent central administration and in the financial organisation which de Boigne had created and which ensured a contented and well-paid army. The obvious choice for a successor was Robert Sutherland, formerly of the Royal Highland Regiment, an able, educated professional. Unfortunately for him Daulat Rao did not know him well and in any case he was engaged in some remote operation with his brigade. With him in Poona was Perron, whose First Brigade lent teeth to his diplomacy in Mahratta affairs, who was always at his elbow and who acted as his military adviser. The young Daulat Rao had seen Perron in action when he had routed Raymond and Nizam Ali Khan at Khardla. Perron was ambitious and persuasive and succeeded in obtaining from his master the tremendous appointment of both Commander-in-Chief and the Governorship of Hindustan which made him virtually the Mahratta regent of the Empire and guardian of the person of the Emperor Shah Alam. Accordingly Pierre Cuiller, now General Perron—'Ekdast Sahib' or 'Sir One-Hander' as the sepoys called him since he had lost his hand through a prematurely bursting grenade at the siege of Kanaund—handed over his brigade to another French officer called Drugeon and set off for Delhi. He arrived in March, 1797, to find that two of his new subordinates, the Mahratta governors of Delhi and Agra were engaged in a quarrel with Daulat Rao Sindia and refused to acknowledge his authority or open their gates to Perron.

It is necessary to pause here and to try to unravel the intricacies of the Mahratta politics of the period. At the best of times the Mahrattas were too lively and too contentious a people to pursue a settled policy for long. The paramount authority of the Peshwa had finally dwindled to nothing with the death of Nana Farnavis and any guiding principle disappeared with the death of the great

Madhaji. In the last decade of the century Mahratta affairs were chaotic to a degree. Thus we see at one moment Lakwa Dada as commander-in-chief of Sindia's Mahratta army, at the next he is in rebellion and then he is reinstated only to rebel again. The Rajput rajas are at one moment allies of Sindia and therefore of Perron but at the next at war with him. The reigning Peshwa is Daulat Rao Sindia's own nominee, but Daulat Rao fights the Peshwa's Prime Minister and then shortly afterwards orders the troops who are actually engaging him to turn round and join the Prime Minister who has fallen out with Jaswant Rao Holkar. Perron, lawfully appointed by Daulat Rao, has to make war to establish his position against his master's own officials. No sooner does Perron put down trouble in one place than it breaks out in another: there was hardly a day from his appointment until the war with the British when his regular troops were not fighting somewhere. It can be understood how George Thomas was able to do as he pleased for so long in Alwar and later in Hariana and the Punjab, for he was at first merely a small eddy in a turbulent sea. There are, however, two clues that give a lead through all these confusing events. They are Daulat Rao's inexperience and folly, and the fact that the Mahratta Confederacy was split into four mutually hostile parties who regrouped and altered their alliances almost from month to month as opportunity dictated. As will be seen, Perron as the civil head of Sindia's richest province and custodian of the Emperor was to find that he could not avoid becoming involved in these dangerous affairs. It was not that he was a man quite different in character from de Boigne, although this is true: de Boigne had been too fastidious to meddle in Mahratta politics and his relationship with Madhaji Sindia had been clear cut. Perron had a weak master who spent all his time at Poona immersed in the affairs of the Confederacy and he inevitably had to take great decisions on his own and so inevitably became more and more independent and exposed to the temptations of power and office.

Daulat Rao Sindia in 1795 could not have been in a more fortunate position. He owned vast territories of his own, he had inherited an invincible army, he was master of what was left of the empire of Akbar and paramount among the other Mahratta chieftains. Tukaji Holkar, his great-uncle's enemy, was dead and had been succeeded by an imbecile in poor health, so the house of

Holkar offered no rivalry. Dead too (in 1796) was Nana Farnavis, the able minister of the Peshwa. The boy Peshwa, Mahda Rao Narayan, whom Madhaji had wooed so assiduously, was also dead. He had been on the terrace of his palace in Poona flying his kite when 'Fate ordained, the string of his life being short, for his foot to slip: he fell from the parapet and the kite of his soul flew away into the air'—a mysterious accident that was announced as suicide. Diplomacy backed by the presence of the First Brigade had secured the accession of a new Peshwa—Baji Rao II—favourable to the house of Sindia, for Daulat Rao had inherited from his great-uncle a shrewd and able minister, Baloba Tantia, who knew how to manage and had the confidence of the tricky and turbulent baronage who followed Sindia.[1] All these blessings Daulat Rao threw away in a series of acts of folly.

It is wrong to pass moral judgements on a young man in Daulat Rao's position, a mere boy when he succeeded. He may well have been cruel, or self-indulgent, or lazy or debauched, but he was the victim of the system. All the politics of an Asian court of that era revolved around the physical or psychological capture of the heir. The system was to indulge him. Warfare, hunting, falcons, horses, women, boys, drugs or debauchery: whatever his tastes, he was plied with them until he was satiated and had become the pliant tool of his ministers. Sometimes he developed a sadistic taste for blood which made court life more exciting, for a jealous whisper from a rival might suddenly cast the reigning favourite from fabulous wealth and power to disgrace and a horrid death. The monarch himself often tolerated this treatment of his heir for, as was plainly seen among the Moghuls, a son was often a rival whom the father was happy to see distracted from any premature and dangerous aspirations. The measure of an Asian ruler's ability was the speed and the ruthlessness with which he could shake off these parasites and assert himself. This Daulat Rao proved quite unable to do. The only man he trusted and longed to have by him was de Boigne, and failing him he saw Perron as his de Boigne; but he had sent him away to Hindustan. Alone, he was unable to resist these pressures. He was eventually 'captured' by a man despicable and cruel even by the elastic standards of an Asian court of that era, one Shirzi Rao Ghatkay. Ghatkay brought off two coups. He married his daughter, a persuasive and attractive woman, to Daulat Rao, and he

Swords for Hire

displaced Baloba Tantia and imprisoned him. The rise of Ghatkay was seen with fear and anger by the chiefs, but what triggered off the rebellion of Lakwa Dada and some of Madhaji's old followers was what came to be known as the affair, or the war, of the *Bais*. (*Bai* is the suffix added to the name of Hindu ladies.)[2]

Madhaji Sindia had left three widows who, happily, had not declared themselves *sat* and followed the revolting Hindu tradition of burning themselves alive on Madhaji's funeral pyre. It was Daulat Rao's duty to provide them with suitable estates on to which they could retire, but for one reason or another this was endlessly delayed and they were kept on in uncertainty at Sindia's court in Poona. Two of these ladies were elderly matrons, but the third was a young and flighty thing who took the fancy of Daulat Rao. To us today an affair with one's great-aunt would seem grotesque rather than sinful, but to the strait-laced Hindus the idea of incest even where no blood-tie existed was infinitely shocking. None expressed their horror more loudly than the two elder Bais. Ghatkay Rao, pretending to be jealous of his master's reputation, arrested them, had them well flogged, and imprisoned them in a dungeon in the fort of Ahmednagar. Both the accusation of incest and the treatment of the two widows of the old Patel, whose fortunes good and bad they had followed since Panipat, disgusted all Sindia's older followers. It also alarmed them. If men of Baloba Tantia's rank could be thrown into prison and high-caste women made to bare their backs to the eyes and the whip of the executioner, who was safe? When Lakwa Dada rebelled he found that he had many supporters.

It is always a mistake to combine cruelty and tyranny with inefficiency. Ghatkay was inept enough to allow the Bais' friends to effect their escape from Ahmednagar, they fled for protection naturally enough to the sovereign of the Mahrattas, the Peshwa. Daulat Rao, or Ghatkay, sent troops to recover them. The splendid First Brigade was now in the feeble hands of Drugeon, who detached an equally feeble officer called Duprat with four battalions for the task. Duprat achieved the impossible by allowing the battalions trained by de Boigne to be repulsed by the Peshwa's prime minister, Amrat Rao, who refused to hand over the Bais. Ghatkay then tried dissimulation. He promised that if the Bais returned to Sindia's protection and dropped the scandal all would be forgiven and they would be granted jaghirs to which they could retire in peace. When, however, Amrat Rao was on his way to a conference to ratify these arrangements he was ambushed by Drugeon and only narrowly escaped. The Bais fled and took refuge with the rajah of Kolapur well out of Sindia's reach. Daulat Rao therefore had provided himself with two sets of enemies: the party of the Bais led by Lakwa Dada, and his own suzerain whom he had been at such pains to appoint and to keep in his own pocket—the Peshwa Baji Rao II and his followers.

The fourth party in the Mahratta civil war was Jeswant Rao, the illegitimate son of Tukaji Holkar. After Tukaji's death in 1797 his followers quarrelled over the succession, some taking the part of the legitimate heir, while the other party, feeling that the times demanded a stronger and more active ruler, wanted to depose him and put his far more able younger brother in his place. Jaswant Rao took the part of the pretender. Daulat Rao who preferred to see the old enemies of the house of Sindia led by the incompetent heir, entered the war on his side. At first all went badly for the rebels. Dudrenac and the regular troops came out against them, the pretender was killed in battle and Jaswant's own brother fell into Sindia's hands and was executed. Here Sindia made a terrible mistake. Jaswant Rao, whom he had thus made his enemy for life, revived the tradition of Shivaji and the last great fighting chieftain of the Mahratta nation. In almost every battle of this period the futile Mahrattas are seen either avoiding battle or flying in panic. This was never said of them under Jaswant Rao. He understood the art of the guerrilla, none better, but he also led his men up the muzzles of the enemy guns. In British eyes, and also in the eyes of his European mercenary officers, Jaswant Rao Holkar was cruel, capricious, a hater of Feringhis and the leader and creator of those mounted armies of atrocious bandits who came to be known as 'Pindaris'; but in Indian eyes he was a hero. After the collapse of his cause he turned outlaw and guerrilla, and in the style of his ancestors he harried all central India from coast to coast.

At an early stage of his career he met a kindred soul. In the days when de Boigne was forming the First Brigade a young Pathan applied to him for a commission but was rejected. He went off and formed his own band of Pathan horsemen, employing them, like George Thomas, as freebooters or as mercenary cavalry as the state

of the market dictated. This was the famous Amir Khan. He and
Jaswant Rao struck up a long-lasting partnership and friendship.
Amir Khan was an excellent soldier. With Jaswant Rao he was to
force Dudrenac's surrender, defeat Sindia's regulars at Ujjein,
recover Indore and the possessions of Tukaji and even inflict on
the British Colonel Monson so severe a defeat that it led to the
recall of the British Governor-General. Jaswant Rao was too astute
a man and too good a soldier to believe he could achieve everything
by guerrilla tactics and his elusive Mahratta and Pathan horsemen.
If he was to maintain a firm grip on what they conquered for him he
needed proper infantry and guns. Much as he hated and distrusted
Europeans he was by no means so foolish as to deny himself their
help. He therefore formed three regular brigades under good
European officers who proved a match for Sindia and were to
teach him some bitter lessons.

There was also one other enemy that all the Mahrattas forgot in
the course of their fratricidal quarrels until it was too late: the
British. In 1798 there arrived in Calcutta as Governor-General of
the Company's dominions the future Duke of Wellington's eldest
brother, Richard, Earl of Mornington. Mornington, or as he shortly
became, Marquess Wellesley, was only thirty-seven years old, the
first really able administrator in a modern sense Britain was to send
to India; highly intelligent and fresh from the European scene and
the war with revolutionary France. He was a man of imperial outlook
and imperial mien: he did not see his task as limited to ensuring an
ample flow of unearned income to the shareholders of the Company.
He had decided before even he landed that his first objective must
be to secure the Deccan and the far south and rid it of French
influence. The Corps du Raymond—the Nizam's regular army—
was now commanded by a Jacobin adventurer called Piron who
flew the revolutionary Tricoleur and was suspected of being in
contact with Perron in Hindustan and also with the Directory in
Paris.

On 22nd October, 1798, two British officers, Roberts and the
famous John Malcolm, arrived in Hyderabad with a small force of
sepoys, ordered the Nizam's army to parade and under the threat
of their cannon disarmed and disbanded it bloodlessly and with the
utmost ignominy. The troops were simply ordered to pile their
arms, right turn and quick march, which they did like a flock of

A Rajput cavalier, helmeted and armed in chain mail and hung with pearls

Amir Khan, Jaswant Rao Holkar's leader of cavalry, seen here riding unarmed and
in state

sheep, leaving all their weapons behind them. The French officers were ejected, the Nizam Ali Khan was sternly warned not to run with the French fox and the British hounds for the future and ordered to keep up a force of 6000 officered by the British and for their use. Mornington next dealt with Mysore. The other great enemy of the British in the south, Haidar Ali of Mysore, was dead, but his son Tipu still defied the British and was full of fight. After a brisk and ably directed campaign the British drove Tipu into his great and intricately defended fortress of Seringapatam, garrisoned by 20,000 men with 287 cannon. Ripples of shock and awe spread across India when the British, on 4th April, 1799, took exactly seven minutes to storm the walls and in the morning's fighting killed the brave Tipu, another British villain but Indian hero, and 8000 of the determined garrison. From that moment the British were the masters of all southern and eastern India. The Governor-General had to stay his hand while the British army under Abercrombie attacked the French in Egypt, where he had been ordered to send a division of his troops. Once this diversion had been successfully concluded and France cut off from India he was able to turn his clear and baleful gaze on the Mahrattas; and also on General Perron. His political agents told him that that officer and his Army of Hindustan was more French than Hindustani.

Such were the chief parties and political factors when Perron left the First Brigade in the south and travelled to Aligarh to take over his enormous responsibilities in Hindustan. He arrived in February, 1797, and it is not surprising that it took him the best part of 1797 and 1798 to get a grip on affairs. He had to do everything himself. He had no civil service and no army staff waiting to present him with briefs and papers listing the decisions they were waiting for him to take, or orderly 'presentations' with maps and graphs showing the military situation, or lectures on the politics of the Rajputs and the Sikhs. He was faced with the impudent resistance of the governors of Delhi and Agra commanding his own garrisons; adherents of the Bais who refused to open their gates to him or surrender their commissions. The Sikh frontier was in its usual state of anarchy, Thomas and the Frontier Governor having come to blows and left it virtually undefended. Now Thomas was squatting illegally in Hariana and waging private wars as he saw fit. The fine army created by de Boigne had been left headless and without proper

12

central direction for over a year. Its best brigade was absent in central India under the useless Drugeon and another was commanded by his rival Colonel Sutherland, deeply chagrined at being passed over for Quarter-Master-Sergeant Perron. His own position, until he consolidated it, was slippery, as it depended on the whim of an unstable young man who was firmly under the control of the infamous Ghatkay Rao. Its opportunities for fabulous enrichment —the revenues of Hindustan even in its anarchic state may have been eight millions of rupees—aroused the deepest envy of all the Mahratta magnates. In that quarter he had not one friend and two deadly enemies, Lakwa Dada and Ambaji Angria.

Perron also had to contend with his own origins. European officers in the eighteenth century, especially the British, were terrible snobs, despising anyone of 'low' or ungentlemanly origin. This was even more the case with the Indians. They never knew quite how to place the *Feringhis* according to their status, but they were shrewd enough to make a good guess. In their eyes a man like de Boigne was clearly a *sahib*: however caste was measured in his own country, he was clearly of a good one. A man like Thomas was in his way a *sahib* too, and although he was a terrible ruffian he was also almost an Indian: a sort of less horrible Ghulam Kadir or, better, an Amir Khan but with a white skin. Perron was unfortunately placed. The sepoys might admire their Ekdast Sahib, who could lead a storming column with the best, but there were many Indians over whose heads he had leapt who could remember the out-of-work white *havildar* (sergeant) whose half-caste wife used to chaffer in the bazaar for a seer of atta or a few eggs and rub shoulders with low-caste folk. Who was he to put on airs and give orders and rule the Empire ? All these were handicaps which men of the finest proconsular timber might have found daunting. In the face of them the untrained, uneducated Perron ruled Hindustan virtually as a dictator for seven years, in the course of which he governed, commanded the army and expanded it, undertook campaigns and threaded his way through the labyrinth of Indian politics in which it was an achievement to survive. Until he was seduced by the dotty French plot to reconquer India he seems to have managed affairs with restraint and good sense.

Perron saw clearly that the army was the basis of his power. It was small enough by Indian standards. With the First Brigade permanently detached to the Deccan he had only the newer and so far untried Second and Third totalling some 1600 cavalry, twenty battalions and a hundred field guns excluding the permanent garrisons of the three great fortresses, who were not regular, mobile troops. The army he gradually expanded to five brigades (although there is some doubt whether the Fifth was ever brought up to full strength). So far, except for the squadrons in the brigades, too much reliance had been placed on the irregular cavalry. Accordingly he raised a large force of regular cavalry generally referred to as 'Hindustani' horse. It was not a great success, but this may well have been due more to lack of good officers than any fault on the part of the troops. They proved unable to stand up to Thomas' cavalry or to the British. The contentment and reliability of the army depended on its continuing to be well-administered and well paid. Its pay and financial backing depended on retaining possession of and maintaining order in the rich Jumna Doab which had been allotted for the purpose. Perron made certain of the Doab, virtually his inner kingdom, by cantoning a brigade there and also improving the fortifications and the quality of the garrison in the fortress of Aligarh which protected his main base at Koil. Aligarh was believed to be impregnable.

Perron's real problem was the provision of trained senior officers fit to command the brigades who were at the same time loyal to him. There were plenty of good fighting regimental officers to be had, but for his taste too many came from British India which provided an almost inexhaustible supply, either soldiers of fortune from the King's or the Company's regiments, or the sons of officers or those who were euphemistically called the 'country-born'; men of mixed British and Indian blood. The majority of them had grown up in India and therefore had the qualities essential for commanding troops so sensitive to leadership and so beset by problems of caste and race and religion. They could speak the languages and understood the character of their men. They all possessed another essential quality which Indians admired in themselves and others and was always a passport to their approval: their dash and courage in battle. One or two were perfectly capable of a command higher than a battalion, a force of three or four battalions with guns and cavalry perhaps attached (i.e. a 'brigade' in the ordinary English sense). Unfortunately Perron never made good use of this material.

He disliked Englishmen and when he became involved in his French plot he decided to rid himself of all of them. What is more difficult to understand than his treatment of his British officers is his neglect of good French ones. There were in the Army of Hindustan itself, for instance, Bernier, the future conqueror of George Thomas, and Fleury. Elsewhere there was the able Plumet who had left the Holkar's service because he could not stomach Jaswant Rao, and there must have been more. As it was his senior appointments, it being remembered that the command of one of the brigades would rate in the British service as demanding the rank of a Major-General at least, were atrocious. He relied almost entirely on old mercenary hacks like Dudrenac and Drugeon and Pedron; or on poltroons like George Hessing or buffoons like Louis Bourquin who was unfit to command a platoon, let alone an effective division.

There may have been three reasons for this. Promotions to field rank (major) and above were, it seems, by purchase, and of all systems of promotion, even that of promotion by birth, this is the most inimical to efficiency. However, this could account only for the failure to promote good but poor men, but not for the appointment of really bad officers which under Perron seemed to amount almost to a policy. It may well be that Perron, good soldier though he was and therefore a judge at least of fighting commanders, suffered from that dislike and resentment of the educated gentlemen who had slipped so effortlessly to the rank to which he had had to fight his way, which sometimes affects the promoted ranker. He may have had scores to pay off. Smith, speaking of Plumet, for instance, refers to him as 'a gentleman and a Frenchman', adding that this was an unusual combination to find in India.

Officers from the ranks lacking in social polish who have earned their promotion by hard work and their courage and coolness in battle are quick to detect such attitudes and to resent them. Perron tolerated Englishmen and gentlemen as regimental officers in battalions—as lieutenants and captains—but he did not advance any of them to a rank where they might challenge his position. He treated Colonel Sutherland and Major Brownrigg who had been commissioned by de Boigne with considerable suspicion. Another reason why Perron made such bad senior appointments was that he was a member of the small clique of French mercenary officers; some of them, like Dudrenac and Pedron, dating back to the days of Law and of Madec nearly forty years before; others, like Drugeon, whose reputation derived from their having commanded a battalion under de Boigne at Lalsot or Chaksana. They were much inter-married and formed a little society of their own. Perron's wife, for instance, was the sister of a French-Indian officer called Derridon. Perron must certainly have felt more at home with these French and half-French expatriates than with the British, and his promotions may have been, and indeed many were, simple nepotism. It is significant that he could not bring himself to dismiss one of them. When they failed he merely moved them between posts. Drugeon, for instance, was given the responsible post of Governor of Delhi and Hessing of Agra. The First Brigade had four commanders in six years, Pohlmann moving backwards and forwards between the First and Second Brigades; and Pedron, Bourquin and Dudrenac, who all failed as commanders, were later restored to their commands or given fresh ones.

However, all these errors and their consequences lay in the future. The two commanders he found in charge were Sutherland of the Second Brigade and Pohlmann of the Third. Sutherland, able as he was in battle, was corrupt and unreliable and Perron rightly did not trust him a yard. Skinner tells an odd story about him. When Skinner commanded a battalion in the Second Brigade under Sutherland during the operations against Lakwa Dada he succeeded in rescuing a Mahratta chief from an ambush, who rewarded him, according to the fashion of the time, with some jewels and a fine charger. Sutherland chose to rebuke Skinner for exceeding his duty and threatened to report him to higher authority; with the sinister implication that this was a Mahratta affair into which he should not have poked his nose. Having allowed this to sink in he let Skinner, then a subaltern of only twenty-one, under-stand that if he handed the horse over to Sutherland as a present he might contrive to forget about the matter. It would be interesting to know how Sutherland came to be cashiered from the King's service but whatever the reason it seems clear that the 73rd Foot or whichever regiment he came from was well rid of him. Neverthe-less, except perhaps for Pohlmann he was the ablest officer in the Army and a brave and aggressive commander in the field once he had decided to fight. Pohlmann was a very different character. He was a tough old German from Hanover who had been originally a sergeant in one of the Company's European battalions. Like many of the older mercenaries he was thoroughly Indianised, keeping a zenana full of wives. He lived in style as a great *bahadur*, with his own elephant to ride and his personal cavalry bodyguard to accompany him on ceremonial occasions. British accounts include a 'Pohlmann's Brigade' (by then the First) at Assaye where he, or it, helped to give the future Duke of Wellington one of the hardest fights of his life. Pohlmann and Sutherland respectively were to win the great victories of Malpura and Indore. So for the time being Perron was well served.

During this preliminary period Perron secured himself firmly in the Doab, where he made Koil, now better known as Aligarh from the name of a great fortress there virtually his military capital of Hindustan, leaving Delhi to the shadow Emperor. He built a 'cantonment'; barracks, magazines and gun parks for the troops and a 'Government House' for himself. Not until all this was well on the way to completion did he feel ready to deal with the recalcitrant governors in Delhi and Agra. This in 1798, and he did not recover Agra until early in 1799. Perron was a patient man, preferring always, even with Thomas as we shall see to use negotiation, diplomatic pressure, even a bribe rather than force. In this he showed good sense. Obtaining control of Delhi was rather a delicate business, for the Mahratta official there had the king, so to speak, castled; but eventually Sutherland by a combination of bribery, diplomacy and a show of force managed to take possession. Perron was then able to evict the Emperor's warder, the embezzling and penny-pinching fakir Nizam-ud-Din, whom he replaced by a Captain le Marchant (and later by Drugeon) as governor, Imperial chamberlain and also the goaler of the Imperial Person. Shah Alam II probably considered this an improvement, because he and his poor family were now at least given enough to eat. The Governor of Agra proved more obstinate, being a brother of the fallen Baloba Tantia and strongly of the party of the Bais. He defended the great double-walled fortress for three months in the most obstinate manner, inflicting 600 casualties on the Third Brigade, but at length he surrendered when Perron sprung a mine and prepared to storm. (It is curious that the Brigades, so formidable in the open field, never seemed to do so well in siege operations, which their commanders always conducted formally in the deliberate Asian style. The British and, in his smaller way Thomas, were in marked contrast. They seldom had the time or the numbers and they also believed that the attrition of a long siege was as costly in the long run as an assault, which they undertook with the utmost ferocity. They had an uncanny knack of cracking open the masterpieces of Indian fortification by simply climbing over the wall. Many an active man today would not care to attempt some of their escalades even if he were not being shot at.)

The fall of Agra in the February of 1799 ended any prospects that the Bais might have had in Hindustan, but there remained Lakwa Dada in Mewar. He managed easily to evade or outwit detachments sent against him by the incompetent Duprat in command of the First Brigade. He also succeeded in isolating and cutting up two battalions under a Captain Butterfield. As a result Perron sent the Second Brigade under Sutherland to deal with him, but Sutherland rather conspicuously avoided engaging him. To be fair to Sutherland, while he was not above taking a bribe from Lakwa Dada and probably did, he was in a difficult position. There had been a successful counterplot against Shirzi Rao Ghatkay—George Hessing and Fidele Filose being employed to seize and imprison him. (Unfortunately for the Mahratta cause that evil and incompetent man was allowed to live.) The old minister to Sindia, Baloba Tantia, was released and Daulat Rao took both him and his fellow Brahmin back to favour. Lakwa was immediately reappointed to his old appointment of native commander-in-chief. Sutherland was therefore acting prudently in remaining not so much neutral but actively non-belligerent, even if he did make Lakwa pay him for leaving him alone. Perron, however, was most displeased. He dismissed Butterfield and sent Pohlmann to replace Sutherland. Nor was he pleased to see Thomas whom he regarded simply as a bandit and an outlaw making war so successfully in Imperial territory. For Perron these purely Mahratta distractions were merely an irritation, which could easily have been settled had he been able to direct the campaign himself. He was soon, however, fully occupied by a far more serious threat. In 1799 Zaman Shah, the King of Afghanistan once more appeared in the Punjab, rallying the Sikhs and showing every intention of advancing on Delhi. Like his grandfather he could claim that Afghanistan was a province of the Empire, that Shah Alam II was his suzerain and that he owed to him and to the Faith to release his emperor from the infidel, although in reality his mind was probably more on loot.

This caused great alarm: even the British assembled a field force as a precautionary measure. The Mahrattas despatched no less than 100,000 troops to the north to reinforce the regular brigades. Perron recalled the Second Brigade from the south and having concentrated this enormous force at Muttra disposed it north of Delhi astride the classic invasion route into India. He still felt short of troops without the First Brigade, so he formed on his own authority a new brigade, the Fourth. The Fourth Brigade, like the Fifth, which was formed later in 1802, was not raised by direct recruiting but built up from a nucleus of regular battalions drawn from other mercenary corps. Among the reinforcements from the south was a brigade originally raised by a Neapolitan called Michael Filose, who had bequeathed it to his two sons, Fidele and Jean-Baptiste (also known as de la Fontaine). Perron bought some of their battalions, or bought them over—it is not quite clear which. They were poor stuff, but under Perron's training they rapidly improved, as was to be seen at Laswari. John Hessing, who had been one of de Boigne's original battalion commanders, later left him and raised a corps of his own. When he grew older he was given the post of kiladar, or garrison commander of Agra and handed his corps to his son George. This was absorbed into the Army of Hindustan to become the Fifth Brigade.

However, these precautions turned out to be unnecessary and there was not to be another Battle of Panipat. Zaman Shah was forced to return home to deal with a rebellion and the alarm subsided. This was the last of a long series of disastrous irruptions into India from inner Asia, but the spectres of Taimur and Nadir Shah and the Abdalis remained to haunt the British who as a result embarked long afterwards on one or two misguided adventures west of the Khaibar in an attempt to lay them. Perron dispersed his grand army, but he took the opportunity of his brigades being mobilised and in the field to bring the cis-Sutlej Sikhs to heel. He called in all the major chiefs to a conference at Kurnool, where they agreed to behave themselves for the future, to refrain from raiding and to acknowledge that the Imperial writ, or rather Perron's, was effective up to the Sutlej. For some reason Perron did not at the same time deal with George Thomas, although he had been much annoyed by his rampaging and looting in Sindia's territory on his way from the Mewar campaign. Over Thomas, Perron acted with his usual caution and circumspection. He may have seen him as a useful counterbalance to the Sikhs and as a useful auxiliary, for he certainly tried to buy him over to Sindia's service before they finally and fatally quarrelled. He may not have thought military action was worth the trouble in 1799, not then seeing Thomas and his handful of ragged battalions as a threat to his position or something he could not easily suppress whenever he chose. In any case, he had other things to distract him in 1800.

No sooner had the danger in the north subsided and the Sikhs been pacified than serious troubles broke out again in the west in Rajputana and in the south. In Rajputana the Raja of Jaipur, Pratap Singh, was once again feeling restive under the hated Mahratta yoke. Two years had passed since the terrible defeats at Patun and Mertah. Madhaji was dead and de Boigne had retired. The great Lakwa who had been set over the Rajputs in the stronghold of Ajmir was in disgrace. Daulat Rao Sindia was distracted by the affair of the Bais and Lakwa Dada's rebellion. Pratap Singh saw there was a chance to defy his hated conqueror and to tell him, in effect, that he could whistle for his *chaut*. He may have believed that with the disappearance of de Boigne the brigades were no longer so formidable or efficient, in which he proved to be mistaken. Where Pratap Singh made a greater mistake was in believing that he was challenging Daulat Rao, whereas in fact he was colliding with Perron, a man who would not tolerate the slightest defiance of his authority, or any delay in the payment of revenue. He mobilised two of the brigades and a large contingent of Sindia's Mahratta horsemen, and placed the whole force under command of, ironically enough, Lakwa Dada, who by one of the rapid shifts in Mahratta politics was once more but only temporarily in favour.

Much of what we know about Perron's Rajput campaign of 1800 comes from the vivid but sometimes inaccurate memoirs of James Skinner. He was at the time a youthful battalion commander of twenty-two in the Second Brigade. His father was an elderly but junior officer in the Company's army who had acquired a Rajput lady as part of his spoil after an engagement. In those days the relationship between the races had not been eroded by evangelical Christianity or the arrival of floods of Englishwomen who sternly disapproved of subalterns cohabiting with brown ladies; or by the catastrophe of 1857 after which British and Indians became rigidly separated in social life. The elder Skinner was one of the many poor Company's officers who were forced to make their lives in India and were the founders of the later Anglo-Eurasian population. He married the girl, who presented him with six children. She remained in *purdah* (i.e. in strict seclusion), as such wives often did in that period. She kept her own religion, and so high was her caste and so strong her caste feeling that when Skinner insisted on sending their daughters to school instead of imprisoning them in the women's quarters—the zenana—she committed suicide. James Skinner, the middle son, was violently torn between his British and Indian identities. After an English schooling he ran away from a post in an English firm his father had found for him, to submerge himself, like 'Kim', in native life; but he was detected by a servant of his family who dragged him home. He was deeply conscious of his Rajput ancestry and full of martial dreams. This was discovered by his godfather, a colonel who knew de Boigne and who asked him to give James Skinner a commission. He was appointed a very young ensign in a battalion of najibs in 1795 and there he found his vocation.

In about March 1800 the Second Brigade, by then under Colonel Pohlmann, was ordered to join the force being assembled under Lakwa Dada to subdue Pratap Singh and his fellow chiefs; Lakwa Dada's new post being due to the fact that Daulat Rao had been prevailed upon to arrest his father-in-law and restore his great-uncle's trusted generals and advisers to their proper places. Lakwa's order of battle was two regular brigades—one under Dudrenac and Pohlmann's Second Brigade—5000 of the new Hindustani Horse and the inevitable and useless mob of Mahratta light cavalry. With these he marched to the vicinity of Jaipur city, where Pratap Singh was preparing for a pitched battle in the high, antique style of the Rajputs. He chose a position near the village of Malpura, which gives the battle its name. There he dug trenches and batteries while behind there grew a city of tents complete with a bazaar and a temporary but splendidly appointed wooden palace for himself, for he had chosen to lead the army in person. His army was the usual valiant mixture of tribes and castes, of matchlock-men and Goshais and Bairagis, and it included a force, reputedly 10,000 strong, of the yellow-garbed Rathor horsemen, who now faced the Army of Hindustan for the fourth time.

Lakwa Dada arrived at the Malpura position on the 14th April, and determined to attack early on the following morning. Pratap Singh, whose astrologers had calculated that it was the day for a decisive battle, was agreeable and marched out to meet him. The battle that ensued was devoid of manoeuvre or subtlety and was simply a head-on collision in mediaeval style. Lakwa's own dispositions were also somewhat old-fashioned: more like the seventeenth or even the sixteenth century. He deployed his army in two long lines. In the first he put the infantry and guns of the two brigades, Pohlmann on the right, Dudrenac on the left, with regiments of the Hindustani Horse stationed so as to protect each flank. (The presence of the Chevalier Dudrenac in Sindia's army is puzzling. He certainly joined the Army of Hindustan and in 1803 was commanding the Fourth Brigade, from which he deserted to surrender to Colonel Vandeleur when war with the British broke out. As far as can be made out the Chevalier at the time of Malpura was still in the service of Jaswant Rao Holkar, Daulat Rao Sindia's deadly enemy. He may of course have left earlier and the two brigades at Malpura have been Pohlmann in command of the Second and Dudrenac of the Fourth. Alternatively Dudrenac may have taken his own corps, raised for Holkar's service, to Malpura on contract just for this one operation so as to earn some money on the side; an amusing thought and not at all contrary to mercenary custom.) In the second or reserve line he put the Mahratta cavalry. The whole army advanced in this awkward formation, the gap between the infantry and the unenthusiastic Mahrattas gradually widening until the two sides were within cannon-shot for the preliminary artillery exchange without which no native Indian battle could be said formally to have begun. The next stage, also by custom, was the charge and countercharge of the cavalry.

To meet this Pohlmann, that good German soldier, wasted no time in altering his most unsuitable formation. He quickly put his Brigade into hollow square. (Or possibly, as he had only six battalions, into a three-sided box formation, closing the rear with the cavalry.) In either case it was a complicated evolution from line. According to the tactics of the day the advance should have been made in column of battalions from which any suitable formation could quickly and conveniently have been adopted. As it was the two centre battalions had to continue to advance while the two on either flank broke into column, checked their pace, inclined inwards and while keeping perfect distance took station so that when the orders 'halt!' 'form square' and 'prepare to receive cavalry!' were given each company could pivot exactly into position without leaving a gap and present a continuous line of guns and bayonets on each face of the square. Pohlmann was thus ready for anything, but Dudrenac left his raw troops standing helplessly in extended line and in this formation they took the full shock of the attack of the Rathor cavalry. Skinner from his position in Pohlmann's square witnessed their fate. Massed in their usual dense ghol the Rathors were unchecked by Dudrenac's artillery fire. They rode over their own dead, through the batteries, burst through his infantry and killed or wounded a quarter of them and scattered the rest beyond hope of reforming. Dudrenac only saved himself by falling down and shamming dead.[3] They then went on full tilt into the Mahratta second line who turned and fled, as a matter of course. The sight of their backs and the intoxication of unlimited killing led the Rathors on past any hope of a rally until pursued and pursuers disappeared far away in the distance and out of the battle for good.

This was unfortunate for Pratap Singh, who would have been glad of their help. Pohlmann had in his methodical way persisted in his attack, keeping his box-formation edging forward and hammering the Jaipur army with his guns: those well-served, terrible cannon of the Army of Hindustan, banging away every twenty seconds or so in their steady, disciplined gun-drill. He was gradually gaining the upper hand when in the twinkle of an eye the charge of the Rathors swept away Dudrenac and all the Mahratta support. Pratap Singh then saw that the battle might be his and mounting his war elephant so that he could be clearly seen by his men, led two determined charges that the Second Brigade were barely able to hold. The Rajputs, under the Rajah's eye and banner, fought as they have never done at Patun or Mertah or against George Thomas the year before. At one stage in the battle a few of them actually burst into the square and Skinner, caught in the open, had to run and hide under an ammunition wagon, the horsemen leaning from their saddles and poking at him with their spears until someone shot them. Then a cannon shot brought down Pratap Singh's elephant, poor beast, and the castle-like howdah and his royal rider crashed to the ground. At once this terrible and ominous sight caused the superstitious panic from which those valorous but totally undisciplined armies suffered. Pratap Singh took to his horse and fled to Jaipur followed by the rest of his troops and all the followers of the camp driving, riding or walking leaving Pohlmann alone in possession of the field and all his guns.

The battle suddenly broke out again at midday. Pohlmann's iron discipline had, fortunately for him, kept his troops from scattering to loot the Rajput camp, and under arms. He was therefore still in battle formation and covered by his vedettes when they gave him warning of the return of the Rathors, who had grown tired of hunting the Mahrattas. By some chance the captured standards of the Jaipur army had been collected and, presumably for convenience stuck in the ground by their staffs and were seen by the Rathors floating above the ranks of the Second Brigade. The battlefield was silent and empty. The Rathors, perhaps still bemused by the fear-removing opium and bhang they took before battle, imagined the troops around them were the Raja's and walked their weary horses towards them, kettle drums rattling and with triumphant cries of '*Jai Bhowani*'. To their surprise and confusion they were greeted with a tempest of case-shot and musketry. They were bold and brave enough to try to form up and attack, but after some desperate attempts they rode off, on this occasion not persisting in their ghastly tradition of absolute self-immolation. This was the last occasion on which the chivalry of Rajputana charged in a great battle in their hallowed style. Malpura finally broke the western Rajputs as a military power. They were never the enemies of the British, who found much to admire in that antique warrior-caste and who wisely left their princes more or less to themselves. They later recruited Rajputs into their army and taught them less suicidal methods of warfare.

Skinner, always inquisitive and adventurous and also with an eye for the main chance, wandered off into the great camp of the Jaipur army and looked it over before the sepoys or the thieving Mahrattas were released to plunder it. It was completely deserted; the tents still standing, the cooking fires burning, the stalls of the banias and merchants their produce still on them forming orderly streets in the camp bazaar and, strangest of all, the gorgeous timber-framed pavilion built as a sort of portable palace for the raja himself. Skinner entered it to gaze astonished on the rich hangings and carpets, the gold or gilt images guarding the ceremonial entrance, the scattered wealth lying about abandoned, like one of the Spartans in the deserted camp of the Persians. Not a soul opposed him as he picked over the best of the loot. The entire population of the canvas city had fled; courtiers, astrologers, priests, guards, the mahouts for the royal elephants, the saises for the horses; the butlers, cooks, barbers, the drivers of bullocks and the drivers of camels, the cutters of firewood, the water-carriers for Hindus and the water-carriers for Muslims, scullions, torch-bearers, messengers and sweepers of dung were all riding or running or trudging towards Jaipur and safety. There was no pursuit, for Lakwa Dada was too busy reassembling his scattered and shattered units, apart from which there was the camp to be looted and the spoil to be counted; seventy cannon and all the transport. Skinner was lucky to have some time in the camp uninterrupted. He collected, among other trifles, two gold idols with diamond eyes and a curious object of virtue in the shape of the 'Fish of Authority' conferred by the Emperors on their amirs and rajas; a catfish or a barbel modelled in brass. Skinner tactfully gave it to Lakwa Dada.

Perron when he heard the news of this victory marched down in person to deal with Pratap Singh's submission, the terms of the peace treaty and the amount of the indemnity the Rajputs were to pay. He brought four battalions by way of reinforcement and was splendidly escorted by his new regiment of bodyguard cavalry formed in imitation of de Boigne. All then was feasting and fun. Pratap Singh appeared to show no great chagrin or resentment either at his disastrous defeat or at the bill for 2,500,000 rupees for arrears and for reparation presented to him by Perron. (It is impossible not to wonder if these huge sums that are so often mentioned had any real meaning, or whether the loser agreed to them light-heartedly, confident that another rapid revolution in the political situation would render the whole debt void. Some payments, as Thomas found in Bikanir, were in worthless paper; others may have been mere liens on future and uncollected taxation.) He invited all the officers of the brigades to an audience, a 'durbar', where they presented their *nazzars* and received *khiluts*, robes of honour, in the Moghul style, after which there was an official dinner party, at which, of course, the Rajah could not sit or take part, followed by tiger and elephant fights and attended by bevies of dancing girls. All of this Skinner greatly enjoyed. That was about all the relaxation he had, for some of the outlying Rajput rajas and thakurs refused to submit and Pohlmann was ordered to deal with them. This occupied him in long and troublesome operations involving endless skirmishing and in the systematic reduction of the forts into which the disgruntled chiefs retired. They were made doubly troublesome by the unreliable and understandably reluctant Rajput levies told off to assist him now that Jaipur was once again an ally of Perron's. One fortress in Mewar was defended with peculiar bitterness, the garrison refusing the first summons and driving the storming columns, British-led and six battalions strong, out of the breach with terrible loss. In the second and successful storm two British battalion commanders—one Irish, one English—were killed and added to the long list of those unknown and adventurous soldiers of fortune who occupy so many unmarked graves in India.

Skinner only narrowly escaped joining them. He had been on detached duty in command of a force composed of his own and three other regular battalions together with a contingent of Rajput levies: a striking tribute by Pohlmann to the ability of a subaltern of twenty-two. He conducted a vigorous and successful campaign until he was betrayed and deserted by the Rajputs. He allowed himself to be trapped by superior numbers and his battalion fighting in square formation doggedly to the end was destroyed. Skinner was left badly wounded on the field to die. It was on this occasion that he vowed to become a Christian like his father if he survived. It says something for his stamina that he survived the attentions of the robbers of the dead, who stripped him but left him alive, and two nights and a day of exposure amid the dead and dying of his wrecked battalion with a matchlock ball in his groin. On the morning of the third day after the battle the first aid arrived, from the lowest of the low castes, a *chumar* (a worker in leather) and his wife, who brought water and gave as many as were left alive a morsel of food. A century and a half later the descendants of even a Rajput in such straits, or merely exhausted and hungry in battle, might have thankfully murmured 'where there is no eye, there is no caste', and accepted; but one of Skinner's subahdars (captains) lying by him with a mangled leg and almost dead of fever and thirst, refused. Drink touched by such a hand was absolute pollution and he elected, he said, to die with his caste unbroken. Fortunately for both of them a burial party sent out by their opponents arrived in time to save both their lives. The Subahdar lost his leg, but Skinner with the resilience of youth escaped blood-poisoning and gangrene and recovered in time to be present at the Battle of Sounda. He gave the chumars a thousand rupees and kept his word to the God of his father, building a church, dedicated naturally to St. James, in Delhi, although his Christianity was always to be a little shaky.

Meanwhile, Daulat Rao Sindia was still hopelessly embroiled in the affair of the Bais. A fresh convulsion in Mahratta affairs was brought about by his folly in allowing his wife to talk him into releasing her father and reinstating him. Ghatkay Rao wasted no time in rearresting Baloba Tantia and having him poisoned. He then went on to proscribe and murder every Mahratta of note he could lay his hands on with results that were disastrous for Daulat Rao in the long run, for many of them were fighting chiefs he was to miss in his impending clashes with Jaswant Rao Holkar and with the British after that. Lakwa Dada once more rebelled. His stronghold in Ajmir was no longer safe with Pohlmann in Jaipur with his whole brigade and Pratap Singh once more allied to Sindia. Accordingly he fled to Bundelkhand with 6000 of his cavalry and his regular sepoys under William Tone, avoiding all attempts by Perron to trap him. He chose Bundelkhand as a refuge as the Bundelas, led by the Rajah of Datia and a Muslim chief called Ali Bahadur had long kept up a resistance against Sindia since the days of Madhaji; both Appa Rao and later Sutherland having undertaken long and tiresome campaigns there without ever completely pacifying them. Politically Lakwa was in a strong position. Sindia now depended almost entirely on his foreign mercenaries for support. Even Ambaji, Lakwa's rival and now reinstated as Sindia's Mahratta commander-in-chief, could not stomach Ghatkay and was carrying out his orders to pursue Lakwa with a distinct lack of enthusiasm. The other leaders of the Confederacy were on the side of the Bais, and Jaswant Rao was actually at war with Sindia. Lakwa at this point made a fatal and for him unaccountable strategic error. His best, indeed his only plan would have been to avoid breaking his teeth on the formidable battalions he himself had so often commanded in battle, to keep on the move, to consolidate Daulat Rao's enemies and not to challenge him in the field until he had thoroughly undermined his position: in short, to adopt the same Mahratta guerrilla tactics by which Jaswant Rao had so far kept his cause alive and shown could still be successful. Lakwa himself had shown considerable dexterity in avoiding George Thomas and picking off Ambaji's battalions in Mewar in 1799. Instead he fell back on the hallowed Indian practice of seeking for a strong natural position and, having fortified it, sitting down inside. He found one near a fort called Sounda in some broken and mountainous country affording little scope for the rigid drill of the regular battalions and there he made himself, as he thought, impregnable, and remained unchallenged for months.

By the beginning of that year Perron was back in his headquarters in Aligarh satisfied with his year's work and attending to the essential business of governing Hindustan. Jaipur was pacified and Pratap Singh had invited him to his daughter's wedding to cement their alliance. He had chased Lakwa out of his home territory and he had settled the hash of the Mahratta governor of Saharanpur who had had the impudence to come out for the Bais. Militarily everything seemed well in hand. Ajmir still held out but was under siege by one of his officers. Ambaji was closing in on Sounda with the largest mercenary army yet assembled: the whole of the Third Brigade under Pedron, Ambaji's own mercenary corps under Shepherd and a third corps of najib battalions under one Kaleb Ali, possibly a Rohilla or a Pathan. It was then that Perron was confounded by his own policies concerning promotion and selection for the command of the brigades. The man he had sent to besiege Ajmir was Louis Bernard (alias 'Bourquin'). Bourquin was a French deserter who had served the Company for some time in a European unit rejoicing in the title of 'Captain Doxat's Chasseurs'. He had then been honestly occupied as a chef and later as a manufacturer of fireworks, after which he drifted into Moghul India and was commissioned into the Army of Hindustan. With Napoleon's marshals in mind there is no reason to turn up one's nose at officers of French and humble origin, but Bourquin is unequivocally denounced as an incompetent poltroon by both Skinner and Smith, who were able to observe him at close

13   181

quarters in the fierce fighting that brought down George Thomas. He dawdled outside Ajmir and made no impression on it at all.

Pedron was equally disappointing. It was clear to Perron, as it had been clear to de Boigne and more recently to Pohlmann, that native commanders-in-chief were the focus of acute and conflicting political pressures, often from the enemy. They were conscious that today's enemy might turn out to be tomorrow's ally or tomorrow's victor: this was particularly true of the relations between Ambaji and Lakwa Dada. Sometimes they deferred taking any decision, not from cowardice but because a defeat or a set-back might mean a loss or 'blackening' of face. It therefore always behoved the European commander to take the initiative. Pedron was quite incapable of this. He was a dithering old man who must have been at least in his sixtieth year, for he was from the original source of mercenary officers, the French mission of General Law who had surrendered to the British in 1761. He may have been a capable battalion commander in his day, for he had been commissioned by de Boigne and had reached his majority under him, and he may have had those powers of organisation which are very much part of a soldier's qualities, for it seems that it was he who raised the Third Brigade. In the field, however, he could not bring himself to do anything. Ambaji found that he had business to attend to in Gwalior forty miles off and deputed his brother to take over operations, who did nothing. The mercenary officers naturally did nothing either, except patrol and skirmish and look dolefully at Lakwa's immensely strong complex of positions. This went on from March until the end of April, by which time Perron came down to take charge of operations himself. The fact that he was able to do so outside his own territory, and so obviously and so woundingly to supersede the great Ambaji Angria, reveals the extent of his power and authority.

Reconnaissance showed him that there were three routes through the tangle of jungle and ravines into Lakwa's fortified lines which extended over about seven miles. All were narrow and defended by batteries of guns and trenches and none was wide enough to allow his artillery and disciplined battalions to deploy properly and bring their full weight to bear. He had, however, ample troops, one of the biggest concentrations of the trained battalions ever to take place in the history of the mercenaries. He resolved accordingly to attack by all three routes at once. This was an absolutely sound plan as he could be in superior strength at each point of attack and a success at any would allow the other two to be 'turned'. It was brutal, direct and without any frills. He gave one line of attack to Ambaji's regulars under Shepherd, and divided Pedron's brigade between the two others, and ordered the assault to be made at dawn on 3rd May 1801.

Sounda was not one of those battles in which masses of Asian flesh were mangled according to the best scientific principles of European warfare and by the disciplined fire of the robot-like sepoys and their gunners. It was a bloody affair between equals; the packed columns, probably in 'grand divisions' with no more than two companies on a front some thirty yards wide ranged one behind the other, scrambled forward keeping their formation as best they could and accepting what the defenders had to offer them in the way of shot and bullets until they could cross bayonets and exchange stab for stab. After that sheer primitive combat between man and man had to decide the day. Pedron with four battalions eventually overcame and accepted the surrender of William Tone suffering, according to Skinner who had recovered from his wound and had been posted to Pedron's brigade, a thousand casualties, or a half of his strength, which is hard to believe, but it is not impossible. In the centre Shepherd fought his way into Lakwa's position but slowly and also with heavy losses, including three European officers. On the left, however, the Raja of Datia emerged from his entrenchments and threw himself on a Captain Symes and the other half of the Third Brigade with such fury that their ranks were broken and they were driven back and Symes wounded. Perron then played a general's part, ignored by the British historians who dismiss him so contemptuously on the basis of his later collapse beset by every difficulty in front of Lake. He formed a reserve of two battalions by drawing on Pedron, rallied Symes' battalions and personally led them up again to the attack. In the desperate fighting that ensued the Raja of Datia was killed, and Perron himself, handicapped in combat as he had only one hand, received a stab from a pike. The three columns then pressed into Lakwa's position, Lakwa was badly wounded, his other Bundela ally killed, his regular sepoy force smashed and all his guns taken. Lakwa and the Bais managed to escape, but they never made head again and the rebellion was finally over.⁴

Perron was now at the summit of his extraordinary career. De Boigne had always exercised his politcal power as Subahdar of Hindustan with great discretion and in the field, where he never disposed of more than the original First Brigade, Madhaji Sindia had invariable placed him under a Mahratta general or made him share command. Because Daulat Rao Sindia was so completely absorbed with political affairs in the Deccan and never (as far as can be discovered) even once visited Delhi the whole conduct of military and civil affairs in the north was left to Perron. It was he who mobilised the complete Mahratta army against the threat of invasion by Zaman Shah, put the Sikhs and the Rajputs in their place and ended the rebellion of the Bais. With eventually five brigades owing their loyalty to him personally he was the absolute master in Hindustan. Had he wished he could have made his master Daulat Rao his puppet, just as the great adventurer Haidar Ali had made the Raja of Mysore his puppet thirty years before. Yet in the next two years Perron did not so much fall as slither to disaster. De Boigne long afterwards described Perron as a plain, simple soldier, but he was mistaken. It was de Boigne who was the plain soldier free of ambition or uncertainty about his goal and Perron who was the complex character; at once patriotic and selfish, enjoying power and moved by self-interest and at the same time drawn by soldierly loyalty to support his master Daulat Rao (which in the end he did and lost all), physically brave but in intrigue at one moment prudent, the next daring and then timid.

Perron would have had quite enough to tax his undoubted abilities in maintaining his grip on Hindustan, supporting his unreliable master, managing his army single-handed and defending his personal position. There is evidence he had a further pre-occupation into which he was drawn as a patriotic Frenchman. This was a scheme to exploit Perron's position of power, his military strength and his possession of the Emperor's person together with his link with the Mahrattas to re-establish French influence in India and to make war on the British. Some believe that this plot existed only in the minds of the British. Admittedly the evidence for it is slight and circumstantial but it cannot be entirely dismissed. Raymond, who commanded the regular troops of Nizam Ali Khan, had died and had been succeeded by another French mercenary of ardent Jacobin sympathies called Piron, who was ejected by the British in 1798.

Piron is known to have corresponded with Perron with a view, possibly, to enlisting him in some vague anti-British project, although there is no reply on record from Perron. A slightly more solid piece of evidence is afforded by the Decaen expedition. The Treaty of Amiens in 1802 restored their Indian possessions to the French, and in March, 1803, a young and successful general was selected by Napoleon to take over Pondicherry. This was Decaen, the victor of Hohenlinden. He was briefed by the First Consul himself who said that if he fulfilled his instructions 'he might one day gain the glory which keeps alive the memory of men for centuries', which even allowing for French grandiloquence implies some action beyond re-opening a French trading post. Decaen's expedition consisted of four warships and two troop transports carrying 1250 troops in all, including a strong contingent of un-attached young officers. It will be remembered that the regimental officers in the Army of Hindustan were almost entirely British or of British origin, and the supposition at the time was that these officers were to replace them in anticipation of war with the British.[5]

As against this there is nothing to connect Perron with Paris in the French records of the time. Perron was too good a soldier not to realise that war with the British would be a dangerous enterprise (although in fact when it did break out between the British and the Mahrattas he made quite a good plan for the employment of the brigades in conjunction with the Mahratta irregular forces, which was ignored by the Mahratta leaders and never put into action). It was somewhat optimistic to suppose that a cadre of young officers fresh to India could immediately take over command of troops of whose language and strange customs they were entirely ignorant and who, moreover, had been drilled according to the English manual and using English words of command. As for basing the expedition on Pondicherry this was the equivalent of, say, Tipu Sultan sending a corps of Mysore volunteers to support the Irish rebels of 1798 and landing them in Naples. However, it is a fact that Perron filled nearly all his key appointments with Frenchmen. (Bourquin in command of the Second Brigade, Geslin the Third, Dudrenac the Fourth, Drugeon in Delhi and Pedron in Aligarh.

The exceptions were George Hessing, a Dutch-Eurasian, who followed his father in command of the garrison of Agra and Pohlmann, a German, in command of the First Brigade. The only inconsistent appointment was that of Brownrigg to command the partially raised Fifth Brigade, but Brownrigg was well above the average ability of mercenary officers and perhaps Perron was hard put to find another Frenchman or someone not British to command a brigade. Perron gave the command of his newly raised independent cavalry force to the French Colonel Fleury.)

This still leaves Perron's knowledge of and attitude towards the French plan, such as it was, a matter of conjecture, but there remains his strange action in suddenly turning on George Thomas, whom he had tolerated for so long and who had never challenged him, and whose ambitions and actions had all been directed to the north-west and away from Delhi. It is possible that Perron saw Thomas as a threat to any French plans in the event of war with the English, because he was notoriously and violently hostile to the French, and Perron must have known that Thomas had been in contact with Calcutta. He may have felt that he could not risk having Thomas firmly ensconced in his rear and within a few marches of Delhi. Whatever the reason he fought him and crushed him, but ironically the defeat of Thomas was to lead to his own downfall.

11   *The Last Fight of George Thomas*

TWO YEARS and a half after his victory at the Lines of Sounda Perron had fallen, Daulat Rao was a fugitive, the Peshwa Baji Rao was a British vassal, the trained brigades had been destroyed and the British were the masters of Hindustan. George Thomas was dead, but it was he who unwittingly fired the explosive charge which brought all these disasters for the Mahratta cause in its train. Perron destroyed Thomas, but to do so he had to neglect his master Daulat Rao's business, by doing so he left that foolish young man to be defeated, he himself was then dismissed as a faithless servant and finally the brigades were left without a leader, to be destroyed by Arthur Wellesley and Lake.

In May, 1801, Perron's empire was at peace. Rajasthan was subdued, the rebellion of the Bais quelled, the wounded Lakwa Dada was on the run and no longer a force, Daulat Rao was amusing himself in Poona, Jaswant Rao and Amir Khan off raiding somewhere or other, and the Brigades were unemployed. Thomas, it is true, was occupied in one of his piratical expeditions against the Sikhs, but this served to keep him and the Sikhs out of mischief. Then, suddenly, in July, the whole scene changed. It gradually began to dawn on Perron that Thomas was not simply a prominent bandit but a political force. While he was in his cautious way considering how to win Thomas over or at least to render him harmless, one of Daulat Rao's follies came home to roost unexpectedly. Jaswant Rao, now styling himself Jaswant Rao Holkar, so long a defeated fugitive, burst into Sindia's own territory of Malwa at the head of three 'trained' brigades of his own, complete with European officers and a huge force of Pathan cavalry under Amir Khan. Daulat's inept moves to counter him met with a resounding defeat. The result was that in August, at the very moment when Perron was conscious of the fact he had a rival established within a few miles of Delhi, he was assailed by cries for help from his master commanding and imploring him to march south with the Brigades to his aid at once.

Thomas' last expedition against the Sikhs was not conducted

with any clear objective or any definite plan. His fantastic notion of conquering the Punjab as he described it to Francklin later seems to have taken root in his mind after it was over. His story is that he intended to capture Ferozepur and establish a new base there, to build a fleet of boats and embark his army to circumnavigate the Punjab by floating down the Sutlej and then up the Indus, subduing the country as he went. When he said this he was a dying and disappointed man, his brain inflamed with brandy. In his sober moments he would never have contemplated anything so foolish. He never even attacked Ferozepur and his last great raid was made, like all his others, for plunder. What is undoubtedly true is that at the end of it he realised that the Sikhs were an easy prey and also that the Punjab was divided in religion: for every Sikh enemy he could find a Muslim ally. He certainly had designs on Lahore at least, which was more realistic than his ambition to plant 'the British standard on the banks of the Attock', as he described it in a bombastic message to the Marquess Wellesley. The short history of his last Sikh war was that he set off in about December, 1800, with some 5000 horse and foot and 36 guns with an eye to the main chance and made such a nuisance of himself that the Sikhs bought him off at immense expense. He began by intervening in a quarrel between Sahib Singh and his opponent of the year before, that war-like young lady his sister Kunur whom he was besieging in one of her forts. Thomas came to her aid, secured her neutrality, and then went north to 'levy contributions', as he used to put it. All this was in the usual Thomas style. He attacked the town of Bhat and reduced the fort, with its strong bastions and walls thirty feet high and twelve thick, disregarding a Sikh army threatening his rear. When he felt that the situation was becoming out of hand he wheeled up his usual six-pounder, blew in the gate at point-blank range and led the storming column himself. He had only just before this stormed another strong fort and butchered the garrison in his impatience, so the people of Bhat were only too happy to surrender at once and purchase their safety at the cost of 50,000 rupees without waiting for the Sikh army to relieve them.

He next accepted the offer of a lac of rupees from a young Muslim noble, Rai Elias, the ruler of the neighbouring town of Maler Kotla, to relieve him of the attentions of a Sikh bandit called Sahib Singh Behdi. This was easily done and he had established himself in this Muslim enclave—Rai Elias having offered him 50,000 rupees a year for his protection—when he was forced to retreat. The Sikhs from every village were roused against him like wasps, in their thousands; Sahib Singh of Patiala had 15,000 men in the field, Bhag Singh of Jhind and Lal Singh of Kaital had denounced agreements he had made with them and had risen to cut his route home, Bapu Sindia had invaded Hariana in his absence and Thomas' own little army had been reduced by casualties to a mere 3500 men. Thomas decided to return to Hansi but, from what he told Francklin, only because he was running out of ammunition! Thomas' withdrawal is a supreme example of his insolence and audacity and also of the paralysis which his mere presence and reputation inflicted on his opponents. He marched home thrusting aside contemptuously any attempt to stop him, pausing first to storm a fort belonging to the faithless Bhag Singh and slaughter the garrison by way of a lesson; and then to besiege more formally and capture Safidun, belonging to Lal Singh. Sahib Singh and his confederates, whose army outnumbered him four to one observed each move from a respectful distance, being content to see Thomas retreat. They finally halted on the northern frontier of Hariana. Thomas was in fact not retreating but attacking. He made a dash at Bapu Sindia who, with previous experience of Thomas, promptly withdrew. Thomas only paused at Hansi to pick up reinforcements and to replenish—he was out of powder and shot—and whipping round in his tracks raced north to attack the dismayed Sahib Singh and his confederates. This was too much for him. He decided to make peace and Thomas with the air of a victorious monarch imposed a conqueror's terms.

Thomas said later to Francklin: 'I explored the country, formed alliances and in short was dictator in all the countries belonging to the Sikhs south of the Sutlej.' This was not bombast. Sahib Singh agreed that Rai Elias was to be left in peaceful possession of Maler Kotla and also to stop molesting his sister Kunur Bai and to leave the agreement between her and Thomas to stand. He also agreed to raise and to pay for a border guard to keep watch and ward on Thomas' northern frontier and prevent Sikh raids into Hariana. Thomas was to be ceded a number of frontier districts and he was to be paid two lacs by way of 'reparations' and a further lac to release a number of Sikh hostages he had thoughtfully captured and taken with him. It was in the fit of euphoria provoked by this great success that he came to believe that the Punjab was his for the taking.

By 1801 Thomas' reputation and resources had reached their peak. With the funds accumulated from his raids on Jaipur, Bikanir and Patiala he expanded his small, élite force into a small army equivalent in size and strength to one of Perron's regular brigades. Perron's reaction was understandably one of alarm. He said later in a letter to de Boigne[1] with whom he regularly corresponded: 'A man called George Thomas who had taken advantage of my absence in the Deccan to raise a party (*parti*) of 12,000 men and 60 cannon, seize a considerable tract of territory on the Sikh border and to pillage the whole countryside up to the very outskirts of Delhi. I have been forced to destroy his party entirely and I have permitted the scoundrel (*scelerat*) to leave on condition that he never again enters the territory of the prince' (i.e. Daulat Rao). This was not quite true. He undoubtedly saw Thomas as threatening his own position, the Sikh chiefs had appealed to him to supress Thomas and join in the war against him, and he may have seen Thomas as an obstacle to be removed before challenging the British. What he did first, however, was to try to win Thomas over and to persuade him to employ his troops in the Mahratta service.

Unfortunately for Perron just at this delicate moment he was distracted by this fresh disturbance in the Deccan and urgent demands for help from Daulat Rao Sindia. Until the beginning of 1801 Daulat Rao's defeated rival, Jaswant Rao Holkar and his Pathan colleague Amir Khan had confined themselves to rapine on a grand scale, ranging all across central India. They had not so far dared to threaten Sindia or match themselves against his regular troops. Then, in July, when he was about to make his first moves against Thomas, Perron heard the news that the pair had entered Sindia's territory, inflicted a severe defeat on an independent brigade commanded by George Hessing and sacked Ujjain, Sindia's capital. At that moment Daulat Rao had with him, apart from the Mahratta irregular cavalry, the First Brigade under Sutherland and Hessing's and Filose's independent brigades. Perron had the Third and Fourth Brigades, which he needed to deal with Thomas, and the Second detached under Pohlmann holding down Jaipur. He therefore judged that his master had sufficient force to repel Holkar and that to detach any more to him from the north would be to risk its stability and would also interfere with his own plans against Thomas. This was to prove a political error of the first magnitude. Daulat Rao saw Perron's refusal to come to his aid as indiscipline. Others close to him saw it as something worse, a betrayal designed to bring down Daulat Rao for some sinister purpose of Perron's.

The course of events in the Deccan from June, 1801, onwards was as follows. Daulat Rao was in Poona when he heard that Holkar was raiding in Sindia territory, in Malwa, and was almost at the gates of Ujjain. The news was sufficiently alarming to force him to move at the height of the monsoon when every minor stream is a torrent, and he had to cross two great rivers, the Narbada and the Tapti, in full flood. The operation that followed was a masterpiece of incompetence. Daulat Rao left his most senior and experienced commander, Robert Sutherland, behind in Poona with half the First Brigade to keep the Peshwa Baji Rao in a properly submissive frame of mind. He took with him the other half and most of the guns, part of John Hessing's old independent corps, now under his Eurasian son George Hessing, and also some battalions of Fidele Filose's independent corps. With this mixed bag of troops, which was without any single superior commander, he set off together with the usual collection of Mahratta horse and all the impedimenta of an Indian prince on the march. He eventually reached Burhanpur on the north bank of the Tapti where, receiving news of Jaswant Rao, he halted in an excess of timidity. He first despatched Hessing with four battalions to protect Ujjain. Then, as he received each successive and more discouraging message about Jaswant Rao's movements he responded by sending off another detachment. It never occurred to him or to his advisers to advance with his whole powerful army united.

By the beginning of July the position was that George Hessing with four battalions had arrived at Ujjain. Approaching him were two more of Filose's corps under an officer called MacIntyre, then at intervals two battalions of the First Brigade and behind them again two more under Sutherland's second-in-command, Major Brownrigg. It appears that the leading battalions had left their guns behind so as to march the faster and that Brownrigg's column was escorting the whole of the artillery of the force, some fifty guns or more, creeping on at bullock pace. On the 8th July Jaswant Rao trapped Hessing's battalions against the walls of Ujjain. They were forced into square by Amir Khan's cavalry and then cannonaded to a pulp in close order, being charged again if they opened out to avoid the gunfire—classical tactics. Hessing fled, but seven young officers died fighting round their colours. Their names were Lany, Graham, Montague, Doolan, Macpherson, Haddon and Urquhart, and indicate the strong British element among the junior regimental officers. All, according to Compton, were the country-born sons of officers in the Company's service. The heads were cut from their corpses and presented to Jaswant Rao.

After the battle Jaswant Rao allowed his troops to sack Ujjain thoroughly and brutally and then without wasting any time marched south to meet the rest of Sindia's army. He met and attacked MacIntyre, forced his surrender and continuing the hunt, collided with Brownrigg. Brownrigg, however, was a capable and warlike officer: Lewis Smith speaks of him with great admiration and affection. He had warning of Jaswant Rao's approach and sent a messenger to the commander of his two forward battalions to halt and wait for him. He caught them up near a village just north of the Narbada river called Satwas (Lewis Smith says 'Burkaisur') where he chose a strong position. Jaswant Rao arrived in great strength and had with him the good Major Plumet and a brigade of regular infantry, but they were both to find that the Cheria Fauj was a very different concern from the battalions of Hessing or Jean-Baptiste Filose. After some hours of facing the swarms of case-shot sent hissing into their packed files by fifty massed guns, and the volleys and the immovable hedge of bayonets of the infantry even Plumet's regulars could not be induced to make yet another attack. Jaswant Rao drew off dreadfully mauled; so much so that he retreated to the north and made no further effort against Daulat Rao who sat biting his nails with despair at the news of Ujjain in his rain-sodden camp at Burhanpur.[2]

It never crossed Sindia's mind that Brownrigg had evened the score for him and that he could now act offensively; indeed, that Jaswant Rao was so shaken that he could defeat him decisively. From then on all he could think of was the six battalions he had lost, of the terror of the names of Jaswant Rao and Amir Khan, and that Perron must at once come to his aid. He was, after all, no general, or even much of a prince. He was only a spoiled and extremely foolish young man with only older and wickeder and equally foolish men as his advisers. To him Perron, like de Boigne before, was like a powerful father who could, if he only would, easily rescue him from this disastrous muddle and put everything right. Perron did not feel in this way in the least. His proper concern, he felt, was to hold the far more turbulent and dangerous north in his secure grip. What was more annoying was that this unnecessary panic in the south coincided with the new and unexpected threat from this ruffian Thomas. Suppose Thomas combined with the Sikhs and turned against Hindustan proper ? Perron allowed himself to become hypnotised by Thomas: in the end he never sent Daulat Rao any assistance at all, neither did he visit him or consult with him.

As far as is known Perron and Thomas had so far never met. Perron, always cautious and diplomatic, after an exchange of visits by vakils agreed that a conference should take place on 19th August, 1801, at a place not unaptly named Bahadurgarh—'The Fort of Heroes'—about twenty miles north-west of Delhi. The venue was more or less on neutral ground and flattered Thomas, but Perron counterbalanced this by bringing the whole of the Third Brigade into the field. Thomas on his side brought his bodyguard cavalry and two battalions as an escort. Everything was done with protocol; it was like the meeting of two sovereigns which, of course, in a way it was. Perron sent an English officer, Lewis Smith, to meet Thomas, guide him to his camp-site and act as his temporary aide-de-camp and possibly interpreter: Perron did not speak English fluently, judging from Skinner. The initial meeting was devoted entirely to an exchange of courtesies and in the evenings the officers of both armies entertained each other to dinner. The ever-inquisitive Skinner took the opportunity to inspect Thomas' troops; not very strictly disciplined by the Brigades' or by British standards, he thought, but the artillery excellent and its cattle very well kept and strong. (As for discipline, the attitude of Thomas' Pathan troopers towards this half-*Feringhi* officer from a rival army can well be imagined: lolling and lounging in their own peculiar manner of amused insolence and rising and saluting with just that hint of hesitation required to show their independence.) He met three young English officers in Thomas' camp; Hopkins, a find of Thomas' who by courage and ability during his Sikh raid had virtually become his second in command, Birch and Hearsey. Skinner and Birch were to do their best to kill each other in the near future. However, eighteenth-century military manners never allowed business or 'ideologies' to interfere with the pleasures of life, and neither thought any more of the incongruity than if they were opponents in a game.

Thomas' other visitor from Perron's camp was Lewis Smith, an older and more experienced soldier who, although only a captain, was frequently entrusted with an independent command. He turned his shrewd gaze on Thomas and later recorded his impressions. Generous, he said, hospitable, full of charm that he knew how to exert ('often insinuating from inclination', is how he puts it). He also perceived that he was a man of tremendous arrogance and insatiable ambition. 'His exertions towards station, power, riches and glory were uncommon. He would be all or nothing. To serve under the orders of another was an inglorious dependence in his estimation.' If Perron consulted Smith he ignored his advice, for his diplomacy foundered exactly on these characteristics and because he failed to recognise the kind of man Thomas really was and what lay behind his apparent good humour and easy address. Each man knew roughly what the other wanted. Perron wanted to draw Thomas into Sindia's service and into his own orbit, as he had already drawn Jean Filose's battalions and was to absorb Hessing's. He had a tidy military mind and he disapproved of rival, independent corps. Thomas was equally determined to keep his independence. Perron must have known that Thomas had been intriguing with the British and had been in touch with their agents. Thomas probably knew that his Sikh enemies had offered Perron five lacs of rupees and a large contingent of troops if he would rid them of Thomas once and for all. Perron knew that Hariana could never pay for Thomas' army and that he was perenially short of cash. Thomas had heard the news of Ujjain and had divined Perron's dilemma. The cards were evenly distributed and at first all went smoothly as ideas were exchanged; but Perron's final proposals when he tabled them which seemed so generous and realistic in his own eyes were in fact calculated to enrage Thomas. He combined their offer with an ultimatum which enraged Thomas still further. Perron told Thomas that he must render Jhajjar back to the Imperial authorities, but he could keep Hansi. Thomas was offered a colonelcy in Sindia's service in the Army of Hindustan but under Perron's orders, with a salary of 60,000 rupees. When agreement was reached Thomas was to send four battalions forthwith to reinforce Sindia against Jaswant Rao Holkar.

This was by no means an ungenerous offer. Thomas could hardly hope to challenge the whole Army of Hindustan, backed by the resources of the Doab, from his little tract of desert. Even if he was suspicious of Perron and believed this to be only the first move to reduce his power, it was always open to him to prevaricate and delay if Perron showed signs of treachery, and above all he had to retain his freedom of movement. The trouble was that Thomas was becoming increasingly irrational, through incessant strain, through illness and perhaps through drink. He was, in fact, absolutely ungovernable, and the berserk rages and refusal to tolerate the slightest repulse which served him so well in the field were now a disadvantage in any form of transaction requiring coolness and prudence. Any suggestion that he should give up territory that he had once seized upon drove him frantic, and Jhajjar in particular was the apple of his eye. Every argument was in favour of his temporising with Perron, who was in a most difficult position, but instead he flew into a passion, broke up his camp, and marched off without a civil word. Perron immediately ordered the Third Brigade to engage Thomas at once, destroy his army and reoccupy the stolen districts. He himself did not waste any further time on the matter. He had the vast affairs of Hindustan to attend to and in any case, good as Thomas' loosely disciplined troops might be, he did not believe that they could stand up to the battalions of Hindustan.

Whom he did not reckon with was the commander of the Third Brigade. It is not unheard of in the best military circles for officers of unbelievable ineptitude to rise to one high appointment after another by some uncanny form of persuasion, but this is usually in peace.

In an age when for both moral and practical reasons generals had to have physical courage Bourquin went to such lengths to be out of cannon shot that he could not even see the troops he was commanding. He was despised by the regimental officers. What possessed Perron when he appointed this creature to the equivalent of a major-general of a division remains a mystery. At first Bourquin was buoyed up by the thought that Thomas was easy meat and was afraid of him. He began operations by detaching Lewis Smith and two battalions with all the heavy artillery to take Jhajjar and Thomas' fort of Jehazgahr while he himself set off to bring Thomas' field force to book. He had heard that Thomas had gone to Jhind and decided to follow him there, although why he thought that Thomas would at this juncture flee into the country of his bitterest enemies is a mystery, unless he too believed a rumour that he was secretly in league with the Sikhs. Having reached Jhind he heard that Thomas was on his way to Patiala but when fairly on his way there he learned that Thomas was in fact far to the south of him, and racing with his whole army for Jehazgahr. Thomas had in fact humbugged Bourquin completely and had opened in the best classical style. He had divided his powerful opponent and was about to descend with his whole force on Lewis Smith and his two battalions, the bulk of Bourquin's guns and all his baggage and reserve ammunition. De Boigne's First Brigade had beeen nicknamed the Cheria Fauj—the 'army of birds'—because of its fast marching: Thomas' was as fast, if not faster. He advanced towards Smith at the prodigious rate of thirty miles a day, covering the last seventy-six miles in forty-eight hours, leaving the Third Brigade's cavalry regiment a day behind and its main body two. The whole staff College at Camberley could not think of a better manoeuvre, and had Thomas' campaign taken place in Europe or had he been a respectable British general, reams would have since been written about his brilliance. Campaigns are not decided by clever strategems, however, but by hard fighting and luck. As for luck, Thomas' famous *iqbal* was to run out at last; and as for hard fighting, he was to be foiled by a native officer called Puran Singh.

Lewis Smith had occupied Jhajjar without difficulty, but Jehazgahr with a garrison of 800 Rohillas was a tougher nut. He had settled down to a formal siege operation when his picquets brought him warning of Thomas approaching in strength. Smith was a thoroughly capable officer and on receipt of this unexpected and disagreeable news he acted promptly. He took the precious guns of the Brigade out of action at once and sent them to Jhajjar, hoping to make a stand behind its walls until Bourquin arrived to relieve him. Next went the baggage, which included all the reserve ammunition wagons, or 'tumbrils'. He drew up his two battalions as a rear-guard, with Puran Singh and his companies as the rearmost echelon or 'rear-party' of this. Some time in the blazing afternoon Thomas' vanguard battalion under an officer called Martaza Khan came in sight, the men staggering with fatigue after their long march and parched with thirst, their formation ragged and the companies strung out. Martaza Khan quite rightly attacked at once. It was his duty whatever the risk to fasten his teeth into Smith's battalions and grip them where they stood while the rest of the army came up. He pushed his men into action as they arrived. Puran Singh saw his opportunity. The tall crops around Jehazgahr afforded him ample cover for an ambush which he used to good effect, surprising Martaza Khan while he was still strung out. There was a fierce fight between ancient enemies—the Rajput Puran Singh against the Pathan Martaza Khan and Muslim against Hindu—in which Puran Singh broke Martaza Khan's battalion and captured its guns. He then held his ground against Thomas himself and his main body, losing the guns he had captured and all his men and being himself wounded and captured, but giving Smith time to get the guns and the rest of his troops away, although he lost the ammunition and baggage. But for the brave Puran Singh's rapid move and self-sacrifice the Third Brigade would have been 'defeated in detail', and fought the next battle short of two battalions and most of its heavy guns. The next day Felix Smith, an ex-regular officer of the 36th Foot (a 'King's' or a 'Royal' regiment as opposed to one of the Company's) commanding a regiment of the Hindustani Horse, arrived to join his brother Lewis, and Thomas' opportunity had gone. He wisely paused to collect and rest his troops and to prepare to meet Bourquin whom he knew was hot on his trail.

Thomas had with him about 6000 men and therefore was outnumbered in infantry by about three to two, but including the pieces in Jehazgahr he had over 50 guns, having stripped the defences of Hansi. He decided to fight a defensive battle and for this he carefully chose and dug a prepared position linked to Jehazgahr fort, which was firmly held by the Rohillas under one of his most trusted officers, Shitab Khan. His right front was anchored to the fort, his left on a redoubt he threw up for the purpose, and his rear was protected by a large walled village which he turned into a strong-point. The position and its approaches was in an area of sand-dunes which cushioned the effect of round-shot, which achieved much of its lethal effect by bouncing and skipping over hard ground. This was important in view of the excellence of the Army of Hindustan's artillery. The whole front was covered by emplaced batteries and a trench and parapet. The exact strength of the opposing sides is uncertain. Thomas' whole army is said to have been eight battalions of infantry of 750 men (this figure including the battalion gunners) or 6000, 1500 Rohilla irregulars, 1000 horse and over fifty guns, altogether 8,500 men. Of these he left some 1200 regulars and irregulars to garrison Hansi. At Jehazgahr he may therefore have had 4500 regular infantry, the 800 irregular Rohillas under Shitab Khan but only, apparently, 300 cavalry, and all his guns; 6-pounders in the battalions and some heavier guns, possibly 12-pounders, as well.

The Third Brigade, assuming that its establishment was on de Boigne's old model may have had some 8000 men in eight regular and two irregular battalions, 50 field guns and some siege pieces and in addition Smith's regiment of 'Hindustani Horse', 1000 or perhaps even 1500 strong. It was accompanied by 600 irregular Sikh cavalry contributed by the chiefs of Patiala and Jhind. It arrived exhausted from marching in front of Thomas, now firmly in position, at about midday on 29th September, two days after the skirmish between Thomas and Lewis Smith. Bourquin in his besotted way still seemed to be under the impression that Thomas might once more try to escape. In spite of the protests of his more experienced junior officers he determined to attack him at once without resting the troops or reconnoitring the enemy position.

Jehazgahr is an example of what happens when two confident armies each with a long history of unbroken success and who have never fought a well-trained enemy finally meet. Bourquin made no attempt at manoeuvre, except for sending two battalions to try something against Thomas' rear who achieved nothing and do not seem even to have made contact. The main body of the Third Brigade attacked frontally in line of battalions in column of companies with the batteries in the battalion intervals, the gun-bullocks left behind and the kelasis straining at the drag-ropes in the sandy soil. Then, following the tactics which had in the past been so carefully instilled into them, when they were within musket-shot they began to deploy into line for the few preliminary volleys of musketry and salvos of grape and case-shot that were to be the herald of their irresistible assault.

At this moment Thomas' long line of batteries exploded in flame. There was one tremendous salvo and then each detachment settled down in its own rhythm to bang away systematically every twenty or thirty seconds and send its swarms of bullets hissing into the packed files of Bourquin's infantry: the leading companies having to stand fast under this murderous hail while those in the rear ranged slowly in succession up alongside them. They staggered, and then for the first time in their history fairly broke and streamed to the rear. Never before had they met troops who were not morally shaken by the sight of their battle-line unfolding in the orderly, ceremonial manner of Europe, and never had they faced artillery fire like this. For a quarter of an hour or so while their officers tried to rally them, all that stood between them and Thomas' counter-stroke were their own gunners, who manfully continued to exchange shot for shot. They were in the open, however, and their opponents were in well-built emplacements of soft sand. The loose sand itself was an embarrassment, for it prevented the free recoil of the guns, and in the shock of discharge the pieces either jumped from their trunnions or smashed the axles. Between enemy fire and this damage, soon half were silent. To add to the noise and confusion one after another twenty-five of their ammunition 'tumbrils' full of cartridges and loose powder were hit and blew up.

For Bourquin the battle was as good as lost: not that he could see, for he himself was so far in rear that he had virtually relinquished command. Behind the entrenchment Thomas was forming up four battalions to attack. At this moment of disaster Bourquin's second-in-command, the French Major Bernier, who was up with the troops, grasped control and as an immediate, desperate measure ordered Felix Smith to charge with all the cavalry and try to silence the terrible guns; even if only for a few minutes and at any cost until the infantry could be rallied and reformed. They responded with great courage, but for cavalry to charge well-emplaced and unshaken artillery is suicide and they soon fell back, being followed out of Thomas' lines by Hopkins on the right and Birch on the left, each with two battalions in column of companies as they passed through the intervals of their own batteries and then deployed into line with bayonets fixed ('as if they were on parade', said Skinner admiringly). They delivered one volley and then charged and drove back Bernier at the head of his battalions, who broke once again. Felix Smith and the cavalry again charged to relieve them, but Smith fell mortally wounded and Thomas now let his own horsemen slip, who drove the shaken Hindustani Horse from the field.

At this absolute crisis of the battle, with once again only the indomitable gunners of the Third Brigade still fighting, Thomas suffered an extraordinary stroke of ill-luck. Hopkins was a young officer whose courage and ability had quickly earned him the respect and loyalty of his troops. As he resumed his advance his leg was shot off. His sepoys, men of a race so prone to become devotedly attached to a good officer, suddenly and fatally forgot all their discipline and reverted to type. Picking up his body they cried with dismay in the old manner of Indian warfare when the champion had fallen and retired in disorder to their own trenches. Birch had to fall back as well: and the battle was over. Bernier, that determined man, tried to persuade his troops to make another attempt but they would not face Thomas' batteries again. The guns on both sides gradually became silent, the dust settled, the dense fog of powder-smoke rose into the air in clouds and gradually drifted away to reveal the sand-dunes covered with dead and dying men and horses, smashed guns and smoking wagons. The two armies, equally shocked and stunned by the mutual slaughter they had inflicted on each other, remained motionless until night fell.

It had been the most bloody affair. The lowest and probably the most reliable estimate of Bourquin's casualties is Lewis Smith's, and it is 1100. If Bourquin had committed all eight regular battalions of the brigade to the operation, less the two to the encircling attack which seems to have faded out or lost its way, he had six battalions or some 3500 men in the main assault, and to lose thirty per cent was a severe loss, even by the standards of the day and of the era of close-order fighting. Felix Smith died of his wounds, and three of the infantry officers were casualties. Thomas lost some 700, and Hopkins. After a terrible night, during which the wounded lying out in front of Thomas' trenches provided a chorus of moans and cries for help and water which became gradually *diminuendo* as voice after voice at last fell silent, Bourquin decided to break off the operation. He sent forward a flag of truce to ask for a cease-fire so that he could collect his casualties, which was granted. The morning wore on without his making any further move and then the watchers in Thomas' entrenchments saw the Third Brigade limber up their guns and go, leaving them in possession of the field. Both Skinner and Smith agree that their force was now in a position of considerable danger. Bourquin had lost his nerve completely, half the guns were disabled, the cavalry cut to pieces and, worst of all, the sepoys were cowed and apprehensive. At any moment they expected to see Thomas emerge and fall upon them, in which case Bourquin would have been forced into a withdrawal and possibly a rout. Had Thomas struck then he would have achieved far more than a tactical victory. It would have been a terrible blow to the reputation of the Army of Hindustan for invincibility. In a country where face and *izzat* counts for so much the political reverberations would have been loud and long, and for Perron very dangerous. It was not however to be. Thomas' magic, his luck, his *iqbal* had finally run out. His first stroke of ill-luck was the apparition of the brave Puran Singh, who foiled his attempt to defeat Bourquin in detail. The second was the death of Hopkins. The third was that, sometime in the night of the 29th September, the fibre of his will snapped. On the 30th he remained in his tent, with the brandy bottle as his only companion, refusing to speak or to give orders.[3]

There is nothing very mysterious about this sudden collapse. It was only luck in so far as in the moment at which it took place. Thomas had drawn for far too long on his reserves of courage and energy, and the debt had to be paid sooner or later. Warfare is an exacting business and this sort of psychological injury can happen to the best of commanders under far less severe strain. More commonly there is a slow decline. The self-confidence is eroded, decisions are less firm and made less rapidly, and the touch becomes less sure. Military history is full of such examples. If a flaw exists in the personality, however, there is more likely to be a sudden breakdown. Thomas had a fragile and unstable character of which his manic energy and his aggressiveness—increasing to fits of homicidal rage—are clear indications. There are unmistakable signs of megalomania. He was also ill: he was dead eleven months later. (Possibly from a combination of causes, exhaustion, untreated malaria, persistent dysentery, cirrhosis of the liver; anything.) He could not have been an alcoholic in the sense that he was a 'soak', because of the sheer physical demands his life made on him; but it would be in conformity with his character to take refuge from time to time from incessant strain, and rest a madly active mind in the oblivion of drink. The trigger for this at Jehazgahr could have been the shock of reality induced by fighting regular troops, although to be sure Thomas was used to casualties and was callous enough, or sheer exhaustion. It may possibly have been the death of Hopkins. It is not at all uncommon in the purely male society of any army for an older commander to form a strong attachment to a brave and gay young subordinate, and this was especially the case in Asia where women were little regarded and cooped up in zenanas. Thomas had for years been an expatriate seldom speaking English and dependent entirely on himself. Hopkins had joined him in time for his Sikh campaign at the beginning of the year, and had instantly made his mark: 'an amiable man and a brave and gallant officer', is how Thomas described him through the medium of Francklin. He had been wounded twice in the Sikh campaign, always being found where there was a crisis and where the fire was hottest; and he was gallant enough, but he was also capable. By his death Thomas lost both a friend and a second-in-command whom he could trust.

However, this is as it may have been. Whatever the cause, mourning for a friend, despair or a nervous breakdown, Thomas kept to his tent doing nothing and refusing to do anything for two whole weeks. Then he suddenly emerged, full of hope and vigour again, and of expedients. He reassumed command and tried to reassure his bewildered troops, but it was too late. Virtue had gone out of him. His soldiers were as discouraged as if they had suffered a defeat. A huge army had been assembled against him for the kill, and although it stood at a respectful distance, it was all round him. He was trapped.

News in ancient India travelled slowly enough, but it lost nothing in colour or impetus as it progressed from court to court and from bazaar to bazaar. The battle was fought only forty miles from Delhi and a hundred from Aligarh. The news of Bourquin's repulse could have been in the capital by the following evening and Perron in Aligarh must have known the worst by the 1st October. For the first time in its history a full brigade of the Army of Hindustan, the sole instrument which insured his own rule over Hindustan and his master's over all the Empire and Maharashtra had broken and run and had left the battlefield in possession of the enemy. Its face was 'blackened', and with it Perron's. In forty-eight hours the bullock carts full of maimed sepoys and the walking wounded began to arrive in Delhi with fearful stories of the terrible guns of *Jahaj Jung*—George the Invincible—and his fierce Afghan troops, soon to be repeated and magnified in the streets and in Shah Alam's palace. If Thomas broke loose he would not only gather momentum but allies. No one in Indian politics wasted a second thought on a loser.

Accordingly Perron decided that scotching Thomas was more important than anything else; even the succour of the agitated Daulat Rao Sindia. He ordered Drugeon, the Governor of Delhi, to send reinforcements from his garrison to make up Bourquin's losses at once. He sent Pedron with the Fourth Brigade to join him and to take command of the whole force, together with George Hessing and four of his battalions that had not been engaged at Ujjain, and two battalions from Somru Begum's corps. This, with the exception of the garrisons of his three great fortresses of Delhi, Agra and Aligarh, was the whole of the reserves that he had at hand. All that was left was Pohlmann, fully occupied in collecting land-tax in Rajasthan and discouraging Pratap Singh of Jaipur from entertaining any thoughts of rebellion or independence. (According to Skinner some battalions from Pohlmann's Second Brigade were sent to Jehazgarh which presumably explains why Perron did not use this obvious source to placate Daulat Rao.)

As for affairs in the south, by a purely military appreciation Perron was perfectly correct. Daulat Rao had, as well as the First Brigade which by itself should have been able to deal with Jaswant Rao and Amir Khan (as it was to prove), Fidele Filose's corps, his thousands of Mahratta light cavalry and, under Ambaji Angria his commander-in-chief of Mahratta troops, James Shepherd's good brigade of trained regulars. It was true that Jaswant Rao's success at Ujjain had rallied all Daulat Rao's enemies to him, and that even the Peshwa was showing an inclination to shake himself free of Sindia's control; but all this could be put right by one victory. Nothing could be more orthodox and according to the best principles than to concentrate first on one enemy and then on another. What ruined

Perron's plan was his own misjudgement in trusting operations to such good-for-nothing creatures as Bourquin and Pedron, both of whom had previously betrayed their incapability and reluctance to make a single offensive move. It was inexplicable why he did not promote Bernier, who was French, or take command himself. What he urgently required, strategically and militarily, was for Thomas to be crushed at once with a single smashing blow so as to destroy both his power and his reputation.

Instead Pedron with the utmost Oriental deliberation settled down to blockade Thomas in his lines. He captured his main water supply which was an outlying 'tank', and established a ring of trenches and batteries to contain him. Against them Thomas' most determined sorties battered in vain. Outside, the cavalry patrolled ceaselessly, cutting off Thomas' foraging parties and messengers to the outside world, and preventing any supplies from entering the lines. Vaman Rao tried to reinforce him and to restock his supplies, but his men were turned back and the convoy captured; its camel-drivers having their noses cut off so as to discourage any others who might be bold enough to make the attempt. A war of nerves was conducted against Thomas' native officers. They were pressed to desert, and promised good treatment if they did, even employment, and they were offered bribes; if they remained loyal to Thomas they were threatened with punishment as rebels, and the families of those who lived locally in Hansi or Jhajjar were seized as hostages. All this was in the tradition of Asian siegecraft and a technique Pedron understood very well. He had no intention of attacking Thomas. It was a slow but sure process and saved casualties. It defeated Thomas, but as October wore on into November it also helped to ruin Perron.

Down in the south this inactivity continued to encourage Daulat Rao's enemies. What was the reason, they wondered, for Perron's refusal to come to Sindia's aid? To men accustomed to making the nicest calculations of how to remain on the winning side Perron's strange behaviour, not even sending a battalion or two, could only have one meaning: the most powerful man in Hindustan had judged that the star of Daulat Rao Sindia was setting and was waiting to see who his new master was to be. Some such idea may indeed have passed through Perron's mind, but is more likely that he believed both Daulat Rao's paramount position, his own future and the future of his own half-considered and half-baked plans for re-establishing France as a power in India all depended on the Army of Hindustan's reputation for invincibility and on holding Hindustan and the Emperor. Also, absolute power, whether it corrupts or not, does tempt its possessor to underestimate both friends and enemies. For four and a half years Perron had ruled Hindustan and Rajasthan like a monarch whose real warrant came not from feeble Daulat Rao or blind Shah Alam II but from the guns of his brigades. He treated Daulat Rao and his alarms with indifference and behaved not even as if he was the Regent but as if Daulat Rao was his inferior ally, who could wait upon his convenience. For so politically alert and sensitive a man—he had always paid the most correct and formal attention to the old Emperor as the nominal fount of all authority—it was an inexplicable and a fatal error; as inexplicable as his not going to Jehazgahr as he had to Sounda to take command and order a general attack. He was not, in the event, in the least helped by his military appreciation turning out to be correct: quite the reverse.

When the weather had improved and the rivers were fordable and nothing had arrived from Perron, Daulat Rao decided to move on his own; probably impelled by Sutherland; that devious man, but a man who could fight when he saw a profit so doing. Sutherland came up to Burhanpur from Poona with the rest of the First Brigade and took charge of operations. The best strategy Daulat Rao could devise was the spiteful one of capturing his rival's capital, Indore, and putting it and its population to the same indignities as had been suffered by Ujjain. This in fact acted effectively enough as strategic bait as Jaswant Rao moved his whole force to defend it and in the afternoon of 14th October Sutherland, handling his brigade with great dexterity in ground broken by ravines where Jaswant Rao had taken up a strong position, attacked him and smashed his army to atoms, pausing in mid-attack to change front and drive off Amir Khan and a determined charge by his Pathan cavalry. Amir Khan had his horse shot under him and fell. His men, believing him killed, as usual fled. The First Brigade was not even checked by the treachery of Fidele Filose, who had been bribed by Jaswant Rao to turn his coat and who opened fire into them as they were actually advancing. (This was completely against the honourable mercenary tradition. Fidele was captured and arrested after the battle. He committed suicide to avoid a firing squad, or some even more unpleasant end at the hands of Daulat Rao's executioners.) The Battle of Indore was Robert Sutherland's great achievement. There cannot have been many soldiers in history who have been cashiered and later risen to be victorious generals: Cochrane is the only one who comes to mind, but his story was rather different. He thus relieved Perron of any anxiety he may have felt about the south, but he exposed him to the taunt made to 'Brave Crillon': Daulat Rao had conquered and he had not been there. Nor, perhaps, did Sutherland and Brownrigg, the only British senior officers in the Army, waste any time in contrasting their own loyalty with Perron's selfish indifference and pointing out the difference to Sindia. Perron, they felt, should be dismissed.

Jehazgahr finally succumbed on 10th November. Sieges are dreary enough affairs at the best of times when there is some patriotic purpose or some hope of relief. Thomas' men had neither. Pedron left them severely alone, not even attempting an assault. He confined his military efforts to making his investing lines continuous and impenetrable, ringing Thomas with no less than three hundred guns. All of Thomas' sorties withered under this tremendous fire, and each was pressed with successively less determination by his disillusioned battalions. All that the dwindling garrison had to contemplate between attacks was the brassy sky with its ever-wheeling kites, the sand, the distant redoubts, the dwindling rations, the condition of their families and, worst of all, the diminishing level of water in the village wells inside the perimeter—never meant to support a whole army. Rumours of help from Vaman Rao, from Lakwa Dada or from Jaswant Rao buzzed round the camp and came to nothing. Thomas' sepoys had always felt free to come and go, to straggle or to disperse to loot, provided they turned up for battle. Men gradually began to sneak away by ones and twos at night to see if Pedron's promises of quarter were true, and found it was, and the news went back to their friends. All the bullock drivers, and the kelasis, not after all really soldiers, prudently melted away. Their cattle were slaughtered to eke out the rations; not that this was of much benefit to the Hindu troops for whom it was forbidden food. Towards the end of October two complete battalions deserted, and then two more. All were led by the recently joined Afghan sirdars who had joined Thomas for fame and, of course, loot and not to be shut up in a fort. A last, desperate night attack failed and by the 10th November Thomas knew the game was up. Except for the hard and loyal core of his old guard he saw that he was about to be deserted by all his Muslim troops. Even his trusted Shitab Khan was about to betray him.

That night he galloped through the investing lines at the head of his still faithful cavalry and escaped. From Jehazgarh to Hansi is sixty miles as the crow flies, rather longer if turning and dodging to shake off Bourquin's cavalry is taken into account. After a wild ride and a close pursuit Thomas and his remaining British officers, Birch and Hearsey, reached Hansi on the evening of the 11th. Thomas with still enormous reserves of energy immediately began to organise its defence. All the guns had been taken out to equip his expanded army and its garrison consisted of 1200 men, mostly Rohilla garrison troops but also 300 Rajputs, in all probability some of his original regulars, specially chosen to guard his vital base as men traditionally loyal to their salt until death. He put the Rajputs in the inner fort and the remainder on the city walls and in three redoubts he threw up to protect the approaches to the unfortified city gates. His tremendous energy returned as he worked on his defences: he even found time to cast some cannon in his arsenal to replace those he had lost. He was given plenty of time for these preparations as Bourquin took a leisurely three weeks to close up to Hansi, delayed by the need to pull some big eighteen-pounders across the desert for the siege. He also had trouble over water, as Thomas had taken the unpleasant step of putting dead pigs and cows in the desert wells which effectively barred them to all Muslims and to high-caste Hindus. He arrived at the end of November. This time there was to be no question of starving Thomas out or of applying what we now call 'psychological' warfare on his troops: Perron had left him in no doubt about that. He began by driving the Rohilla garrisons from the outworks after a hard fight and then mounted his heavy batteries to breach the walls.

The bombardment lasted a week. On the 9th December the breaches were 'deemed practicable' and at dawn on the 10th three powerful columns stormed the outer wall and after a morning's violent fighting drove the defenders first back into the town and eventually into the citadel. Bernier was killed; Mackenzie, the leader of one of the columns was wounded and the two Skinners,

James and his younger brother Robert, alone were left to command
the attack. Birch and James Skinner, dinner companions in their
messes in August, to dine amicably together again in another ten
days met face to face. Birch fired both barrels of a sporting gun at
Skinner, fortunately missing him, and Skinner, who affected the
Rajput costume and weapons in 'battle-dress', threw a spear at him
and knocked his hat off. A final bloody struggle took place in the
town square below the walls of the fort as the three columns
converged on it. This provides the only glimpse of the Jehazi Sahib
in all the terror of his berserk fury. Robert Skinner had reached the
square, which was full of his men and the enemy all mixed together
in the confusion of the fight, all shouting and thrusting and hacking
at each other; when there was a murderous blast of case-shot from
a six-pounder pushed up by hand and fired from a few yards away.
With it was a huge man in native dress, armed with sword and
buckler, his face contorted with fury, and roaring like a bull. He
was white: his arms bare to the shoulder and entwined with tattoo
marks. Robert bravely but rashly stood in his path and crossed
swords with him, upon which Thomas turned on him in a fury
and chased him after his fleeing sepoys: Robert having to run for
his very life. For Thomas, however, it was all in vain. There were
nine battalions in the town, and he retired beaten but defiant into
the fort to watch the eighteen-pounders to which he now had no
reply brought into the square to batter its walls.

Even so, with Bernier dead, Bourquin relapsed into his usual
ways and ten more days passed without any attempt to carry the
citadel. The affair was finally resolved by the British officers in the
brigade. There was a freemasonry among the mercenaries and a
degree of chivalry: obscure and humble as some of their origins
were, they adhered, quaintly enough, to the polite and civilised
conventions of eighteenth-century warfare. Thomas was a man they
admired: in their eyes he was honourable: he had never stooped to
being bought or to assassination: by their standards he was a true
soldier. They persuaded a sulky Bourquin to allow them to offer
Thomas honourable terms.[4] He and his men were allowed to keep
their weapons and to march out of the fort as free men, and he
himself to reside in the fort until he had made arrangements for
his goods and his large family. On 20th December he capitulated
and surrendered to Bourquin with great dignity, being compli-

mented by his officers on his resolute defence and in turn praising Robert Skinner for his courage in the assault, embracing him and showing him a sword-cut Robert had made in his belt. Nothing could have been more correct, even genial, than his bearing in defeat. Perron was not vengeful. He agreed that Thomas with his wives and modest fortune should be allowed to leave for British territory under escort of a complete battalion. Its commander was Lewis Smith, and it was during the journey to Anupshahr of a week or more that he was able to talk to Thomas and get to know him. Unfortunately the good mood was not to last. Before leaving Thomas was invited to dine in Bourquin's mess with all his officers. All at first went well. Thomas rode out from Hansi in great state accompanied by his bodyguard to be received with all ceremony in Bourquin's camp and at his table. He was paid every compliment and his health was drunk. It was, of course, a drunken age and it was also specially the habit of Europeans in India to drink heavily and sit long at table; and everyone, except James Skinner (who says he was field officer of the day) got very drunk. Bourquin, ill-bred fellow, so far forgot himself as to taunt the guest at his own table and called for a toast to the 'success of Perron's arms'. Thomas was one of those men who became first sullen and then aggressive in his cups. He had had two or three days for the realisation of his defeat and impending exile from the only life he knew to sink into his mind, and his neighbours at table had been hard put to keep him cheerful. They were unable to cover up this tactless remark. Bourquin was detested, and several officers protested and made matters worse by turning their glasses upside down in a gesture of refusal. Thomas, silent and glaring with fury, for a moment wondering if he had heard correctly and then leaped to his feet and drew his sword. (It was a sound rule in British messes, still continuing, that swords were unbuckled and left outside.) *'One Irish sword'*, he yelled, *'is still sufficient for a hundred Frenchmen!'* With this battle cry he rushed round the table at Bourquin, who, terrified, sprang from his chair and fled from the mess-tent. Thomas' escort, who had been squatting on their hunkers outside in their patient Indian way, on hearing the hubbub drew their swords and burst in, believing that their Sahib was about to be assassinated. 'It's all right,' said Skinner, 'he's only drunk,' an explanation they seemed used to, as they withdrew docilely enough. Bourquin was persuaded that it was safe to come back and peace was restored, but Thomas remained in a brittle and dangerous mood. When he finally took his leave he had to pass through one of the town-gates, now controlled by the Third Brigade's quarter-guards. Unfortunately orders to admit Thomas unchallenged had not been passed round properly and when Thomas replied to the traditional 'Who goes there?' with 'Sahib Bahadur!' the sleepy sentry said he didn't know anything about 'Sahib Bahadur'. Sentries in those days were not merely ornamental: they went in peril if they admitted an unauthorised person and endangered their post. This sentry obstinately repeated that he had his orders and no one was allowed to enter, giving the absolute and unanswerable reply of the literal-minded Indian soldier: '*hukm hai!*'—'it's the order!' Thomas, crazy with rage and humiliation at being refused entry to what had been only a day before his own capital, drew his sword and went for the sentry. He was only prevented from killing him by one of his sirdars seizing him from behind by the belt and hanging on; as it was he cut the wretched man's hand off. Skinner and Hearsey then managed to pacify him and take him off to bed. It is sad that the few living and vivid glimpses we have of that truly remarkable man are only of his final downfall and disgrace. A few days later having wound up his affairs, he left Hansi with his family and property and Lewis Smith as his escort for Anupshahr in British-controlled territory.

Thomas was allowed to take his portable wealth with him, not much compared with the fortunes others amassed but still a useful sum—a lac or more, according to Compton. From this he provided for Hopkin's sister, an orphan and dependent on her brother and pensioned off his native wife and family who following the custom of the time were either discarded or refused to go to Europe. Mrs. Thomas returned to Sardhana and the Somru Begum's household whence she had come. Thomas also gave five hundred rupees to the sepoy he had maimed. These affairs settled he set off on the long, slow journey to Calcutta and eventually, he hoped, to Ireland. Thomas broke his journey in Benares, possibly to sit out the worst of the monsoon rains, where he was entertained by Mr. Hamilton— later Sir John Hamilton, Bart.—of the East India Company's Civil Service, who bought the famous Persian charger which had carried Thomas on his desperate night ride from Jehazgahr to

Hansi. He also met Hamilton's future brother-in-law, Captain William Francklin. Francklin, an assiduous chronicler of the contemporary Moghul scene, happily persuaded Thomas to tell him his story and allow him to write it down. Thomas was only too willing, although he at first protested that he would prefer to do it in Persian or Hindustani as his English was so rusty.

This is the last sight we have of Thomas, talking away to Francklin; boozy—he was drinking hard—boastful and heart-broken by turns; the occasional proud or fine phrase flashing out to contrast oddly with the brutality of his narrative. He is devastatingly candid about himself. The massacre of the defenders of Bairi, the trail of pillage, the town burned by mistake over its inhabitant's heads, the 'contributions' extorted at the muzzles of his guns from the wretched, half-starved peasants are recounted without a particle of shame. Then he mourns his grand design to conquer the Punjab; 'to plant the British standard on the banks of the Attock river': he boasts of his kingdom and his dominion over the Sikhs; 'I was the Dictator': or he haughtily refuses to give way before great odds or in the face of disaster, so as not to dishonour 'my progenitors, who had never turned their backs on an enemy'. He could still fascinate. The priggish Francklin deplored his drunkenness and lack of polish but even his stilted prose reveals that he fell under Thomas' charm and that he admired him intensely.

The pity is that Thomas said nothing whatever about his origins or early life and it is also odd that Francklin never questioned him on this. If he did, he suppressed it. The memoirs begin at the point when Thomas is engaged by Appa Khandi Rao. There is one small clue, although it depends too greatly on coincidence to be anything but faint. Francklin had a drawing made of Thomas to illustrate his memoir of him (see page 85). For some reason or other the artist has decorated the shield at the centre of the stand of arms below the medallion with the rosettes of the Hamilton coat of arms. This line of Hamiltons was (and is) a distinguished family of soldiers and administrators and had an Irish connection. It may have been the artist's whim, but in any case the scent is long since cold. Thomas took his secret, if there was one, with him to this grave. He died on the next stage of his journey at Berhampore, near Murshidabad in Bengal, on the 22nd August, 1802, forty-six years old, of which the last twelve had been spent incessantly at war.

12 *The Destruction of the Brigades*

EARLY in 1802 General Perron decided that it was time to visit his master whom he had not seen for five long years. Thomas was safely out of the way, Rajasthan was quiet and his faithful Louis Bourquin was occupied on the northern marches keeping the Sikhs in order and collecting revenue, a task well suited to him. Perron had a strong reason for his visit. His agents at Sindia's court had told him that there was a plot to dismiss him and replace him by Sutherland, whose influence over Daulat Rao had grown since his great victory. Sindia's court was by then established at Ujjain and there Perron arrived in March, accompanied not only by his splendid cavalry bodyguard regiment but by the whole of the Second Brigade under the loyal Pohlmann—as a counter to Sutherland and the First, in case that officer was by any chance becoming ambitious or entertaining ideas above his station. With the Second there came Captain Skinner whose lively eyes observed the ensuing comedy.

Perron's information was correct: there was indeed a plot. Daulat Rao and his minister, the infamous Shirzi Rao Ghatkay, had planned to seize and possibly to butcher Perron in full Durbar. It did not, however, directly involve Sutherland or the regular troops. They had hired a large band of Afghan toughs for the purpose. (This seems to have been almost a traditional method, following the Indian plan of exploiting the specialty of each caste or race: Ghoseins for forlorn hopes, Brahmins for administration, Jats for doggedness, Rajputs for loyalty and, of course, Pathans for assassination. Appa Khandi Rao, it will be remembered, tried to get rid of Thomas in the same way.) Perron probably received all its details from Gopal Rao Bhao. Gopal Rao Bhao was an old Mahratta warrior, a survivor of Panipat and a former comrade in arms of Madhaji Sindia. Madhaji had dismissed him from his post of commander-in-chief of the Mahratta troops when he caught him intriguing against him with the Peshwa in 1795 and his neck was in danger. He had taken sanctuary with de Boigne and his gratitude extended to keeping his successor informed of what went on at

Daulat Rao's court, to which he had been readmitted. Apart from this, like all Madhaji's old followers he loathed Shirzi Rao Ghatkay.

The ambush was to be sprung at an audience or Durbar, which, by tradition, Perron would be expected to attend with his senior officers. A Durbar was, of course, like a levee or an investiture of today. New officers were presented, older ones graciously noted, all would present their formal *nazzars*, and those who had distinguished themselves would be given *khiluts* or robes of honour to don: literally an investiture. All was governed by rigid protocol and ceremonial. Now, by Indian convention to be put down on such an occasion was as humiliating as it was joy to be lifted up. When the great day came Perron led his officers, all in full dress uniform, to the huge pavilion in which the Durbar was to be held and was ushered into the Presence. As he entered he saw, as he had been warned, a solid block of Pathans all armed to the teeth sitting on the right, or honourable, side of the throne. He was significantly directed to the left. Perron accepted this slight and sat down unmoved while his officers filed in behind in order of seniority. After the last European there followed, most unexpectedly, all his Indian officers as well, three hundred or so, each carrying a pair of pistols; an unusual addition to full dress. There was a long and embarrassing silence. Both the Pathans and Perron's sirdars knew perfectly well why they were present, and Perron's men amused themselves by twirling their moustaches and glancing significantly at each other and the Pathans and ostentatiously hitching their sword-hilts and holsters round to a convenient position as they squatted down on the carpeted floor. Finally Daulat Rao blurted out that he had been expecting only the European officers. Perron, straight-faced, apologised by explaining that the native officers had always been included on Madhaji's day. There was then another long and uncomfortable silence with a lot of whispering between Sindia and his chief minister and Gopal Rao. Then the Pathans were told to leave. 'They all got up,' said Skinner, who obviously enjoyed the whole affair, 'looking as if they could eat us, while our men sat laughing at them with the utmost unconcern.'

Typically, the atmosphere became at once as relaxed and cordial as if nothing untoward had been intended. Perron was loaded with compliments, the ceremonies took place as was customary, betelnut was handed round and every nicety of Indian civility observed

15   213

before Sindia uttered the polite words of dismissal. '*Tashrif lijiye*
—pray remove your honourable presences.' On this Perron rose
and addressed him in carefully chosen terms and with calculated
dignity. He had served the house of Sindia too long and too well,
he said, to endure the humiliation just inflicted upon him. Turning
to his assembled officers (this piece of rhetoric, it will be understood,
was all in high-flown Urdu) he told them to look no longer to him
for orders or honours or promotion for he was laying down the
sword, and with these words he unbuckled his own and laid it
respectfully at Sindia's feet. This caused a great stir. Daulat Rao
rose from the *gadi* and embraced him, calling him 'uncle' and
begging him to explain how he had offended him. Perron, pretending to be mollified, agreed to resume his sword and then with a
bluntness which shocked but also delighted the Mahratta courtiers
he told Sindia that he should learn to distinguish between his true
friends and his enemies; he should be especially on his guard, said
Perron pointing at the livid Shirzi Rao Ghatkay, against wicked
advisers. Having thus put his young and rash master in his place
Perron left for his camp. There, to rub in his ascendancy, he
summoned the victors of Indore and Saswat, Sutherland and
Brownrigg, accused them of disloyalty, dismissed them and put
them in close arrest. Transferring Pohlmann on whose loyalty he
could depend to the command of the First Brigade he placed
himself at the head of the Second and marched home to Hindustan.

Perron was now at the summit of his career. On top of his already
enormous power and influence he had won, and in public which was
so important in India, a diplomatic and political victory which was
to be discussed earnestly in every court and bazaar. It was clear
who was the real master in the Empire now. It was, however, only a
tactical step and was incomplete. Not to follow it up was dangerous,
for both Sindia and his minister had had their faces 'blackened'. No
Indian, certainly no Mahratta, could have thought of anything
thenceforward except revenge.

At that moment Perron could have seized Shirzi Rao amid the
applause of all the Mahratta nobles he had wronged or robbed
and made Daulat Rao his own puppet as much as the Peshwa was
Daulat Rao's. He could have become King-maker over the whole
Confederacy. Indeed, many people thought that he was planning
to desert Daulat Rao for Holkar, and that was why he had allowed

Holkar to defeat him, only to be foiled by Sutherland. Although it was probably not true it was a natural piece of Indian reasoning. Had he been supremely daring he could have demanded for himself the great office of Vakil-ul-Mutluq then vested in the Peshwa: the captive Emperor could not have dared to refuse him. This would have made him, already the regent *de facto*, what was enormously important in both Muslim and Hindu eyes; the ruler *de jure* over all the nominal Empire. Then indeed he could have established the French presence in India again. It was for these dizzy stakes that he had packed his senior ranks with indifferent but loyal French officers, devoted every effort to crushing Thomas, abandoned Sindia in his need and alarmed the English, eventually to the point of their making war on him. In the event, this ambitious, capable, resolute man did absolutely nothing. After his démarche at Ujjain his nerve did not suddenly snap, like Thomas', it slowly drained away. The fact is that Perron, a remarkable man, a brave soldier, a crafty politician, the administrator and ruler for five years of a territory as big as France or Spain lacked the final streak of dominating ruthlessness required to take the final step to establish himself. He became incapable of taking a decision. Perhaps, long exertion, unrelieved and unshared responsibility, illness and the climate of India had at last worn him down as it eventually wore down or killed every other European in a high place.

Whatever it was, it led him to be once more fatally inactive when Jaswant Rao Holkar again appeared in arms in the Deccan; that fierce and resilient man having fully recovered from the trouncing he had suffered at Indore. He had sacked all his French officers, being enraged by Plumet's desertion just before Indore and had engaged three good British ones; Vickers, Harding and Armstrong, who each raised three regular brigades of four battalions. With these new troops and his co-general Amir Khan's Pathan cavalry and his own Mahratta horse he now set out on a campaign to detach the Peshwa from Sindia and to bring him under his own control. Perron remained indifferent and aloof from the operations that followed. Sindia and his advisers behaved with the same ineptitude they had displayed on the previous year, parcelling out the trained troops here and there instead of letting Pohlmann handle the First Brigade as a complete battle formation. The culminating action took place on the plain of Kirkee outside Poona, where Holkar's

215

new army came up with the Peshwa's own regulars stiffened by a
detachment of four battalions under the English Captain Dawes
from the First Brigade.

The battle at first went badly for Holkar. His cavalry made the
old mistake of charging Dawes' unbroken infantry and were murdered by salvos of grape and case. Standing firmly round their
colours and by their guns they continued to repel attack after attack
until Holkar's troops began first to wilt and then to fall back.
At this crisis Holkar showed himself a soldier. From Lalsot onwards
the record of the Mahratta troops proper and their leaders is one
of unbroken poltroonery. Now at Kirkee under a leader in the
tradition of Shivaji they recovered their spirit. Instead of fleeing or
leaving matters to his Feringhis Holkar sent for his horse, mounted
and rallied his shaken followers with a cry still remembered by
the Mahratta nation: 'Now or never,' he shouted above the roar of
battle, 'now or never for Jaswant Rao!' Then with Harding, his
best English brigadier, riding knee to knee with him he crashed into
the erupting batteries of the First Brigade. Harding was killed at
the gun-muzzles and Jaswant Rao was wounded three times, but
after the bloodiest of close combats in which Dawes and his British
officers were killed, the square was broken, the guns captured and
the sepoys of the Hindustan battalions were slaughtered where
they stood fighting in their ranks to the bitter end. Holkar, that
pitiless and Feringhi-hating man, mourned Harding deeply and
saw that his body was properly buried—in what was later the gar-
den of the British 'Government House' on the north side of the
plain.[1]

This action had the most historic and momentous consequences,
for it led immediately to the final British conquest of the Moghul
Empire. It is part of their history and not merely of the obscure and
forgotten story of the mercenaries. Baji Rao II fled to the British
for the protection that neither Sindia or his distant general Perron
would, or could, afford, and on 31st December, 1802, he agreed
the terms of the Treaty of Bassein which placed all Maharashtra
under British suzerainty. It was the refusal of the great chieftains
of the Confederacy to ratify what Baji Rao had signed away without
their leave or agreement that led to the Second Mahratta War.
The sting in it for Perron was that one of its heads stated that the
Mahrattas would never in future employ any foreigners in their

armies who were enemies of Britain. That was the price of his fatal lack of initiative.

The chieftains of the Confederacy, Sindia, Holkar, Bhonsla and the Gaekwar, were all furious, but nevertheless for seven months they negotiated with the British, only to turn down every successive proposal. Sindia, who had been joined by Ragoji Bhonsla was determined not to give way. He only spun the negotiations out in a vain attempt to gain time to persuade Jaswant Rao to call a truce to their ancient quarrel between Holkar and Sindia and join them. The Governor-General was equally determined that he was going to draw the teeth of the Mahrattas once and for all. At last, on 3rd August, the British Political Agent left Sindia's camp and the war began.

The Governor-General had decided on two simultaneous operations. One of these, in the Deccan and directed against Sindia, is probably as well known as any in British military history, for in it the future Duke of Wellington made his brilliant debut as a commander in the field. Every British student of war is familiar with the campaign of Assaye, although almost all are mistaken about the identity of General Arthur Wellesley's opponent. The other is less well known but was strategically far more important. It was perfectly clear to the Marquess Wellesley that Perron and his brigades were the prop of Mahratta power. He laid down as the objectives of the campaign in Hindustan the destruction of the Brigades, the occupation of the Jumna Doab, whose revenues provided their financial support, the removal of Perron and all the French senior officers (whom, rightly or wrongly, he was convinced were a threat to the British) and to take the Emperor under British protection. Such was the importance he attached to the northern operation that he ordered his commander-in-chief in India, General Lake, to take command in the field in person.

Lake mobilised in Oudh. His field army consisted of eight regiments of cavalry organised in three brigades. Three of these were British Light Dragoons—'Royals' or 'His Majesty's' of the British Army—and five native cavalry. The infantry consisted of thirteen battalions of native foot and 'His Majesty's' 76th—later the Second Battalion of the Duke of Wellington's Regiment. Of artillery Lake had some forty-odd light guns distributed among the cavalry and infantry; those with the cavalry being drawn by a pair of horses in shafts and known as 'gallopers'. They had been introduced into the Bengal army by Lake. There were as well six-teen heavier pieces and three howitzers. After the inevitable detachments for guarding the lines of communication and so on had been made the whole force was not much bigger than one of Perron's brigades but through Lake's efforts it was highly trained and full of fighting spirit. The Bengal artillery was an efficient arm, the cavalry were exceptionally well led and while all the infantry were good the 76th proved to be one of the finest battalions of foot in the long and glorious history of the British infantry.[2]

The leader of this formidable body, Gerard Lake, is a general whose reputation has been naturally overshadowed by that of his brilliant subordinate Wellesley and also, in the eyes of many, tarnished by the brutality with which he suppressed the rebellion in Ireland in 1798. He is often dismissed as a brainless officer whose only idea of tactics was a costly frontal attack. His claim to fame was his conduct at Lincelles in 1793 in the war against revolutionary France, when he restored an adverse situation by leading three battalions of the Guards in a dashing attack. Big, jolly, red-faced, fond of wine and the company of pretty women he appears a stereotype of a British army officer. This is quite a mistaken view. Although sixty years old he could stay in the saddle all day and think and decide quickly at the end of it unmoved by fear or fatigue. He was crazily brave; he once killed a tiger with a pistol. It is true that he did not flinch from the prospect of a frontal attack and was undeterred by the fear of incurring casualties, but he was a capable professional soldier. He believed in offensive action and in speed and he was ruthless in pursuit: the hall-mark of a good commander. His frontal attacks, always delivered with great dash and often led by himself, were only made after the most careful reconnais-sance and planning. As for being callous, he was not wasteful of human life—no British general can afford to be—but he understood that a general must feel about his army as a fox-hunter feels about his horse: 'he must care for it in stables as if it were worth five hundred guineas and ride it as if it were not worth half-a-crown.' This was the port-drinking, fox-hunting, ex-Grenadier Guardsman the Marquess Wellesley chose to deal with the Army of Hindustan and whom Perron was destined briefly to meet in the field.

The order of battle and dispositions of the Army of Hindustan in early 1803 were as follows. The First Brigade under Pohlmann was with Daulat Rao Sindia in the Deccan. To reinforce it on the threat of war with the English Perron had, at last, despatched the Fourth (Dudrenac) and the Fifth (Brownrigg) together with four of Somru Begum's battalions under Saleur.[3] Immediately available near Delhi he had the Second Brigade, now under an obscure and ineffective French officer called Geslin, and the Third under Louis Bourquin. As well he had 4000–5000 Hindustani Horse in a fair state of efficiency under the French Colonel Fleury. Separate from this field army were the established garrisons of the three great strong places: Delhi, commanded by Drugeon, Agra, under George Hessing and his own Aligarh under Pedron. He could therefore, if he chose, concentrate a large force of cavalry, twenty battle-hardened battalions and twenty batteries, or 200 guns and howitzers, against Lake's nine regiments of cavalry and fourteen of infantry and 65 pieces of artillery.

Perron's army had, however, one great weakness which the Governor-General was quick to note and to exploit. The majority of—perhaps all—the best regimental officers were British, or Eurasians of British parentage, like Skinner. He calculated with great wisdom and also great cunning that as mercenaries they would be torn between loyalty to their country and to their contract, and between honour and their livelihood, for they depended on Perron's favour for their salary and their pensions. He neither exhorted nor threatened them. He merely let it be known that any officer who was prevented by his conscience from engaging in the war that was imminent need not fear the loss of a career or of fortune. If they left Perron's or Sindia's service and reported to the British authorities the Company would guarantee their pensions, and generously. It sounds both simple and venal, but it was a shrewd stroke. The British officers were already discontented. They had seen what had happened to Sutherland and Brownrigg. They did all the fighting and were frequently called upon to take command of 'brigades' of three or four battalions in the field, a colonel's or major's appointment, but were never promoted above captain. They soon began to trickle out to British territory. Their Indian employers were furious. Amrat Rao, who commanded the Peshwa's troops, tied William Gardner to a gun and threatened to blow him away if he did not swear to serve on, an ordeal which failed to shake him. Later he was able to escape with his usual daring, slipping his guards when in the open and jumping over a cliff and swimming a river. Jaswant Rao considered that the refusal of Vickers, Ryan and Dodd to fight for him was, and from his point of view rightly, a breach of faith and contract—if Mahrattas could fight Mahrattas, why not the British the British?—and, always impetuous, cut their heads off. (If Dodd was the officer who fled to the Mahrattas from Seringapatam in 1800 to avoid a court-martial for murder and extortion he thus kept his 'appointment in Samara'.) Perron acted less drastically, but he discharged all his British officers as potentially disloyal. The measure had another even more profound effect. The sepoys, men both simple and suspicious concluded that their sahibs were about to betray them, and not being sophisticated enough to distinguish between one Feringhi and another, rejected the authority of all of them. Thus at a stroke Wellesley removed the majority of good, fighting regimental officers from the battalions at a moment when it was too late, if it had ever been possible, to replace them from the cadre with General Decaen in far-away Pondicherry, and far too late to train the Indian officers for the positions they were now to occupy. As well he had sowed the seeds of a spreading mutiny. To Lake this move of the Governor-General proved worth a division of troops and a battering train.

The Governor-General also had high hopes of seducing Perron himself, for that officer had for some months been putting out feelers to the British for a safe conduct. This may have been a natural precaution or it may have been the first signs of a breaking nerve and of weakening resolution. Perron's behaviour at this crisis of his career is inexplicable; it seems hardly possible it is the same man who fought at Khardla or Sounda and had out-faced and out-plotted his master at Ujjain the year before. He had just heard that he was to be stripped of all his offices except the command of the regular brigades and was to hand over as Subahdar and as Comman-der-in-Chief to Ambaji Angria. This need not have disturbed him for neither Daulat Rao nor Ambaji could have removed him against his will any more than they could have removed the Marquess Wellesley. Had he decided to resign he had plenty of time to collect his family and his vast wealth and he would have been received by Lake with open arms. Had he decided to fight, then all his training as a soldier should have told him not to challenge Lake except on his own ground and with his two powerful brigades united. As it was he behaved like a man demented with worry and indecision. He sent his family and twenty wagon-loads of treasure to Agra and his British aide-de-camp to negotiate with Lake, who found Lake would discuss nothing but Perron's personal surrender. He allowed Lake to approach unmolested to within a mile or so of his headquarters, merely demanding agitatedly what his intentions were, why he was invading Imperial territory and whether a state of war existed? He made no attempt to concentrate the Brigades: in fact he did the opposite. With no field troops immediately available except his cavalry he detached Colonel Fleury and several regiments of Hindustani Horse in the hope of diverting Lake by a long-distance raid towards Cawnpore, where they overran a small detachment of the Company's infantry near Shekeohabad and kidnapped an officer's wife but otherwise achieved little. Then he, a man who had seen the native irregular cavalry panic on half-a-dozen battlefields, finally challenged Lake at the last moment with a force composed only of Hindustani and of Mahratta cavalry on the outskirts of Koil.

Lake, having mobilised, moved into camp at Kanoje on the Ganges where he amused himself and his officers, and their wives who had joined them while they were waiting to march, with dinners and dances in the evenings, for he was a jolly man, and with hunting by day. It was at this time one of his officers speared a tiger and was rescued from the consequences of his rashness by his Commander-in-Chief pistolling it. When at last the order came to move, however, the tents were struck, the wives sent home—there were to be many widows in the 76th in a month—and he moved fast. By the 29th August, 1803, he was in front of Koil, where he found 20,000 horsemen of sorts drawn up to receive him and attacked at once. Shaken by a brisk cannonade from the galloper-guns they took one horrified look at the Light Dragoons and the Bengal Native Cavalry thundering down on them on their big horses, spun their ponies round and fled. It is sad that Perron's last battle was an absurd rout. He and his troopers did not draw rein until they were some eight miles down the Agra road.

On this very day a party of six dispirited officers were travelling together to Agra, having only just before been dismissed by Perron because they were British.[4] They were anxious because until they found the British they were without jobs or pay and because their families in Agra were in what was for them now enemy territory, and angry because they had been turned off without notice like dishonest servants. They were gloomy, too, because leaving a regiment is not like leaving an ordinary business: it is like a clan or a family and to leave it at the best of times is a great wrench. Among them was a very sullen James Skinner. *He* had no objection to fighting his father's people and he considered that his dismissal was an insult to his Rajput blood and his fidelity to his salt. At noon they camped so as to rest during the heat of the day. Suddenly there was a clatter of hooves and the road filled with a rout of terrified horsemen throwing up clouds of dust and using their whips freely. Galloping along among them they spied to their amazement their Commander-in-Chief of yesterday; exhausted, hatless and in the greatest agitation and distress. They pressed him to halt and refresh himself, and tell them what had happened. Perron groaned that his men had behaved very badly, they had refused to fight, and that he too was on his way to Agra. Skinner went up to him and implored him not to despair, and to play the man. He asked to be taken back, saying that Perron had many friends and that they could still make a fight for it. 'Ah, no,' replied Perron mournfully, 'it is all over. Do not ruin yourself. Go over to the British, it is all up with us.' Skinner persisted. 'Ah, no, Monsieur Skinner. I no trust, I afraid you all go (desert).' He remounted and rode off shaking his head and repeating the same words, 'No trust! No trust!' The words might serve as his epitaph, but the truth is that he distrusted the wrong people. It was not his British captains and lieutenants who were to betray him, but the very Frenchmen whom he had carefully put into the highest posts.

He left Koil confident that the seige of Aligarh would keep Lake occupied for weeks which, now his mind was made up to resist, would give him enough time to gather up the Brigades and to make a fight of it. This brave decision soon evaporated. To his extreme fury and chagrin he learned that Bourquin, his protegé, whose drivelling incapacity to make war he had forgiven three times because he was loyal and French, had betrayed him. Bourquin, on hearing the news that Perron had been dismissed and was to be superseded by Ambaji Angria, decided on a *coup*. The ex-pastry cook suddenly conceived the idea of becoming the commander of the Army himself, and of seizing the Emperor and extracting a *firman* to this effect from him. Drugeon attempted to resist Bourquin by force of arms and only desisted when the Emperor personally begged him to surrender to avoid yet another storm and sack of his capital. Drugeon surrendered to Bourquin, and Geslin also tamely accepted him. Bourquin had sent orders to Agra that Perron was to be arrested. While Perron was digesting this he received another staggering piece of news. Aligarh the impregnable had fallen. Rumours began to circulate among the troops that he himself had betrayed it, and these were redoubled when Fleury's Hindustani Horse arrived tired and discomfited having been chased out of Oudh rather brusquely by one of Lake's cavalry brigadiers. Perron thought that they were about to murder him and Fleury as well. Dipping heavily into the reserves of rupees he had deposited in the fort he bribed the native sirdars heavily to let him go, and with his own faithful bodyguard troops, his family, his English aide-de-camp and Fleury he slipped off to surrender to Lake, leaving an anxious George Hessing to guard a treasure of twenty-seven lacs of rupees with his increasingly unsettled and unreliable garrison. Lake received him cordially and sent him with all the state due to a retiring Governor and commander-in-chief to Chandernagore in what remained of French India.

For five years he had been virtually a king. He rivalled Dupleix, and had he served under Napoleon he might well have ended a Marshal. He had all the qualities of a great man which served to raise him from a pedlar of handkerchiefs and a sergeant of sepoys, save the one insisted on in Acton's dictum: 'great men are almost always bad.' He was not wicked enough; indeed Perron was a good man, avarice apart (but avarice was the disease of Europeans in India). He never murdered or betrayed, and, at the bitter end, decided to fight for Sindia and for France. His exit was inglorious but although a final battle in command of his sepoys would have been more dramatic, it was at least a more comfortable if not exactly a happy ending. He must have been gratified to learn that the treacherous Bourquin was soon to receive his come-uppance at the hands of Lake.

Lake spent four days waiting for an answer to his summons to Pedron in Aligarh to surrender. Meanwhile he examined its defences closely and thoroughly; obtaining what information he could about the plan of its enormously complicated and formidable defences from the British officers who had been recently dismissed by Perron and those who had since slipped out of the garrison to accept the terms. Inside, Colonel Pedron, now the only European, sat reading without the slightest enthusiasm a letter from Perron in the heroic style to which French generals are somewhat prone. It begged him to remember that he was a Frenchman and that the eyes of millions rested upon him, to defend Aligarh as long as one stone rested upon another, but added that this would be unnecesary, because Perron would shortly return with the Army to destroy General Lake. He was, to his relief, denied any opportunity for glory, for he was getting on in years and was not really a very warlike man. His sepoys, incensed by the desertion of the other European officers, deposed him and locked him in a cell. It is a sombre tribute to the Army of Hindustan that they only mutinied at the thought of surrender. In his place they put a Rajput called Baji Rao (no connection with the Peshwa Baji Rao) with orders to defy Lake and refuse his summons.

Baji believed, like everyone else, that Aligarh could be held for ever. It was immensely strong, double-walled with intricate defences and surrounded by a wet ditch wide and deep enough to float a battleship, as Lake said. The only possible route to its interior was through the official entrance, so to speak. This began at the edge of the moat at a fortified gate and gate-house, and then passed over an open causeway into a huge barbican tower standing like an island in the moat between whose double walls it threaded a semi-circular route, out through another strong gate, across another causeway, through a gate in the outer curtain of the main fort, along a passage between the two curtain walls, and finally, after a right-angled turn through a fourth gate, into the bailey of the inner fort. Every yard of the way was covered by a cross-fire from flanking bastions or from inner loop-holes in the double walls. It was like running a gauntlet. In addition Baji Rao dug an outwork for three guns to prevent an approach to or close bambardment of the outer gate-house on the far side of the moat. What he did not know was that the 76th Foot who were to lead the storming column had a lust for combat equal to any Rajput, or that Lake now possessed the secrets of this pathway of death. One of Perron's officers, an Irish captain called Lucan, had offered to turn his coat and act as guide to the forlorn hope.

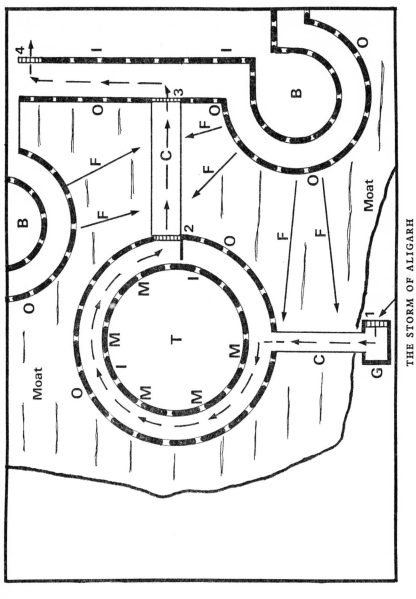

THE STORM OF ALIGARH

G, gatehouse; T, tower; CC, causeway; 1, 2, 3, 4, gates; O, outer wall; I, inner wall; M, matchlock men; B, bastions; F, flanking fire; the arrows represent the entrance route forced by 76th Foot

At dawn on 4th September Baji Rao was aroused by a warning gun from Lake's camp to see the outwork being carried in a single rush by the white soldiers. A twelve-pounder gun was then wheeled up which battered open the first gate. His outer gate-guard fought as Rajputs have always fought. They piked down the escaladers of the gate-house; they actually climbed down the attackers' ladders to fight them outside the walls; they wounded the commander of the storming column and his artillery officer, and killed the adjutant of the 76th and every officer of its grenadier company, but all to no avail. To walk in cold blood, even today, through one of these complex avenues which lead into the great fortresses of ancient India arouses disbelief that any soldiers, however lunatic or heroic, could pass through them alive if seriously opposed; but the fact is at Aligarh the defenders fought at every gate and every turn, and still the stormers came on scrambling over each other's bodies on a front only two or three files wide and heaving and straining at the big twelve-pounder they trundled along the causeways and passages as a key to unlock the succession of gates. In sixty minutes the 76th were inside the fortress and on the ramparts. The garrison refused quarter, or were denied it, and two thousand sepoys were bayoneted inside, killed themselves jumping from the walls, were drowned in the moat or were cut down by the dragoons waiting on its far side if they succeeded in swimming across. When this disgusting business was complete someone found Pedron in his dungeon and dragged him blinking into the light—'a stout elderly officer in a green uniform jacket with gold lace and epaulettes'—and invited him formally to surrender the fort.

The fall of Aligarh, to eight companies of infantry and one gun, sent ripples of shock through Hindustan. Men had often heard that the British were real war-tigers and great crackers of forts. They knew that they had taken Seringapatam in twenty minutes, but that was far-away and against down-country soldiers—but against the Army of Hindustan! Lake won his whole campaign morally before breakfast on the 4th. Next it was the turn of Perron's field army. The only man undismayed by the news was Louis Bourquin. He was as intoxicated by success and dazzling dreams of wealth and power as surely as if he had taken a dose of bhang. As the new Commander-in-Chief and supreme in Hindustan he placed himself, figuratively speaking that is, at the head of his

Third and the Second Brigades and set off to destroy the presumptuous invader. He crossed the Jumna near Delhi and there, reverting to the old traditional ideas of Indian warfare, chose a strong position and ordered the whole army to dig in deeply and establish its batteries. The cavalry was sent out in front. At about noon on the 10th September it came scurrying back, red-coated troopers in chase, and reformed behind the main position. When the front was clear a troop of officers arrived attending a big man in a red coat with a red face, who slowly and insolently rode from end to end of the line inspecting it at close range as if it was his own army paraded for him, disregarding a hot fire directed at him as he passed down the line as if it were a *feu-de-joie* in his honour. Next a long line of enemy cavalry formed in front of the watching sepoys of the Brigades and made one or two tentative dashes at their entrenchments, to be greeted by a crescendo of shot which soon halted them. There they continued to stand, horses and men falling, unwilling to fall back and unable to advance. After an hour of this they appeared to loose heart and still keeping their order they began to withdraw by squadrons until they were out of range.

No one knows what part Bourquin or Geslin played in the action. It seems highly likely from the way the force was deployed and how it was handled at this stage that the fighting line was left to the control of the Indian sirdars and under-officers. When they and the sepoys saw the enemy cavalry beat a retreat a chorus of jeers ran along the trenches and there were loud demands for an immediate advance. With great enthusiasm the infantry left their position and formed up in column, the light artillery was dragged out of its emplacements and limbered up and shouting their war-cries the whole line strode forward in triumph, or the anticipation of triumph; but they had been hoaxed.

Lake had been merely 'amusing' them, in the old military phrase. He had been anxious to entice them from the protection of their strong field-works and heavy batteries and had succeeded. Once the two brigades were fairly in the open and beyond hope of turning back the cavalry turned right and left from the centre in column of troops and rolling back like the curtains parting at a theatre, revealed a line of enemy infantry advancing upon them with the same perfect dressing and measured tread that they themselves had been taught by de Boigne. With their accustomed speed and precision, however, they deployed while their gunners dashed to lift the trails from the limbers, spin the three- and six-pounders round to face the enemy, grab cartridges and case-shot from the limber-boxes and open fire. Prompt as they were, they had been caught on the wrong foot and even though their gunners opened a blistering fire of case which brought down scores of the 76th and the Indian sepoys in front of them they were already too close to be stopped and again in the style they themselves knew so well. Lake's infantry fired a single volley at close range into the faces of the leading ranks of the brigades and raced in to cross bayonets. Bourquin's battalions were sent staggering back and away from their guns. While their officers were trying to rally and reform them their opponents deliberately paused and, surprisingly, closed up into column so leaving large gaps in their front. It soon became apparent why. The battalions who had advanced from the trenches had now been deployed hastily and unless they were given time were irrevocably drawn up in line to meet Lake's infantry. Now while they were in this unsuitable formation, through the gaps in the enemy front came galloping the squadrons of the enemy cavalry they believed defeated, sabring the gunners, crashing through their line and then pelting them from their galloper-guns as they broke and ran. Their order and cohesion collapsed and it was soon all over. Bourquin and Geslin bolted at the first shock and the leaderless battalions dissolved. They died hard. A series of disconnected little fights took place in the ravines and the scrub jungle on the banks of the Jumna where the remorseless 76th and the Bengal sepoys hunted them down, but by sunset the last yells of defiance or terror and the last scattered shots died away, and the field army of Hindustan of fourteen battalions and sixty-eight guns had been killed or captured. For this battle Lake, having made provision for garrisons on his lines of communication, cavalry to deal with Fleury, etc., deployed a brigade of cavalry, the 76th Foot and five battalions of native infantry.

Lake's victory outside Delhi was one of the decisive battles of India, much more than Assaye. There, Arthur Wellesley defeated a limb of the Mahratta power, but on 10th September Lake bit out its heart. He had one more terrible, and as it turned out unnecessary and irrelevant battle to fight after the whole campaign was over, but after Delhi it was all mopping up. A day or two later Bourquin, quickly cured of ambition or any thirst for glory, Geslin and the remaining officers came in to surrender and on 16th Lake entered Delhi in triumph but not altogether as a conqueror. He asked for an audience with the Emperor as if he were his country's ambassador, to convey the respects of the Governor-General, to express his gratitude at being privileged to free him from his captivity and to offer him British protection. He was received by the Emperor in pathetic state; the poor, blind, thin old man, now eighty-three, in shabby clothes and seated under a hastily erected and dingy canopy of state. Ali Johur, Shah Alam the Second, 'The King of the World', no longer had any Persian thoroughbreds or jewel-hilted swords or rich robes of honour to present in Durbar, but he was still the fount of honour and conscious of his high dignity. He conferred on General Lake a string of pompous Moghul titles; one, *Fateh Jung Bahadur* —the 'Victorious Hero in War'—being not at all ludicrous or inappropriate. These formalities concluded Lake turned his attention briskly to the third of the great fortresses; from the point of view of prestige the most important of all—Agra.

There, from his point of view, everything was in a satisfactory state of confusion. With a mixture of cajolery and bluff—and force if necessary—he hoped to liquidate the last resistance there without too much bloodshed or at all costs a formal siege, for which he had neither the men nor sufficient heavy artillery. Fortunately for Lake after Perron's hurried departure the garrison had begun to think about his twenty-seven lacs of rupees under their guard, and who was to have it. Their discipline and their order soon broke down; some wanted to surrender, some wanted to fight the British, some frankly wanted to lay hold of the treasure and share it out and run. Inside the fortress they held as prisoners their commander George Hessing, Robert Sutherland, Perron's brother-in-law Derridon and three British captains. There was also Brownrigg, who had turned up from the Deccan with the small Fifth Brigade (which had been sent back for reasons that will be explained shortly). This was an added complication for the mutineers. The Fifth were in a puzzled and resentful mood having marched to the Deccan and back for no purpose and now had been deserted, like the other Brigades, by all their officers. On top of this their comrades inside Agra would not admit them, fearing they might learn of the twenty-seven lacs. They were camped uneasily outside without leaders or any settled idea of what they should do. There they were

16   229

joined by some of the survivors of the battle near Delhi whose stories added to their gloom and alarm. Lake arrived on 7th October and demanded that everyone should surrender forthwith, promising that all the sepoys would be allowed to go away peaceably to their homes and none be treated as prisoners of war. His difficulty lay in the fact that there was no single person in authority inside or outside the walls to speak for them. On the 10th, as he could get no sense out of the sepoys of the Fifth Brigade he attacked them and after some quite sharp fighting in which he lost over two hundred men drove them away from the walls of Agra, killing or wounding 600 and capturing all 26 of their guns. On 12th October they surrendered. They did more, they asked to be taken under Lake's command. After all, they were mercenaries, following the profession of arms to earn their daily bread. Their loyalty was to the profession and to their paymaster whose salt they ate. They had absolved their izzat by not tamely surrending, and as for a master, they no longer had one and in any case the Mahrattas meant little to these northern men. Many of them later entered the ranks of the Company's army, some in whole units.

With the Fifth Brigade out of the way all that remained was the fort itself. Inside the mutineers' counsel was even more divided. George Hessing's troops were not of the best, and they now had had a grandstand view from the ramparts of the fort of Lake's methods and of the quality of his troops. They alternatively abused their Feringhi prisoners for recommending them to capitulate and pitifully asked them for their advice or to negotiate with the British for them. Sutherland, who seems to have taken charge, told the leaders to forget the treasure and save themselves and their lives. If they meddled with the money, he said rather cynically, the British general would certainly parade them with their backs to the muzzles of his guns. Eventually after much dissension the leaders of the garrison agreed to receive Lake's emissary and to listen to his terms but others rushed to the battlements and opened fire. Lake had already invested the fort and established his batteries, and he immediately ordered the bombardment to start in reply. On this, the defenders, the stories of the storm of Aligarh still fresh in their minds, the twelve-pounder shot knocking on the shuddering curtain wall and with Sutherland's lively persuasion in their ears, decided to surrender without further argument.

The Destruction of the Brigades

The campaign in Hindustan was now over. In forty-two days Lake had carried out all the tasks given him by the Governor-General: Perron had been removed, the Emperor freed, the Doab placed under British control, and the three great fortresses of Delhi, Agra and Aligarh were occupied by British garrisons. There were no more European officers in Sindia's service in Hindustan, and all the infantry and cavalry were destroyed or disbanded and all their guns taken. All that remained unaccounted for were some officerless battalions now dissolving into gangs of freebooters without order or cohesion. These were no military danger, or so Lake was led to believe, but he could not regard his task as complete until they had been rounded up. It was, he decided, an operation in the nature of a pursuit—a cavalry task—so he dumped two battalions and all his artillery except his light cavalry and battalion guns, and set off with three complete cavalry brigades, leaving five battalions to march after him with their best foot forward. In fact, what he believed to be disorganised freebooters was the Fourth Brigade, complete except for its European officers, who had been joined by three or four battalions who had not been engaged or who had escaped from the Battle of Delhi under a sirdar called Sarwar Khan. There is also a possibility the survivors of the First Brigade may have joined with them. Before relating what happened to them, however, it is necessary to turn back in time for a moment to the 23rd September and south to the Deccan.

As has been said, Perron had despatched at some date early in the year two brigades and also four battalions from Somru Begum's brigade under Colonel Saleur to reinforce his master in the Deccan. The fatuous Daulat Rao, who always reacted to every threat by making a detachment to meet it and so scattering his armies in every quarter had, at some date, possibly when he heard the news of the disasters in the north, ordered them to counter-march, so they arrived back in Hindustan in October having been of no use in either the Deccan or in Hindustan. The Fifth surrendered at Agra and disbanded, as has been told. The commander of the Fourth was that ineffective old war-horse Dudrenac. When he heard, while still on the march, the news of Assaye behind him and of Delhi and Agra in front he slipped off with all his officers and surrendered on 30th October to one of Lake's brigadiers, leaving the masterless Fourth wandering about somewhere north of the

Chambal river.[5] There they were joined by Sarwar Khan. Of the Hindustani brigades only the First now remained as part of Sindia's army in the Deccan.

The battle of Assaye has been described so often that it seems unnecessary to do it again, but every writer has been so dazzled by Arthur Wellesley's daring and brilliance that the point of view from the Mahratta side has been completely neglected. (So much so that Arthur Wellesley's opponents are invariably described as 'Mahrattas', whereas in fact we know that the vast horde of Mahrattas were useless in any pitched battle.) Assaye was fought between more or less equal numbers of the King's and the Company's regiments and de Boigne's old battalions recruited in northern India, that great home of warriors. No student seems to have remarked, even Fortescue, on the very odd dispositions and handling of Sindia's regular infantry. It may give a clue to the fate of the First Brigade.

There is no factual account of Assaye from the Mahratta side, but it is possible to reconstruct it from British evidence. On the 23rd September the joint host of Daulat Rao Sindia and Ragoji Bhonsla (without apparently any 'professional' Mahratta general in supreme command: no Gopal Rao Bhao or Ambaji Angria; or Lakwa Dada, who in fact had died) were with 40,000 or 50,000 Mahratta irregular horse bivouacked in a long straggling camp extending for about seven miles along the north bank of the Kaitna river covering the ford leading to the strategic Ajanta pass, or 'Ghat'. Here Arthur Wellesley came upon them, looked at the main crossing and their strength and accordingly turned aside to attempt a flank movement against Sindia's left. He advanced surrounded, but unmolested, by swarms of hovering light cavalry. Of regular infantry Sindia had the First Brigade (described as 'Pohlmann's') estimated as 6000 strong. This figure is not of a full brigade; the reason almost certainly being that the four battalions lost at Kirkee had never been replaced. It therefore consisted of four regular battalions plus the two matchlock battalions, who may well have been the dogged defenders of Assaye itself, this being their typical role. There were also four battalions of Jean-Baptiste Filose's corps under an officer called Dupont who is never heard of before or after the battle. (Jean-Baptiste himself was a mercenary in the old tradition who knew when to avoid a battle, which was usually always, and who was pointedly not engaged in the war.) There were also the four battalions of the 'Begum Somru's' brigade, who as we know were also not exactly gluttons for combat.

While Arthur Wellesley was having his flash of intuition of the existence of the Pipalgaon ford and approaching it all these regular battalions were observed standing in line facing south at the north-eastern end of the camp, a position of no tactical significance whatever. It is perfectly clear what they were doing: they were parading under arms and waiting for the information that the useless cavalry never brought, and for the orders the infatuated Sindia and Bhonsla were incapable of giving. Two miles away on their left they could hear some gunfire. This was from the single unsupported battery which harassed the unopposed crossing by the British of the Pipalgaon-Warur ford: perhaps it was a battery whose lines were near by and saw the whole enemy force defiling in front of them from their gunpark and came into action. The British then advanced, still unopposed, for two clear miles and the next thing Pohlmann, Dupont and Saleur saw, to their astonishment, was a long line of white and brown faces and red coats topping the low ridge on their left, almost on their parade ground and 'crossing their "T"', to use the naval term. In their consternation the various commanders embarked on two quite unrelated manoeuvres. One part of the force changed direction to its left to face the advancing British finishing with its left anchored on Assaye village, its guns to the front. The other withdrew pivoting back in not only a bad but an irrelevant position with its back to the steep banks of the Jewah stream, not facing the British at all and with its left flank pointing at them. Nothing looks odder than this L-shaped formation: what, if anything, was its purpose? (Lewis Smith says Somru Begum's Brigade had three battalions guarding the baggage. Perhaps the rearward branch of the 'L' was the Somru Brigade, evading combat as usual, and the story about the baggage was Saleur's subsequent excuse for survival.) Clearly no single officer was in command.

The portion of the line which turned to face the British attack was observed to deploy in a clumsy and unorthodox fashion. Instead of breaking into column of companies by battalions and so flexibly and conveniently changing front, the battalions already in line facing south were shuffled round to face east remaining in line

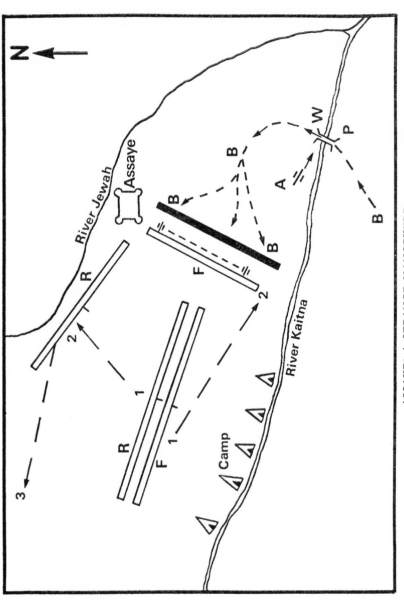

ASSAYE: A STRANGE MANOEUVRE

F, front; R, rear line of regular infantry; 1, 2, 3, successive positions; PW, Pipalgaon-Warur ford; BBB, advance and deployment of British opposed only by guns at A

while moving, as if they were unable to drill properly, or as if those in command did not know the correct orders. It is highly significant. It was absolutely axiomatic in manoeuvre, French or English, to move in column and fight in line. To be technical, had this been a deliberate drill movement the order would have been (perhaps) 'battalions will advance in line in succession from the left, right shoulders forward: at the halt, on the left, form line of brigade'; an immensely difficult operation to carry out correctly. However, it was done somehow and this eastward-facing limb of the 'L', and especially the troops around Assaye, fought like demons until they were finally broken. The limb along the Jewah remained passive throughout the battle. Even when attacked by the enemy cavalry it remained immobile and in line: fortunately for it the exhausted British did not charge home. It was seen to retreat and after a brief stand three miles off marched off the battle-field and disappeared. Colonel Saleur, we know, arrived safely back in Sardhana with three out of four battalions intact.

What are we to make of all this? One likely explanation is that Pohlmann was not present at the battle at all.[6] If he was, we have to believe that the victor of Malpura sat on his horse like a dummy listening to gunfire a mile or so away without investigating it, allowed an enemy force to advance to within musket shot of his flank and deploy there, and that he could not handle his brigade. Alternatively if he was in command of the rearward line, that he did nothing when one effort on his part could have turned the battle, did not form square to meet the cavalry, and treacherously left the battle-field before the fight was over. The front line behaved exactly as it might had the First Brigade been suddenly deprived of all senior direction: uncertain handling but tremendous courage. If (as Fortescue suggests) it escaped from the slaughter, where did it go? Some stragglers might have gone north, but Lake's opponents at Laswari can be fully accounted for, and there is no mention of it or of Pohlmann at Argaum or elsewhere. If their past form is any guide the survivors of Assaye were undoubtedly those professional survivors, Walter Reinhardt's old troops, preserving their non-belligerent tradition to the last; followed perhaps by some of Filose's troops, who were much of the same stamp. The gunners and infantry of the forward line and of the centre around Assaye were de Boigne's old First Brigade, the Cheria Fauj—the Army of

Birds who flew to battle on eager wings—the 'Deccan Invincibles', the victors of Lalsot, Chaksana, Agra, Patun, Mertah, Lakhairi, Khardla, Satwas and Indore and it was they who died round their guns and colours at Assaye. It was they who gave the Duke of Wellington the hardest fight of his life, as he always declared.

When Lake set off from Agra on 27th October in pursuit of the remnants of the Army of Hindustan he believed that he was looking for no less than seventeen battalions commanded by a Mahratta called Abaji. This would only be possible if Abaji's force consisted of two complete brigades, but if the argument above is accepted the other brigade could only have been the First, which had already ceased to exist. In actual numbers Abaji had 9000 with 70 guns, and this almost exactly works out, the guns giving the clue at five per battalion for one complete brigade, the Fourth, reinforced by Sawar Khan's battalions with their guns. Its commander, Abaji, was probably only the senior of a committee or syndicate of Indian officers whose objectives were uncertain and changeable; this is evident from their behaviour. They first departed in purposeless flight into the rugged country of Mewat, Thomas' old stamping ground, making every effort to avoid Lake, then they fought him, then they offered to surrender and then when their terms were actually accepted decided to fight after all. Clearly there was among them a peace and a war party, and as Lake was an impatient man the result was a tragic holocaust. Abaji and his men after Dudrenac's departure had almost immediately slipped back into the bad old habit of looting villages and towns or holding them to ransom; which indicates perhaps that their intention was to set up on their own as bandits, varying robbery with mercenary assignments on the model of Amir Khan or Thomas. Lake, marching prodigiously along the trail of depredation they left eventually heard the sound of cannon where Abaji was bombarding some recalcitrant Mewati village and guessed correctly his quarry was near by. He resumed the march with all his cavalry at eleven at night on 31st October telling the infantry to follow. Twelve hours later he found the marks of gun-wheels at a ford by a little village called Laswari about sixty miles due west of Muttra. Beyond him stretched a jungle of tall elephant grass above which were rising dense clouds of dust from an invisible column of marching troops a mile or more long.

The Destruction of the Brigades

Lake was firmly convinced that Abaji had only one aim, which was to escape him. Accordingly, for once without wasting any time on reconnaissance he ordered his cavalry brigadiers to circle round the right, or northern, flank of the enemy and to attack them immediately and pin them down until his infantry could come up and complete their destruction. Abaji, or whoever was commanding the Fourth Brigade, reacted promptly and effectively. He simply halted his long vulnerable column of route and faced it right as it stood to meet the British cavalry, the guns in one long line in front, in some places with chains or ropes between the wheels so that they formed an obstacle, and behind them another obstacle formed of all the baggage and ammunition wagons which was hastily manned by the infantry. So dense and tall was the grass that Lake's mounted men could see nothing of Abaji's position until they were within twenty yards of the guns and salvos of grape and case were scything into them. They jumped the chains connecting the guns as if at a steeple-chase only to be repelled by the infantry. Nevertheless they achieved Lake's aim of fixing the enemy. British cavalry have the reputation of being rather like the Rathors, with more dash than skill—'good for nothing but to gallop' as Wellington once said unkindly—but the action at Laswari of the Light Dragoons and the Bengal native cavalry was a model of control; indeed, Laswari in both its phases can fairly be called a cavalry victory. Macan's 29th Light Dragoons and the 4th Bengal Native Cavalry charged across Abaji's gun-line no less than six times, three forward and three back, each time rallying and never losing their compact formation: a tremendous, unheard of feat of combined courage and perfect discipline. Colonel Macan was about to go in again when Lake stopped him. The line of wagons was unshakeable and the gunners after each attack crawled out from under their pieces as soon as the horsemen had shot past them, and opened fire again. The tremendous, sustained fire of artillery revealed to Lake that he had a tiger by the tail and he called the cavalry off.

At this point he received two welcome pieces of news. Abaji sent in officers under a flag of truce requesting terms and offering to surrender his guns, asking in exchange to be allowed to go in peace; and the infantry had come up. Lake, that practical man, ordered them to have breakfast and gave Abaji one hour to ratify the agreement. Abaji may have been playing for time, or it is equally possible that the more warlike members of the Brigade's leaders forced a change of mind, for when the hour was up Abaji had gone and was a mile and a half off, having deployed with speed and precision into a strong position in two lines anchored on the walled village of Mohalpur. There Lake, incredibly, with only five battalions and ten guns, smashed them. Tactically he fought the battle as cleverly as he had fought at Delhi, using the cover of the jungle grass to file up and attack Abaji's flank and so avoid the frontal fire of his huge array of cannon, while his cavalry encircled and enveloped from right and left. He gripped Abaji's exposed right: the attacks of the 76th Foot forcing it to stay in line, and then sent the dragoons crashing into their vulnerable, extended ranks. Abaji's sepoys and gunners fought, as Lake said, 'like devils, or rather heroes'; but they knew not for what purpose, their ordered military world had fallen about their ears, and they were marching away from their homes and families who were in Agra and Muttra and Meerut, whence came terrible news of defeat. They stood and fought, but only like blocks under the chopper, held to their colours and guns only by the habit of discipline and their izzat. They hardly knew their new leaders. Lake's men were elated by victory and led by a skilled general whom they trusted. Wherever there was trouble or danger the tall figure on the tall horse—called, typically, 'Old Port!'—was there; cheering, directing and supporting. They would would not, as old writers say, 'be denied'.

The result was a fearful, a disastrous, display of unnecessary heroism and one of the bloodiest battles for the numbers engaged in the history of British warfare in India. The 76th Foot alone lost 43 killed and 149 wounded. Lake lost his deputy General Waring and one of his aides-de-camp killed, his other, his own son, wounded; his deputy quartermaster-general, his adjutant-general, his military secretary, his political adviser and his escort commander were all wounded, 'Old Port' was shot under him and he himself took a matchlock ball through the skirts of his coat fired by a man so close that the flash burned the cloth. Altogether he suffered 824 casualties. On the other side, of the 9000 men who deployed around Mohalpur 7000 fell. This was not during the slaughter of a rout, for there was none. Even when the line was broken the last survivors of the Army of Hindustan formed square and tried to march away in order, dragging their guns off and blowing up the ammunition wagons they

left to deny them to the enemy. Only when they were finally surrounded, their ammunition exhausted and too tired to lift a musket
and bayonet, did they ask for quarter, which was thankfully granted.
'I was never in so severe a business in my life,' said Lake afterwards,
'or anything like it, and I pray God I never may be in such a
situation again.' As he rode slowly across the battlefield when it
was all over a group of soldiers cheered him. He took off his hat and
thanked them in his polite, Guardsmanlike way, but pointing to the
heaps of dead lying around the enemy guns bade his men to admire
their foes and their devotion.

As evening fell the two sides, utterly exhausted and dazed by the
shock of their mutual slaughter lay down together without enmity.
That night one of the tremendous storms of Asia broke over them,
remembered by all who fought at Laswari; the rolls of thunder
drowning the sustained chorus of moans and cries from the
thousands of wounded lying out in the grass and scrub. Their
voices fell silent as the night wore on. In the blessed cool of the
Indian dawn, when all is still except for the green pigeons flashing
in the trees and the little babblers chirping busily among the thorn
bushes, the wretched peasants of Mohalpur, who had also suffered,
crept out of their hiding places in the jungle and back to their
ruined village to rake over the smouldering ashes of their homes and
to gaze with horror at the carpet of dead men and dead horses which
stretched over their peaceable fields in every direction. It took
Lake's men a whole week to clear the battle-ground and bury the
dead. Such was the end of the Army of Hindustan.

Epilogue

THE WAR did not end with Laswari. Jaswant Rao Holkar, who had so perversely refused to sink his difference with Sindia and to join his fellow chiefs, took up the Mahratta cause and led Lake a dance for another two years, inflicting one shattering defeat on a detachment commanded by Colonel Monson, the man who had led the storming column at Aligarh; but in the end Lake hunted him remorselessly and drove him—'his whole kingdom on his saddle-bow'—across the Sutlej and into the Punjab.

The war ended in December 1805. The Marquess Wellesley, that archetype of imperialists, had been relieved by a gentler ruler, and the peace treaty restored to the Mahratta chiefs all their proper territories south of the Chambal. This policy of clemency and conciliation was made without regard for the Mahratta tradition or for the characters of Jaswant Rao or Daulat Rao. They saw no reason for meekness or gratitude at being restored to their own property by a foreign invader. It proved in Fortescue's words to be 'the concession of all that had been gained by great expenditure of blood and treasure in order that more blood and treasure might be expended in fighting another war for the same object in the near future'.

Under the lax Mahratta rule their armies degenerated into huge bands of mounted raiders called 'Pindaris' who recognised neither law nor frontier and raided across all India, not sparing the rich and peaceful dominions of the Company; ransoming, pillaging, killing and raping and 'carrying off the young girls tied three or four, like calves, on their horses'. Another great war against the Mahrattas had to be fought in 1817. The Peshwa was pensioned off, the Mahratta dominions annexed, and the Sindias and Holkars dwindled into the Mahrajas of the shruken states Gwalior and Indore. Jaswant Rao had died, of the brandy-bottle, it is said, in 1811. His comrade Amir Khan, still riding hard and at war in 1817, was persuaded into respectability by being created Nawab of Tonk in Rajputana, where his successors still ruled in 1947. Lake was made a viscount and died soon after returning to England. He is remembered today, if he is remembered at all, as the cruel suppressor of Irish freedom in 1798 and as the man who failed to 'bully Bhurtpore', i.e. to take the great Jat fortress, the only one ever successfully to resist a British assault; but in three years by sheer energy and skill he first defeated a formidable orthodox army and then a master of evasive, mobile guerrilla warfare.

De Boigne remained carefully aloof from any French schemes to intervene in Indian affairs. He confined his activities to endowing two hospitals, a school for poor girls, a library and a lunatic asylum. In 1814 Louis XVIII made him an honorary field-marshal and appointed him Chevalier of the Order of Saint-Louis. In 1822 Victor-Emmanuel appointed him lieutenant-general in the army of Sardinia and created him Comte de Boigne. He died in 1830. In 1853 an old Indian lady called Helene Bennet (Benoit) died and was buried in the parish churchyard of Horsham in Sussex. This was the Begum de Boigne, his first, probably legal and certainly undivorced first wife.

Perron left India in about 1805, disgruntled at the Governor-General's heartless refusal to entertain his claim to the twenty-seven lacs of rupees he had deposited in Agra fort. Lake, that old-fashioned officer, had wasted no time in observing one of the most agreeable usages of formal war in claiming it as booty and distributing it as prize-money among his delighted troops; a practice whose passing modern soldiers cannot but regret. Nevertheless, he left India with a sizeable fortune and settled down in a château near Vendôme in his native Loir et Cher where he lived in obscurity until his death in 1836. Pierre Cuiller Perron has not been treated fairly by history. His French subordinates spread stories of his absolute rule and his unquenchable avarice—as if *they* were innocent—and English writers have been either Francophobes or have dwelt on his ignominious fall. He never used the leisure of his embittered old age to set down the story of his remarkable climb from quarter-master-sergeant to uncrowned king and commander-in-chief.

The lesser mercenary officers, those lieutenants and captains whose bodies had filled so many graves in Hindustan and Rajasthan, in Malwa and the Deccan, were soon forgotten. One great event followed another; the Sikh war and the arrival of British rule on the Indus, the Mutiny (where the last stab of the Mahratta dagger was inflicted: Nana, or the 'Nana Sahib', the hero or villain of that terrible episode, was the adopted son of the last of the line of the dispossessed Peshwas), and the Proclamation of British rule instead of the Company's. The India of Warren Hastings was transformed into the India of Simla and Mrs. Hauksbee, to the solemn, whiskered, Bible-reading administrators and soldiers of the mid-century who 'fell first on their knees and then on the natives'. The men of the eighteenth century with their uninhibited appetite for 'native' women, for wine, for rupees acquired by force or fraud, and for combat, were like beings of a remote age or another planet. They were also sadly disreputable. As a result, with one or two exceptions, the lesser mercenaries disappeared without record into the vastness of India which to many was their only home. Nearly a century elapsed before Compton was inspired to piece their story together.

Some of the French officers who had actually been in arms against the British were deported, among them Louis Bourquin and Drugeon. The two Hessings, father and son, Robert Sutherland, the Chevalier Dudrenac, Derridon, all left their bones in India after living out their lives on their savings or on their British pensions. Fortunately for history Lewis Ferdinand Smith, who had quitted the Fourth Brigade at the same time as Dudrenac, wrote down all he could recollect of his colleagues and their corps while it was still fresh in his mind. Some transferred to the Company's service. One of them was Pohlmann, which strengthens the argument that he never bore arms against the British although he does not appear in the list of officers who received pensions. Another was Brownrigg, who was killed during the campaign against Jaswant Rao Holkar.

Amir Khan captured Lucan, the man who betrayed Aligarh, and he died a prisoner, of wounds, or neglect, or possibly from an act of revenge. Birch, after serving Thomas, was employed by Perron and then later by the Company, as was Hearsey. James Shepherd, the ex-batman, went over to the British who accepted his whole corps as auxiliary troops. Colonel William Gardner had a distinguished career in the British service. He too settled with his Muslim wife in India as his home.

James Skinner ended as a Companion of the Bath and the Colonel of Skinner's Horse, which he formed from the squadrons of Perron's Hindustani cavalry he brought over with him when he opted for the British. His life is well known. He built, as he had vowed when he survived his wound at Uniara, the church of St. James in Delhi, was confirmed into the Church of England, read his Bible assiduously and had fourteen wives and concubines; thus rationally compromising between his Scottish and Rajput blood.

The wicked, as ever, flourished like a green bay tree. In November 1804, Jaswant Rao, racing through Sardhana solicited Somru Begum to join her forces to his and resist the British, but that crafty lady could smell a loser a long way off, and in any case the urgent Lake was on Holkar's heels. On the 16th November Lake, having marched twenty-four miles in the day, arrived in Sardhana and the Begum fervently assured him of her new found loyalty to the British. The gallant Lake, a little carried away, forgot protocol so far as to give her a hug and a smacking great kiss. Her bevy of ladies-in-waiting were scandalised but she calmed them by explaining unblushingly that the exuberant *general sahib bahadur* was also a Christian priest and it was the custom in her religion for a priest—a *padre*, or father—to salute the females of his flock as if they were his daughters. She did not, apparently, offer to let Lake kiss any of the other Christianised and younger ladies in her court. The arrival of the British was a deliverance to the Begum she had long awaited. Her vastly expensive incubus of an army could, under their protection, now be reduced and disciplined. It was finally disbanded. The British at the same time attached her to their side by confirming her in her jaghirs. With no army to pay she became immensely rich.

She also began to prepare for heaven, making enormous donations to the Pope and building a Roman Catholic church in Meerut and, following the sound principle of hedging her bets, made another to the Archbishop of Canterbury and built an Anglican one there as well. To her eternal credit she gave a home for life to the families of her dead friends and enemies. The daughter of the treacherous Jafar Yab Khan, or Balthzar Sombre, the son of the mistress of Reinhardt she had displaced so long ago, lived with her, inherited much of her wealth and married a British officer. Thomas' wives and children also spent the rest of their days under her protection. One of his sons was for a time an officer in the Sikh service. Zib-el-Nissa Joanna Nobilis Reinhardt, the ex-dancing girl and by-blow of a passing Arab trader, now so satisfyingly rich and so hospitable, was believed by the British to be of the bluest Moghul blood and

even descended from the Prophet, and they flocked to her enter-
tainments. She died in 1836, if not exactly in the odour of sanctity,
at least in that of the best Anglo-Indian society.

In 1843 the State army, as it had become, of the Maharaja Sindia
of Gwalior became troublesome and was attacked and broken up
by the British at the battles of Maharajpur and Punniar. Just before
hostilities its Commander-in-Chief, who had a life-long aversion
from the cruder side of military life, went over to the British. He
was Jean-Baptiste de la Fontaine Filose, who was therefore the
last survivor of the European mercenary soldiers of Hindustan,
outlasting the gallant Skinner, who had died the year before.

As for the brave Indian soldiers the European mercenaries had
trained and had led in so many hard-fought battles, those whose
bones had not been picked by hyaena and jackal went back to their
villages and fields, or lingered on in the diminished armies of the
princes, or joined the British; all except the men of Thomas' old
guard, the band of picked warriors who had ridden with him from
Tijara to the fall of Hansi. They, the story goes, elected to become
sannyasis. After Thomas, they said, they could serve no other,
so they tore their uniforms, broke their swords, forswore the world
of action and devoted the rest of their lives to prayer and contemplation, tramping the roads and begging for their daily bread.

Sources

The principal source of information of the European officers in the service of the various rulers in the closing years of the Moghul era is Herbert Compton's *A Particular Account of the European Military Adventurers of Hindustan* published in 1893. Compton was a man of enormous industry who assembled between its covers all that can be found on the subject, both first-hand and hearsay. The two great obstacles he faced and which subsequent students also face is the time that elapsed before he began his researches and the fact that almost all the history of that episode is based on British evidence. 'Free' India, beyond the encroaching pale of the East India Company, was in anarchy and there are hardly any contemporary Indian accounts. Compton, although invaluable, is unsatisfactory for other reasons beside the fact that he is openly and unpleasantly contemptuous of the 'natives', is a violent Francophobe and is writing what is not so much an historical work as an adventure story and an imperialist tract. He barely mentions his sources. 'It would be tedious to give in detail the names of all the works from which fragments of information have been gleaned,' he says in his introduction, and he ends his sketchy bibliography with 'etc., etc., etc.'! The book itself is not a finished or coherent work. It is a collection of biographical sketches loosely thrown together and overlapping in time and is full of inaccuracies and inconsistencies: different dates are given for the same event, often two conflicting accounts of the same battle or incident are given, and questions like, e.g. the date of Sounda, or the ultimate fate of the First Brigade are left unresolved. To be fair, however, these errors seem to be slips due to editing which would have disappeared had he written the book his material deserved. To follow up each of his statements to the original would be a labour of Hercules, but as far as I have been able to check he was an honest workman and is almost invariably correct as to essentials.

His and all other accounts of the Indian mercenaries are based on only five works of contemporary, written, first-hand evidence: the only exception being the late Brigadier Desmond Young's life of de Boigne for which he had access to the de Boigne family papers. All others are compilations borrowing from these or from Compton.

They are as follows: Lewis Smith, an officer who served under Perron, often acting as a temporary brigadier, who mentions some of the mercenary officers and provided the details of the establishments of de

Boigne's infantry and knew him and Perron well. Compton relied extensively on him, often quoting without acknowledgment.

William Francklin took down Thomas' recollections at Benares just before his death in 1802.

Baillie Fraser did the same for James Skinner, but long after the events Skinner so vividly and amusingly described.

Ali Bux, or Charles, Comte de Boigne, wrote an account of his father's life.

Grant Duff, the historian of the Mahrattas, visited and consulted de Boigne, and the footnotes to his History contain a complete biographical sketch and an outline establishment of his Brigades taken down from his own lips.

To these must be added James Tod's fascinating *Annals and Antiquities of Rajasthan*. He, like Duff, knew men contemporary with the events described.

The monumental *Imperial Gazetteer of India* is a mine of information on topography, local history, tribe, caste and religion.

The authority for contemporary tactics is *The Principles of Military Movement* of Sir David Dundas ('Old Pivot'). I was encouraged by the fact that the battalion organisation he describes in such detail coincides exactly with de Boigne's, except for de Boigne's special arrangements for artillery, animal transport, and for Indian 'followers'.

I must confess to using Colonel Alfred Burne's weapon of 'inherent military probability' once: in my description of Lalsot. If Tod's account, quoting Charles de Boigne, of that action is correct and if de Boigne used the old British system of manoeuvre, as we know he did, then that is what happened.

General Hughes' is the authoritative work on artillery performance.

For the war of 1803 I have replied implicitly, except for one or two details, on Fortescue, the historian of the British army. I have only dared to differ from him over the Mahratta side of the battle of Assaye. (As a matter of interest, the maps of Aligarh, Assaye and Laswari in Fortescue were almost certainly copied from Lewis Smith.)

Select Bibliography

COMPTON, H. *A Particular Account of the European Military Adventurers of Hindustan*. T. Fisher Unwin. London. 1893.

DE BOIGNE, CHARLES, COMTE. *Memoire sur la Carrière Militaire et Politique de Monsieur le General Comte de Boigne*. Chambery. 1829.

DUFF, J. G. *History of the Mahrattas*. 2 vols. Times of India Office. London. 1878.

DUBOIS, THE ABBE J. A. *Hindu Manners, Customs and Ceremonies*. 3rd Edition. Oxford. 1928.

DUNDAS, COLONEL DAVID. *Principles of Military Movement*. T. Cadell in the Strand. London. 1788.

FORTESCUE, SIR JOHN W. *History of the British Army*. Vol. V. Macmillan. London. 1910.

FRANCKLIN, COLONEL WILLIAM. *The History of the Reign of Shah Aulum*. 1798. *The Military Memoirs of George Thomas*. Cooper and Graham. London. 1803. (Bound in one volume.)

FRASER, JAMES BAILLIE. *The Military Memoirs of Lieutenant-Colonel James Skinner, CB*. 2 vols. Smith, Elder. London. 1885.

HOGG, BRIGADIER, O. F. G. *Artillery: Its Origins, Heyday and Decline*. Hurst. London. 1970.

HUGHES, MAJOR-GENERAL B. P. *British Smooth Bore Artillery*. Arms and Armour Press. London. 1970.

MALLESON, COLONEL G. B. *The Decisive Battles of India*. W. H. Allen. London. 1885.

MONTGOMERY, OF ALAMEIN, FIELD MARSHAL. *A History of Warfare*. Collins. London. 1968.

SAINT-GENIS, V. *Un Page Inedite de l'Histoire des Indes*. Poitiers. 1873.

SEN, S. P. *The French in India, 1763–1816*. Mukhopadhyay. Calcutta. 1958.

SETON-CARR, W. S. *Selections from 'The Calcutta Gazette', 1784–1788*. Calcutta. 1864.

SMITH, CAPTAIN L. F. *A Sketch of the Rise, Progress and Termination of the Regular Corps Formed and Commanded by Europeans in the Service of the Native Princes of India*. Calcutta. 1805.

247

Select Bibliography

SMITH, VINCENT. *The Oxford Students History of India.* Oxford University Press. 3rd Edition. 1962.

TAYLOR, MEADOWS. *A Student's Manual of the History of India.* 4th. Edition. Longmans, Green. London. 1879.

TOD, COLONEL J. *The Annals and Antiquities of Rajasthan.* 2 vols. Higginbotham. Madras. 1873.

Various authors: The Imperial Gazetteer of India. Volume I: *The United Provinces of Agra and Oudh.* Volume II: *The Punjab. Asiatic Annual Register, 1800,* Debrett. London. 1801.

YOUNG, BRIGADIER DESMOND. *The Fountain of the Elephants.* Collins. London. 1958.

Notes

Chapter *1*

1 Dubois, 674 *et seq.*; Vincent Smith, 219, 234; Montgomery 402–6.
2 Malleson, Chapter I.
3 Hughes, 44–5, 78.
4 Meadows Taylor, 410, 456–8; Sen, 35.
5 Malleson, 155; Meadows Taylor, 459; Compton, 400 *et seq.*
6 Madec (sometimes 'Madoc'), Lewis Smith, 14; Compton, 371; Sen, 128–43.
7 Bourquin (also Bourgien and Bernard), Lewis Smith, 32; Compton, 341.

Chapter 2

1 Smith, 81.
2 Compton, 372–6.
3 St Genis, 48. 'Le prince Hindou (*sic*, he was, of course, a Muslim) ne borna point la ses actes de munificence en faveur de protegé du redouté Warren Hastings.' Quite so! Young (Appendix) suggests that de Boigne was a British intelligence agent, but why should he have been treated so lavishly?
4 Madhaji Sindia (correctly Mahadaji), Francklin, 119; Grant Duff, vol. II, *passim*; Vincent Smith, 265–6.
5 Dundas, 56. This was the old drill. The British changed from three to two ranks in the firing line early in the nineteenth century.

Chapter 3

1 Meadows Taylor, 524, 508–10.
2 Tod, I, 390.
3 Meadows Taylor, 509–10: Seton-Karr, 263–6; Francklin, 173–9; Grant Duff, II, 9.
4 Compton, 368.

Chapter 4

1 Lewis Smith, 64; Compton, 64 *et seq.*; Grant Duff, II, 215, 406; Fortescue, 67. N.B. The artillery ratings were the British 3, 6 and 9 pdrs. as opposed to the French 4, 6, and 8 pdrs.; see Hughes, 124.
2 Compton, 53, 60.
3 Tod, II, 650. 'Ghora, joora, pagri/Mootcha, kug, Marwar/Panch rekma mel-lida/Patun myn Rhatore.'
4 Tod, II, 553.
5 Tod, 652.

Notes

Chapter 5

1 Compton, 347; Sen, 545–6.
2 Compton, 358. This was James; not William Gardner, the Irish ex-regular officer who served in Jeswant Rao's and the Peshwa's armies, married a daughter of the Sultan of Cambay, and after a romantic and adventurous life joined the Company's service. His story lies outside the scope of this work, unfortunately.
3 Also 'Khurdla', near Ahmednagar. Vincent Smith, 279; Compton, 226; Meadows Taylor, 531.
4 Young, 101, 186, 213 *et seq.*

Chapter 6

1 Thomas' early history is unknown or conjecture. The date and place of his birth is from the *Dictionary of National Biography*, which quotes Compton as the authority.
2 Dubois, 677. Authorities differ about their exact status but they were Hindu petty chiefs, each ensconced in his own hill fort, who remained in possession of their lands after the Moghul conquests in the Carnatic and south of the Tungabhadra river.
3 Francklin, 165–9, 3.
4 Francklin, 34.
5 This account of the Begum and her rescue by Thomas is from the unsupported evidence of Compton, who appears to have drawn on Sleeman's *Rambles and Recollections of an Indian Official*—not quoted in this bibliography—and based on hearsay and native sources long after the event. There is no reason to believe it to be untrue.

Chapter 7

1 *Imperial Gazetteer of India*, I, 223, 244–5.
2 Francklin, 27.
3 *Imperial Gazetteer*, 261.
4 Francklin, 34, 44.
5 To be strictly accurate Goshais were Shivites and Bairagis were Vishnuvites, but sometimes these loyalties were reversed. Hinduism is never simple. Dubois, 112–20; Malleson, 190–1.
6 Zaman Shah threatened invasion on two occasions, 1796 and 1799. Meadows Taylor, 540, 549; Vincent Smith, 279, 290.

Chapter 8

1 *Imperial Gazetteer of India*, I, 223, 244–5. The memory of Thomas, or his legend, was still fresh in 1901. There was a mosque called *Jahaj* ('George') masjid in Hissar. Also Francklin, 93–4.

Notes

Chapter 9

1 Francklin, chapter X of the *Military Memoirs of George Thomas*.
2 Hogg, 246–8.
3 *Asiatic Annual Register*, 7.

Chapter 10

1 Tod, I, 354.
2 Grant Duff, II, 327. Shirzee Rao Ghatkay 'personally invaded the privacy of the zenana, flogged and barbarously degraded them'.
3 Compton, 349.
4 Compton, 245.
5 Sen, 562–3.

Chapter 11

1 St Genis, letter No. 4 in Appendix.
2 On this one occasion Compton differs from the older sources, whom he quotes. He says that Brownrigg's victory preceded the fall of Ujjain, but Grant Duff and Lewis Smith say the opposite and I have followed them.
3 Francklin does not mention Thomas' inactivity at Jehazgarh, naturally.
4 Jehazgarh to the fall of Hansi, Fraser, II, 229 *et seq.*

Chapter 12

1 Grant Duff, II, 367; Lewis Smith, 25; Meadows Taylor, 547; Compton, 279.
2 British operations and order of battle, Fortescue, Chapters I and II.
3 Lewis Smith, 37.
4 Fraser, II, 250.
5 Grant Duff, II, 406.
6 The truth probably is that Assaye was so confused and bloody an affair and events moved so rapidly after it that these interesting details never attracted any attention. A senior European officer was found among the Mahratta dead—could he have been 'Dupont'? Compton in his Appendix states that Pohlmann was subsequently employed by the Company in command of an irregular force. Lewis Smith lists all the officers pensioned by the Company after deserting the brigades, and Pohlmann's name is not included. The bad handling of Sindia's regular troops at Assaye must remain a mystery.

APPENDIX

De Boigne's Establishments

(based on Lewis Smith)

De Boigne's brigades were organised on establishment tables as precise as those of modern armies, laying down tables of manpower, equipment, transport and animals. Omitting much interesting detail they were as follows:

A BATTALION

HQ

Captain (comd),† Lieutenant,† Adjutant (native captain, or *subahdar*), two colour bearers, corps of drums: 27

COMPANY

(Two sub-divisions of 15 to a platoon, two platoons to a company.) Native lieutenant, or *jemadar*; native sergeant-major, or *havildar-major*, N.C.O.'s and *sipahis*, or sepoys: 62

Six line, one light and one grenadier companies: Total 496

ARTILLERY

(Two 3 prs, two 6 prs, one light howitzer, five ammunition wagons, or tumbrils; 400 rounds per gun, 100 rounds per howitzer; 100 bullocks.)

Sergeant-Major,† five gun-Sergeants,† *jemadar*, *havildar*, seven gunners and seven kelasis per gun*: 83

Total under arms 606
(excl. irregulars)

* Excluding drivers and non-combatants.

ATTACHED

Armed irregulars for baggage guards, etc. 50

Non-combatants: surgeon, water-carriers, transport drivers, clerks, accountant, armourers, smiths, pioneers, carpenters, messengers, etc. 81

Total animals: bullocks 120; camels 18.

Appendix

A BRIGADE

Colonel, commander†	I
Brigade Major†	I
Eight battalions regular infantry	4848
Two najib battalions	2000
Cavalry regiment (uncertain)	800
Armed irregulars	500
Total under arms	8150

† Europeans; total 24 officers, 60 artillery N.C.O.'s.

NOTE:

1 Rank did not go with the appointment, but by an arbitrary system of promotion; e.g., Skinner commanded a battalion and more as a lieutenant, Brownrigg a full Brigade as a major.
2 Contemporary writers, including Thomas (Francklin) sometimes counted armies by effective weapons, which is confusing; e.g., they would describe a brigade as 3840 bayonets, 50 cannon, and so many sabres and matchlocks. Alternatively the whole host of camp followers was sometimes included leading to the most inflated estimates.

Index

Note: Where an officer's rank is not known, the words 'merc. officer' have been inserted in each case.

254

Index

Index

Index